Transsscalar Critique

For Oscar Bay and your endless wiggling across scales

Transscalar Critique

Climate, Blackness, Crisis

Henry Ivry

EDINBURGH
University Press

Edinburgh University Press is one of the leading university presses in the UK. We publish academic books and journals in our selected subject areas across the humanities and social sciences, combining cutting-edge scholarship with high editorial and production values to produce academic works of lasting importance. For more information visit our website: edinburghuniversitypress.com

© Henry Ivry 2023, 2024

Edinburgh University Press Ltd
13 Infirmary Street
Edinburgh EH1 1LT

First published in hardback by Edinburgh University Press 2023

Typeset in 11/13 Adobe Sabon by
IDSUK (DataConnection) Ltd

A CIP record for this book is available from the British Library

ISBN 978 1 3995 0646 5 (hardback)
ISBN 978 1 3995 0647 2 (paperback)
ISBN 978 1 3995 0648 9 (webready PDF)
ISBN 978 1 3995 0649 6 (epub)

The right of Henry Ivry to be identified as the author of this work has been asserted in accordance with the Copyright, Designs and Patents Act 1988, and the Copyright and Related Rights Regulations 2003 (SI No. 2498).

Contents

Acknowledgments   vi

Introduction: Ecologies of Crisis   1

1. Crisis Realism: Writing Economically, Thinking Ecologically   43

2. Global Weirding: Climate Crisis and the Anthropocene Imaginary   76

3. Transscalar Blackness: Race and the Long Anthropocene   110

4. Improbable Metaphor: Jesmyn Ward and the Asymmetries of the Anthropocene   140

5. Unmitigated Blackness: Paul Beatty's Transscalar Satire   173

Works Cited   208
Index   222

Acknowledgments

The majority of this book was written while I was searching for a permanent academic job. This meant sneaking research in during lunch breaks from my 9-to-5, during holidays, or, as has been the case for the past year, in the wee hours before my son woke up. Trying to engage in scholarship while also figuring out how to make ends meet was a humbling experience and a constant reminder to rethink the own scales of my work – quite often recalibrating the occasional grandiosity of my thinking with the smaller scale of a quick close reading. As I write this now in the later winter of 2022, I know how privileged I am to have found that supposed golden goose, but I also know that I will never quite shake the sense of precarity that early career academics are forced to embody and navigate. I hope that all my colleagues and friends who are doing important work outside of the academy are able to sound out scales inside and outside of institutions that allow you to think in the ways you need.

This book benefited hugely from the conversation, feedback, and SoundCloud reposts of people across the globe. Thank you to Max Karpinski, Thom Dancer, Paul Downes, Naomi Morgenstern, Kate Marshall, Michael Cobb, Tim Lem-Smith, Kyle Murdock, Norman Mack, Jordan Howie, Amy Coté, Veronica Litt, Christina Turner, David Farrier, Philip Sayers, Dana Seitler, Cannon Schmitt, Avery Slater, Alan Ackerman, Heather Murray, Stefan Krecsy, Laura Dosky, Kyle Kinaschuk, Kurt Bruekner, Mia Schwartz, Ami Padykula, Cody Hicks, Andrew Huehle, Katie Plazier, Joel Friedman, Sarah Corey, Michael Hessel, SJ Okemow, Heidi Støea, Rowan Spencer, Andrew Ryce, Amy Noon, Gabe Thomas, Mark Webster, and everyone else that watched OB monster walk, tried to restrain Frank, read job application materials, watched me train wreck mixes on Tyndall, or shared a conference panel with me. A special thanks to Chris Crosbie, Courtney McLarnon-Silk, Naomi Blech, Sam Hege, and Fiadh who spent countless hours dissecting dating shows with me via video message over the course of the pandemic.

Over the course of writing this book I lost my two biggest heroes, Barbara Ivry and Rosemary Lacey. They were the two most comprehensive readers I know and the criticism that I put forward on the pages that follow is written in homage to them. As is the way of the world, alongside this loss, I also gained a second family. I've been so lucky to get an extra mom, dad, and sibling. Meg, Colin, and Oly: thank you for the endless encouragement, the infinite reservoirs of love you each have, and your patience while I learn it's OK to be touched.

The kernels of this project started 6 months after I met a wide-eyed beauty in Berlin. I am now submitting the final version of this manuscript eight years, three therapists, two transatlantic moves, one pug, and one baby, later. The depths of your kindness, patience, and puttanesca watermark every page, Anna.

Finally, thank you to my dad who taught me to think, my mom who taught me to critique, Oscar who taught me to slow down, Frank who taught me to speed up, and Sam who taught me to look for the breaks.

Introduction

Ecologies of Crisis

In an early moment in Don DeLillo's quickly canonized *Harper's* essay on 9/11, "In the Ruins of the Future," DeLillo takes stock of the attacks. Written ten days after the collapse of the World Trade Center buildings, DeLillo tries to find a narrative frame adequate to capture the immensity of the event at both a literary and a historical level:

> The cellphones, the lost shoes, the handkerchiefs mashed in the face of running men and women. The box cutters and credit cards. The paper that came streaming out of the towers and drifted across the river to Brooklyn backyards, status reports, résumés, insurance forms. Sheets of paper driven into concrete, according to witnesses. Paper slicing into truck tires, fixed there.
> These are among the smaller objects and more marginal stories sifted in the ruins of the day. We need them, even the common tools of the terrorist, to set against the massive spectacle that continues to seem unmanageable, too powerful a thing to set into our frame of practiced response. (n.p.)

What begins as a material inventory of the detritus emanating from the towers quickly morphs into an allegory for mediating 9/11. DeLillo is looking for a narrative frame of reference, a way to represent and mediate the "unmanageable," but his analytic frameworks are frayed at the borders of "practiced response." Equally striking about this passage is that people are conspicuously absent. While DeLillo starts with a nod to "running men and women," they are the background furniture upon which we encounter "mashed" handkerchiefs. As a counterpoint to the bodies jumping out of the towers and the final cellphone calls played on a constant loop, DeLillo offers a reflection on the nonhuman import of crisis. DeLillo starts with the objects of

9/11 – "cellphones," "shoes," "box cutters and credit cards" – before we see the paper darkening the September sky.¹ DeLillo focuses on these "smaller objects" to suggest that understanding 9/11 requires a synthetic perspective incorporating the "marginal" and the "massive spectacle." He is darting between frames of mediation, what I will call throughout this book "scales," trying to find the right narrative form and critical vantage at which to write "too powerful a thing." In miniature, then, this scene rehearses the problem at the heart of *Transscalar Critique*: how do we narrate crises when crisis move across so many scales, from the human to the nonhuman, from the marginal to the massive, from the big to the small?

And while the focus of this book is on literature and the ways in which literature grapples with the scales of crisis, I want to suggest in these opening pages that the problem of mediating crisis is not restricted to novelists. There is a similar scalar confusion in an unlikely yin to DeLillo's yang, the *9/11 Commission Report*. The authors of the *Report* argue that 9/11 was an issue of "*the scale* of the threat [bin Laden's] organization posed to the United States" (National Commission 342; emphasis added). The 9/11 Commission is arguing that 9/11 originates in part from a problem of scale: the United States was not prepared for the attacks because it did not understand the size of Osama bin Laden's threat, that there was a scalar incommensurability between a network of terrorists and a global superpower. But, more than this very literal problem of scale, the 9/11 Commission argues that the event presented a crisis to our cultural understanding of scale more broadly conceived. The event felt unprecedented in part due to the fact that, as they write, "[Al Qaeda's] crimes were on a scale approaching acts of war, but they were committed by a loose, far-flung, nebulous conspiracy with

---

1. Burning paper will quickly become a recurrent trope (to the point of cliché) in narrative accounts of 9/11, most prominently in literary fiction, from Jess Walter's *The Zero*, where "burning scraps of paper" are imagined as "little birds" (3), to Amy Waldman's *The Submission*, where her protagonist sits in "moonlight" picking "out a strange fine dust clinging to leaves and branches; his toes rested on a paper scrap with charred edges" (35). Coming to terms with the lack of physical bodies after the terrorist attacks, it was as if novelists tasked with creating paper novels as paper eulogies of 9/11, reenact this lack of bodies by using burning paper as metonyms for human remains. Ken Kalfus takes this literally in his *A Disorder Peculiar to the Country*, claiming that paper and people become entirely fungible in 9/11: "They were human body parts, yes, and with them whole bodies scattered on the slate pavement blocks. Charred memos, reports, printouts, balance sheets, and Post-Its eddied around them like departing spirits" (13).

no territories or citizens or assets that could be readily threatened, overwhelmed, or destroyed" (348). The Commission realizes that 9/11 occurred on two scales: at once "acts of wars," but unlike the sovereign nations who usually authorize those acts, there are "no territories or citizens or assets" that underpin them. It is this uneasy cohabitation of scales that makes the event so "nebulous."

The understanding of the world in these two accounts of 9/11 is, despite vastly different political agendas, similar. I start with these two readings as I want to argue that both DeLillo and the 9/11 Commission make the claim that 9/11 marked a watershed moment for what we understand by both crisis and scale in contemporary American culture. As the *9/11 Commission Report* has it, "In the post-9/11 world, threats are defined more by the fault lines within societies than by the territorial boundaries between them. From terrorism to global disease or environmental degradation, the challenges have become transnational rather than international" (361–362). In this reading, 9/11 becomes entwined with a future of "global disease" and "environmental degradation," suggesting the emergence of an ecology of crisis, a rethinking, as I will suggest throughout this book, of the scale of crisis. As the "fault lines" and bounded areas of society start to fray, both DeLillo and the 9/11 Commission ask: how are we able to confront and represent contemporary crises?

Across this Introduction and the chapters of *Transscalar Critique* that follow, I argue that thinking crisis in the contemporary requires a transscalar form of narrative. Crisis is a central concept to this book, as crises, I contend, are moments that reveal the inextricable layerings of myriad scales. In this sense, I argue that crisis has a pedagogical element to it, alerting us to our interconnection with a world that constantly exceeds human metrics of measurement. This is why, for example, DeLillo's nonhuman catalogue and the Commission's accounting for "environmental degradation" become crucial for mediating 9/11. More than just these nonhuman and ecological questions, however, thinking at the level of the transscalar is, as DeLillo and the authors of the *9/11 Commission Report* also suggest, a question of thinking about the discursive at the same time that we are also thinking about the material. To understand crisis in the contemporary, we have to read crisis as encompassing the material weight of "small objects" at the same time that it exerts the discursive and formal weight of "massive spectacles." At the risk of trivializing the very real tragedy of 9/11, if there is something to be learned, it has nothing to do with the ostensible goal of the 9/11 Commission to learn "how to protect our nation in this new era" (361), but rather with thinking about crises in new ways.

Before I go any further, I want to underline that this is not a book about 9/11. It is, however, a book about contemporary crises in American literature and culture, and starting with 9/11 has a twofold effect. First, the reading of 9/11 I offer in this Introduction moves centrifugally, alerting us to the nonhuman/human interstices and ontological/epistemological couplings that I've quickly glossed in DeLillo and the 9/11 Commission. Second, 9/11 moves centripetally, collecting work of literature and criticism around it as a periodizing marker. These two features of 9/11 can be extrapolated onto crises more generally. As I will show in the first two chapters that follow, crises spawn their own literary archives and genres in attempts to make sense of what it is that makes the contemporary feel contemporary. Said another way, contemporary history is a history of crisis and, even more pointedly, contemporary literary history is a history of contemporary crisis literature. This is even more true as awareness of the current epoch we now know as the Anthropocene enters our cultural, political, and geological horizons. This is something we glimpse in germinal form in the *9/11 Commission Report* as the authors describe how 9/11 and "environmental degradation" activate a scale that moves outwards. In this very actual sense, then, the 9/11 Commission themselves have begun to anticipate the scalar dysphoria we experience in the Anthropocene. This is, I will argue throughout this book, part of the condition of living in the perennial crisis of the Anthropocene, a moment where our sense of the contemporary is now stretched not just across years and decades, but across millennia.

While a substantial portion of the second half of the book will detail the complexity of thinking through the uneven terrain of the *Anthropos* that constitutes the Anthropocene, asking who the subjects of the Anthropocene actually are, an underlying premise of *Transscalar Critique* is that no matter what originary point we ascribe to it, as Christophe Bonneuil and Jean-Baptiste Fressoz put it, the Anthropocene is a reality that we now have to contend with. "We already live in the Anthropocene," they write, "so let us get used to this ugly word and the reality it names" (11). Temporarily bracketing the vexed and politically fraught questions of where, when, and how we can measure the Anthropocene,[2] the fact is, they argue, the Anthropocene is here to stay, both conceptually and geologically,

2. A lot of this debate is centered around what Clive Hamilton has derided as a "spike fetish" (that is, the placement of Global Boundary Stratotype Section and Point markers) that has been a red herring for scientists and philosophers alike trying "to find a marker when there is no event and to ignore an event when they cannot find a marker" ("The Anthropocene," 106). This spike fetishism, as Kathryn Yusoff argues, is part and parcel of an attempt to elide a history

whether we like it or not. While it is important to be increasingly vigilant of its temporal specifics, geological textures, and, most importantly, the type of racialized abstraction that are performed by the very name "the Anthropocene," this does not obscure or lessen the fact that "this ugly word and the reality it names" is a reality we have to contend with. If anything, this reality requires us to focus with even greater force on what both that "ugly word" and "the reality it names" actually mean for all of us living through this new and precarious epoch.

The force of this reality, in part, requires an acknowledgment that the Anthropocene has become so effective in distilling the complexity of past, present, and future planetary crises into what Axelle Karera christens a "single authoritative word," acting as a metonym for the myriad valences of climatic and planetary anxieties that plague all of us daily (38). Karera is pointing to two interrelated ideas. First, there is an effective whitewashing of the violent anti-Black and colonial history upon which the Anthropocene is structured. But, second, she is also suggesting that the ascendancy of the Anthropocene, as both material and cultural entity, has forced a recalibration of our critical imaginaries, requiring us to understand the contemporary as always inflected with the conceptual and material weight of the Anthropocene. What this means for contemporary literary studies is that any account of the contemporary needs to reckon with how our sense of being contemporary has been altered by the Anthropocene. Theodore Martin offers a critique of the pervasive anxiety in marking out the contemporary in contemporary literature. Martin describes the basic problematics of thinking about the contemporary as a literary period as an effect of its closeness:

> What makes the contemporary such a "déclassé" historical period is the fact that it is neither historical nor a period. Unfinished, ongoing, and altogether too close, the contemporary's history remains to be written, while its status as a period waits to be retrospectively bestowed. ("Contemporary," 133)

Martin goes on to describe how this is particularly true when questions of climate change are brought to bear on literature, arguing

> of antiblackness underpinning geology more generally. While searches for these spikes, she argues, "endeavor to geologically map the material relations of space and time according to stratigraphic principles and scientific precedents, these spikes are not real places as such; they are trace effects in material worlds that infer the event/advent of this most political geology" (33). I will cover this in detail in Chapter 3.

that the "extended timescales of climate change seem to stretch the notion of the contemporary to its breaking point" (*Contemporary*, 126). And while this may make it difficult to try to think of the solidity of the literary period that we have cleaved to in times past (for example, Victorian or Modernist), what I think is equally important to argue is that it has become impossible to read contemporary literature without reckoning with its place in the Anthropocene. I don't mean this in the sense that all contemporary fiction is *de facto* Anthropocene fiction.[3] What I do mean, however, is that for literary critics invested in thinking through what it means to live in the contemporary requires a reading of contemporary crisis literature, even when it is not specifically concerned with climate or the environment, with and through the Anthropocene. Said another way, this book takes the climate of its subtitle in two directions. There are explicit moments when I will discuss the climatic implications of certain texts and policies, dealing with a very material and very real crisis of anthropogenic climate change. But equally important to this book is an understanding of climate in slightly more ambient terms, thinking about the Anthropocene as a surround, an ever-present background: a climate, in other words, upon which these texts unfold.

With this as a starting point, this book translates this focus on climate into ecological terms in two interrelated senses. First, I am invested in articulating an ecological and antiracist politics through transscalar critique.[4] This is straightforward enough: living in the current moment of twinned environmental crisis and anti-Black violence means that we need to account for all human and nonhuman

---

3. Or the even more radical form of this argument: all fiction has always been Anthropocene fiction. For more on this, see Matthew Griffiths or David Higgins.
4. Backgrounding the ecological and antiracist politics throughout this book is the work of Bruno Latour and Sylvia Wynter. Latour argues that a transscalar understanding of the Anthropocene is necessary for contemporary politics: "It is not that the little human mind should be suddenly teleported into a global sphere that, in any case, would be much too vast for its small scale. It is rather that we have to slip into, envelop ourselves within, a large number of loops, so that, gradually, step by step, knowledge of the place in which we live and of the requirements of our atmospheric condition can gain greater pertinence and be experienced as such" (*Facing*, 286). Searching out this "large number of loops" is what, as I will argue, it means to perform transscalar critique. In explicitly antiracist terms, Wynter argues, "[All] our present struggles with respect to race, class, gender, sexual orientation, ethnicity, struggles over the environment, global warming, severe climate change, the sharply unequal distribution of the earth resources [. . .] these are all differing facets of the central ethnoclass Man vs. Human struggle" ("Unparalleled," 260–261).

life in equitable and politically viable forms. But this book is ecological in a second sense: *Transscalar Critique* thinks about ecology topographically. This book reads contemporary crisis literature and the criticism of that literature as forming a nexus of representation and critique. This is a subtler sense of ecology, what the *Oxford English Dictionary* describes as ecology's "interrelationship between any system and its environment." In this way, I am modeling methodologically what I mean by the transscalar. I am thinking about the ontological, questions of what and who counts as being in the Anthropocene, and the epistemological, the way representations of crises interact with one another. This is, then, a book that offers an ecological account of crisis and an ecology of crisis.

Although the majority of this book will be a discussion of literary texts, I have chosen intentionally to start not with a passage from one of DeLillo's novels but with a piece of his criticism alongside the *9/11 Commission Report*. Using DeLillo's critical thinking as an opening into this book underlines a point I will make throughout about the relationship between crisis and narrative form. Forms, I will argue, move across literary, political, and critical spheres, constantly animating and informing one another. This is a point that I take in part from the work of Caroline Levine. Forms, she argues, are not "reflections or expressions of prior social forms" but a site "for identifying and tracking the unfolding relation among different terms" (122). Levine is making an ontological claim rather than a representational one. Forms, she argues, are continually in flux, disidentifying with themselves: "The space of formal collision is in this sense an aleatory one – an unpredictable event as each form tries to preserve its own logic – because it is not clear at any moment which form organizes all the others" (92). This "aleatory" element is precisely what is captured by the transscalar as it claims that literary forms themselves reform the world that they interact in.

Of particular interest is the intersection between popular culture, criticism of that culture, and public policy. This is not to say that there is a one-to-one causal relationship between Don DeLillo and the 9/11 Commission, for example. But it is to say that there are moments of symbiosis and osmosis as narrative representations of crisis, public policy, and literary critique try to understand the crises that constitute the contemporary. This is another place where *Transscalar Critique* models what I mean by the transscalar. Although fiction will remain the grounding point of this book, I have called this book *Transscalar Critique* rather than, say, *Transscalar Literature* to signal the ways that this is as much about the literary representations of these crises as the criticism that has sprung up around them.

As I will make clear in the remainder of this Introduction, the relationship between literature and criticism is largely a formal problem. I argue that 9/11 inaugurates a new mode of thinking about crisis and prompts a critical reconsideration of the relationship between crisis and form. In the next section, I explore how 9/11 precedes and participates in a general crisis of literary and critical scale. This scalar crisis is symptomatic of a larger trend in literary criticism. More and more critics have become invested in trying to locate the right unit of analysis for literary and critical questions. From the transnational and the planetary to new materialism and the biopolitical, I argue that contemporary literary criticism is defined by its oscillations of scale. But often missing in this search for a new scale of reading is the second term of this book's subtitle, Blackness. After having set out the thematic concerns that will dominate the first half of the book, I then turn my attention to the question and crisis of Blackness in the Anthropocene, looking at the ways in which Black Studies and Black fiction offer us an alternative perspective to think the transscalar. As Ian Baucom puts it in a book that tackles the question of race and climate together, "[Any] liberatory politics of the present must be routed through the force of black reason" (24). This is also foundational to this book. To locate a transscalar mode of critique requires thinking across all three terms that make up the subtitle of this book – climate, Blackness, crisis – as simultaneously operative and inextricable from one another at all times. This is where I argue that transscalar critique is a way to describe and incorporate continual and necessary vacillations in units of analysis. The transscalar, I contend, is a way to think across and with the multiple scales of temporality and spatiality, materiality and discourse, ontology and epistemology, race and politics that constitute life in the Anthropocene. It is a way, said simply, to think about the big and the small at the same time.

9/11 and the Realist Novel

In an attempt to periodize a contemporary that increasingly feels fractured and disjointed by ever more distressing economic, political, and environmental conditions, Lauren Berlant examines the relationship between 9/11, crisis, and literary form. Berlant argues that the contemporary is defined by a "generic impasse," what they describe as "the waning of genre, and in particular older realist genres whose conventions of relating fantasy to ordinary life and whose depictions of the good life now appear to mark archaic expectations about having and building a life" (6). Berlant is offering up a eulogy for realism. Realism, they argue, is no longer a tenable mode of representing the economic, material, ecological, and affective realities of the present. This "waning of genre" is an effect of a contemporary riddled with crisis, what Berlant describes as a "crisis-defined and continuing now" (54). For those living in this contemporary, especially racialized and marginalized peoples, crisis is no longer an irruptive or eruptive event: crisis has become identical with "ordinariness itself" (100). To live in the present, Berlant argues, is to live through this crisis "ordinariness." For Berlant, this ordinariness begs a formal question: in a present defined by the continual historical demarcation and diffusion of crisis, what type of literary forms might be able to articulate an understanding of crisis-as-contemporary-history?[5]

Berlant goes on to suggest that one place to trace this negotiation between the proximate relationship of crisis and literary form is in the inchoate category of the 9/11 novel. As DeLillo's essay articulates, from the moment the towers fell it was as if a huge burden was foisted onto novelists. Arin Keeble argues this point, claiming that both the academy and popular media outlets sought out writers, hoping that "literature would provide answers and give meaning to a newly uncertain world" ("Marriages," 6).[6] But, as Berlant implies, with this demand came a concomitant anxiety about narrative form. Returning to DeLillo's *Harper's* essay, he reads this anxiety as a provocation. "The writer wants to understand what the day has done to us," he begins, before pausing and asking, "Is it too soon?" His initial answer seems to be a resolute and simple, "Yes." The essay goes on to lament the media saturation of the events and how

---

5. In a searing polemic appropriately titled *Anti-Crisis*, Janet Roitman describes the historicizing homogenization performed by crisis in the contemporary: "Through the term 'crisis,' the singularity of events is abstracted by a generic logic, making crisis a term that seems self-explanatory [. . .] [Crisis] serves as the noun-formation of contemporary historical narrative; it is a non-locus form from which to claim access to both history and knowledge of history" (3–4). If the stakes are not clear enough, Roitman goes on to denigrate the narrative mode activated by crisis as a "transcendental placeholder" that becomes the be-all-end-all for periodization (9).
6. Alex Houen captures this moment presciently as he satirizes the cultural undertow trying to rope in novelists as purveyors of level-headed cool: "Call in the novelists: This was the response of many newspapers in the immediate aftermath of September 11. Call in the novelists – experts at imagining the unimaginable, the masters of other worlds of possibility" (419).

this impacted both aesthetic sensibility and larger generic questions about representing crisis:

> The events of September 11 were covered unstintingly. There was no confusion of roles on TV. The raw event was one thing, the coverage another. The event dominated the medium. It was bright and totalizing and some of us said it was unreal. When we say a thing is unreal, we mean it is too real, a phenomenon so unaccountable and yet so bound to the power of objective fact that we can't tilt it to the slant of our perceptions. (n.p.)

The events of 9/11, DeLillo claims, are an encounter with an inhuman sublime.[7] The terrorist attacks stretched across scales of perception as a moment of the "unaccountable." Describing the attacks as "expressions of the physics of structural limits and a void in one's soul," DeLillo sees a recalcitrance to scale. DeLillo is attempting to think outside of a strictly anthropocentric scale after being confronted with a "totalizing" distortion of the "too real" that can't be mediated to fit within the bounds of "our perceptions." Later in the essay, he continues: "In its desertion of every basis for comparison, the event asserts its singularity. There is something empty in the sky. The writer tries to give memory, tenderness and meaning to all that howling space" (n.p.). DeLillo, again, returns to the scale of the novelistic imaginary, asking how can we give form to that "howling space"? When confronted with the "singularity" of crisis, we are confronted with the "primal terror" that comes before "politics, before history and religion." In this moment of encounter with crisis that is outside human conjugation, DeLillo is trying to theorize what new aesthetic forms crisis narrative might, indeed, can take. He wants to find a new form for crisis that can capture, in his words, the very "air around us."

In this sense, DeLillo acts as a bellwether for the conversations that will dominate discussions of contemporary literature in the decades that follow. In querying the scale of realism, DeLillo throws his hat in with a then fledgling reading of contemporary fiction in general and contemporary realism in particular. As more and more critics began to critique the resurgent rise of realism in the early 2000s following

---

7. As will become clear across this Introduction, the tropes established in the immediate wake of 9/11 had a remarkable staying power. For more on this question of media and mediation, see Jacques Derrida's interviews in Giovanna Borradori's *Philosophy in a Time of Terror*, Marc Redfield's *The Rhetoric of Terror*, and Richard Grusin's *Premediation: Affect and Mediality After 9/11* for some of the most insightful examples of this line of critique.

the high postmodernism of the 1990s, two schools of criticism quickly established themselves as competing orthodoxies. One school put forth a capacious and insurgent definition of realism as a way to claim that realism has undergone a "productive transfiguration" (Plotz, 434). In these defenses of realism, the basic argument is that the generic expectations and operations of what realism is have shifted.[8] This is where DeLillo seems to place himself in trying to create a realism outside the bounds of the human, stretched to new scales. Similarly, Peter Boxall argues that it is specifically a shift in scale that has become the defining trait of contemporary realism: "[What] the contemporary novel witnesses is a growing disjunction between the material conditions of contemporary being and those spatial and temporal forms in which such conditions become collectively meaningful" (*Twenty-First*, 9). Against the proliferation of contemporary crises, Boxall, DeLillo, and others are looking for a mode of realism that might be able to interrogate and mediate "the emergence of new kinds of realism, a new set of formal mechanisms with which to capture the real" (*Twenty-First*, 10). And, as Boxall's claim about the "disjunction" of "spatial and temporal forms" suggests, this means an expansion of the scale of the literary. What is being constellated here are the tentative outlines of a transscalar approach to literary form and criticism, a way to read realism outside of any one dominant scale.

As exciting and promising as this not-quite-realism sounds, this was, sadly, the path not taken by the novels and critics of 9/11. The other emergent school, that is, sought out realism as a reversion, implicitly, and sometimes explicitly, to conservative, reactionary, and predominantly white, narrative forms. This came to bear across the post-9/11 archive.[9] It was a shame, therefore, to see the foreclosure

8. These run the gamut from Frederic Jameson to Ramón Saldívar, but pulsing through most of these is a speculative dimension. As a literary movement and moment, Jeffrey T. Nealon has called this a "realism redux" that coincides with the return of philosophical realism and signals "the cultural or academic return of what looks like several unrelated strands of realism" (72).
9. The best-known essay capturing these two schools is Zadie Smith's "Two Paths for the Novel." In this essay, she critiques what she describes as a post-9/11 "lyrical realism" in authors like Joseph O'Neill. A related strain of thinking has congealed to critique "capitalist realism." The term emerges from the work of the late Mark Fisher and is best encapsulated in the edited collection *Reading Capitalist Realism*. There, the editors Alison Shonkwiler and Leigh Claire La Berge make a genealogical argument to claim that capitalist realism follows postmodernism but has given up the "skepticism toward systems and paranoia about control" in lieu of a sedated "recognition of the ruling order of capitalism as both more banal and more encompassing" (16).

of any sort of scalar opening as 9/11 gained its own generic logic within the larger cultural memory. As the debris and dust settled at One World Trade Center Plaza, this possibility of an alternate literary form regressed into the very realism that it had initially seemed to disavow, with people like Graydon Carter, the former editor of *Vanity Fair*, proclaiming on September 18 that 9/11 meant "the end of the age of irony" (ironically, on Jon Stewart's *The Daily Show*). This was concurrent with a political shift signaling an even more problematic retreat into entrenched racial, gendered, and nationalistic paradigms led by the Bush Administration.[10] Either which way, by the time 9/11 novels started to appear and make waves in late 2005 and early 2006, the literary injunction of imagining otherwise, hinted at by DeLillo, fizzled out. What topped the *New York Times Bestsellers List* and clogged up the NPR airwaves were a series of sterile and generic novels by primarily white authors that imagined 9/11 through the surrogate lens of familial crises, most often divorce or an extramarital tryst. This was true of writers like Jay McInerney and Helen Schulman but also true of more experimental novelists including Jonathan Safran Foer and even DeLillo himself. "The formula for the 9/11 novel has by now come into its own," writes Georgiana Banita as she takes stock of 9/11 fiction a decade and a half later; "urban and emotional architecture organize an endless loop of marriage, divorce and other prefabricated plots" (154–155). What we see, then, is a huge trove of novels that continually rescale 9/11 down to the level of domestic realism, crudely retroping the terrorist attacks into more manageable units of what Banita calls "micro-realism" (159).[11] The effect of this rescaling is that the more expansive scale of the geopolitical (in other words, the conditions that led to 9/11), the environmental, or the violent racialization that attended 9/11 is evacuated from these texts. It is not that we want or need 9/11 novels that don't have the domestic in them; there is a

---

10. See Gretchen Ritter, Judith Drew, Susan Faludi, Thomas Bjerre, Rebecca Carpenter, and Meghana Nayak, among others.
11. I should add that a domestic rendering isn't *de facto* a bad thing. As critics like Christine Marran argue, a domestic turn in crisis fiction is a way to capture the quotidian violence of the everyday, especially for racialized populations. Marran argues that the domestic turn in environmental writing, for example, signals the way in which environmental crisis (like crisis more generally) has become "no event at all" (101). As we will revisit in Chapter 2, the scale of the domestic is a counterbalance to the ways in which Anthropocene thinking has tended to function only "at the unprecedented scale of a global commons" that does not account for the asymmetries of lived experience (118).

danger in having the domestic as the sole determinant scale, especially when the domestic was so imbricated with racialized and gendered imagery. The 9/11 novel, in this sense, is monoscalar, creating a false choice between the marriage plot, on the one hand, and the political on the other.

Understanding 9/11 as a scalar issue is further fleshed out in the critical debates surrounding 9/11 literature. It wasn't just a question of writing 9/11 fiction, but also a question of reading 9/11. Responding to the first wave of critical accounts centered on trauma theory that located and mapped the impact of 9/11 through an individualized and psychoanalytic lens, a new critical scaling started to appear in 2008.[12] This new scaling appeared as polemics against what Richard Gray called "the desperate retreat into the old sureties" of both content and form in the 9/11 novel (16). This debate took place across the pages of *American Literary History* (and later in monograph form in Gray's *After the Fall*), inaugurating what can be described as a cottage industry of 9/11 literary criticism. In this mode, critics imagined a transnational 9/11 novel, a novel tuned to both the vicissitudes and the possibilities of a globalized and racially diverse world. Gray describes this as a "hybrid" form, internationalizing the realist novel, "seen from an interstitial perspective that resists any oppositional grid of either/or distinctions" (96). For Gray, this 9/11 novel would look to the immigrant experience to craft this "interstitial perspective." Michael Rothberg, Gray's primary interlocutor, supplements this imagined horizon of the 9/11 novel by adding a geographical

---

12. This "first wave" of 9/11 criticism is captured in anthologies such as Ann Kaplan's *Trauma Culture*, Judith Greenberg's *Trauma at Home*, and Ann Keniston and Jeanne Quinn's *Literature After 9/11*, and monographs like Kristiaan Versluys's *Out of the Blue* and Randall Martin's *9/11 and the Literature of Terror*. At the risk of caricature, these texts are focused on the individualized effects of trauma, what Berlant describes as trauma's "fundamentally ahistoricizing logic" (10). It is important to note, however, that traumatic readings of 9/11 do not necessarily imply a scalar model that collapses inwards. In Judith Butler's *Precarious Life* and its companion text, *Frames of War*, for example, Butler argues that there is another way of reading 9/11 that is able to "[furnish] a sense of political community of a complex order [. . .] by bringing to the fore the relational ties that have implications for theorizing fundamental dependency and ethical responsibility" (22). The vulnerability limned by trauma, in other words, points to an interdependent precarity connecting all of us relationally. For more on these more expansive accounts of trauma theory, see also *The Trauma Question* by Roger Luckhurst and the edited volume by Gert Buelens, Samuel Durrant, and Robert Eaglestone, *The Future of Trauma Theory: Contemporary Literature and Cultural Criticism*.

axis. "In addition to Gray's model of critical multiculturalism," he begins, "we need a fiction of international relations and extraterritorial citizenship. If Gray's account tends towards the centripetal – an account of the world's movement toward America – I propose a complementary centrifugal mapping that charts the outward movement of American power" (153). What both Rothberg and Gray are articulating is a mode of fiction and criticism that is transnational in the sense that it accounts for America's own racially multicultural population while also charting the diffusion of America across borders. What remains limited in this account is the ways in which the national remains the determinant scale of 9/11. Both Rothberg and Gray fail to properly describe a world that is not in some way tethered to its Americentric gravitational center.[13]

Somewhat surprisingly, Rothberg turns to Irish-born novelist Joseph O'Neill's *Netherland* as a paragon of this mode that "[explores] the epistemology, phenomenology, and impact of America's global reach; and [reveals] the cracks in its necessarily incomplete hegemony" (158), while Gray searches out immigrant fictions of "deterritorialized America" (72). These gestures, however, merely replicate the aspirational horizon of globalization wherein the form of realism is left intact while the content of the texts merely changes.[14] There is no formal indeterminacy, just the plugging of new data points into an existing algorithm. It is as if a more expansive globalism is the antidote to this post-9/11 crisis in literary fiction. This is to say that both critics and their literary

---

13. The particular problems of the scale of the nation is something I will return to in my readings of Paul Beatty in the final chapter.
14. Not to mention the fact that the champions of this transnational mode were primarily white authors. Even critics of this Gray–Rothberg reading of 9/11 seem to fall unwittingly in line when it comes to their actual aspirations for the 9/11 novel. In their introduction to a special issue of *Modern Fiction Studies* on 9/11, John Duvall and Robert Marzec argue that "Gray and Rothberg are both unwilling to look very closely at what 9/11 fiction sets out do because they are both sure that they know what 9/11 fiction ought to be doing" (384). This is a fair point – a critique of the appropriative hermeneutics that sprung up as a response to the depoliticized traumatic readings of 9/11 (and feels especially true of the championing of the white O'Neill). That said, Duvall and Marzec praise texts that "[contemplate] the larger, global forces at work in the constitution of twenty-first century human subjectivity" (394). From the hindsight afforded by two decades, however, there is not much of a debate here. Rothberg and Gray critique 9/11 texts for not being transnational enough, while Duvall and Marzec celebrate texts that are appropriately aware of "transnational political affiliations" (394). Again, the actual form of the novel remains static and circumscribed.

archives are merely reflective of a desire for a text that is more and more globalized, that captures more and more divergent "spatial and temporal settings" (Gray, 96).

Pieter Vermeulen is precise in taking this genre of 9/11 criticism into his crosshairs:

> Gray's and Rothberg's interventions convey an undiminished belief that the novel form, if only it would begin to live up to its potential, has the capacity to deliver ever more "otherness," and can serve as an appropriate imaginative vehicle for addressing the ethical and political problems that face us in the twenty-first century. (68–69)

Vermeulen locates a latent, fetishized, and neocolonial desire to figure out a way to world 9/11. As any passing survey of the onslaught of post-9/11 monographs and edited collection indicates, this ostensibly requires a scaling outward, a move from the "tendency to linger over the disabling psychological effects of trauma" (Vermeulen, 68) into a larger and larger novel that might be able to incorporate the shifting scales that Rothberg and Gray envisage. This is captured by titles like *Transatlantic Fictions of 9/11 and the War on Terror*; *Fictions of the War on Terror: Difference and the Transnational 9/11 Novel*; *Rethinking Identities in Contemporary Pakistani Fiction: Beyond 9/11*; *From Solidarity to Schisms: 9/11 and After in Fiction and Film Outside the US*; *American Unexceptionalism: The Everyman and the Suburban Novel after 9/11*; and *Post-9/11 Espionage Fiction in the US and Pakistan*.[15] The suggestion seems to be that the 9/11 novel and its attending mode of criticism have become more expansive, and, as the introduction to any of these collections will tell you, more attuned to the vagaries of geopolitics.

That said, the progressive politics that are longed for in these titles are maybe not so progressive when put in dialogue with the very reactive document that I started this Introduction with, the *9/11 Commission Report*. There, the Commission describe Al Qaeda as the flipped side of the globalization coins, the dark underbelly of a new mode of transnational geopolitics.[16] In eerie resonance and thematic similitude to the Gray/Rothberg axis of 9/11 criticism, this transnational rendering of 9/11 carries on throughout the *9/11*

---

15. This is also true of literary fiction. Whereas the 9/11 literary canon was once limited to novels by American and other white, Anglophone authors, more and more articles and monographs now include authors like Kamila Shamsie and Rattawut Lapcharoensap.
16. As they note: "Al Qaeda were more globalized than we were" (357).

Commission Report: "9/11 has taught us," the authors write, "that terrorism against American interest 'over there' should be regarded just as we regard terrorism against America 'over here.' In this same sense, the *American homeland is the planet*" (362; emphasis added). Capturing both the centripetal and centrifugal forces of Rothberg and Gray's imagined 9/11 novel, the *Report*'s authors argue that 9/11 signals a moment when the scale of what constitutes America has changed. The clearly racist undertones of this argument make for an uneasy transference between the neo-imperialist geopolitics of the Bush Administration and the transnational 9/11 novel. While this may be a somewhat hasty comparison, it is hard to shake how questions of 9/11's transnational reading are, at best, troubling and, at worst, a direct perpetuation of American white supremacy and global hegemony. What is equally telling for this book, moreover, is the way in which the *9/11 Commission Report* scales up from Gray and Rothberg by anticipating the Anthropocene's inconvenient reality: the scale of discourse moving from the merely (trans)national to the level of the planetary. What Gray, Rothberg, and the authors of the *9/11 Commission Report* all seem to agree on is that 9/11 was a failure of "the issue of proportion – and imagination" (343). This is, at its core, a crisis of scale. Post-9/11 "proportion" and "imagination" have to be figured at the level of the planetary. These are terms for thinking through scale – proportionality – and literary form – imagination. Even the authors of the *9/11 Commission Report*, then, are invested in this intersection of literary form and scale mediated by crisis that will remain at the center of *Transscalar Critique*.

Scales of Critique

If 9/11 begins a tectonic shifting in the scale of literary and critical form, scale becomes an even more central term in literary criticism in the years that follow. As my glossing of a number of 9/11 monographs and edited collections suggests, there has been a recent push to scale literary criticism outwards, looking for more expansive analytics and vocabularies. Many of the above titles, for example, could be grouped together under the banner of the "transnational turn."[17]

---

17. While this taxonomy is a convenient shorthand, it is important to highlight the asymmetries that constitute the transnational. As Yogita Goyal summarizes, there remain "polemical disavowals of the transnational on one hand and ongoing manifestos for the need for the transnational on the other" (2).

The transnational's more expansive reach of literary criticism is, in large part, a response to the expansiveness of the contemporary itself. As Debjani Ganguly puts it in a book that theorizes "the world" as both a literary trope and a critical category,

> The novel now evinces a capacity, predominantly through a global informational infrastructure, to imagine the human condition on a scale larger than ever before in history and certainly beyond national and regional configurations, which have traditionally marked both its conditions of possibility and its limits. (2)

What Ganguly is making clear is that the contemporary novel is invested in "a scale larger than ever before in history." Imbricated within its aesthetic and historical DNA, that is, there is a way in which the novel is looking for larger representative modes. To read this expanding novel, *ex post facto*, we also need critical modes that can respond to this scale.

This desire for a critical scaling outward is not particularly new. An expansive and encompassing critical scale has been the cornerstone of comparative literary criticism for the better part of two decades. Starting with Gayatri Spivak's call for a "planetarity that we are called to imagine" as an antidote to globalization (81)[18] and moving through Franco Moretti's distant reading methodology,[19] scales of reading have been expanding outwards spatially and temporally to accommodate what Ganguly sees as the expansion of the novel itself.[20] Without diving too deep into any of these specific categories

---

18. In contrast to the rescaling of the planet as the American homeland in the *9/11 Commission Report*, Spivak uses planet as a counterbalance to "the globe," which she imagines as "the imposition of the same system of exchange everywhere" (72).
19. Moretti provides a methodological scale that attempts to account for a much larger cross-section of literary texts, looking at literature as "a collective system, that should be grasped as such, as a whole" (4).
20. Although Moretti (and Frederic Jameson before him) is making a spatial claim in his canonical *Graphs, Maps, Trees* that we should be thinking the literary "*in the direction of width*" (90; emphasis in original), Wai Chee Dimock revises this axis with the suffusion of a temporal scale in *Through Other Continents*. We cannot enlarge one without the other, she argues, and we need to think at both the temporal and the spatial scale in order to conceive of what she calls "scale enlargement:" "Literature is the home of nonstandard time and space. Against the official borders of the nation and against the fixed intervals of the clock, what flourishes here is irregular duration and extension, some extending

and their subtending complexities, my point is that contemporary literature and contemporary criticism have both been drawn to larger and larger units of analysis. One text that highlights this intersection of the literary and the critical scaling out particularly well is Caren Irr's *Toward the Geopolitical Novel*. Irr's book examines a category she christens "the geopolitical novel," a novelistic form that leaves behind national borders as it works towards "the end of history into another time frame altogether" (173). In this sense, she is reading novels like the ones Ganguly cites, novels concerned with a more expansive world. Concomitant with this is Irr's own methodology, one that resonates with Moretti. Irr revises her scale of critique to "read widely and synthetically" to replicate her archive's formal attempt to "move beyond existing national forms" (3). That is, both the scale of the texts and her hermeneutic apparatus expand outwards. This is all to say that whether they fly the banner of the transnational, the planetary, or the world, these modes of criticism are all responding to the problematic of scale by scaling outwards, arguing for a type of literary criticism that can get bigger and bigger.

Concurrent with this outward pivot, however, there is another scale in play for literary critics. Equally important in discussions of contemporary literature has been the scaling down of the units of literary analysis.[21] In a cutting and insightful diagnostic of the present titled *The Official World*, Mark Seltzer argues that the contemporary is defined by its self-reflective nature that "comes to itself by staging its own conditions" (6). This fixation with recursion, according to Seltzer, generates a hyper critical self-awareness that can think critically only at the micro scale, what he cheekily dubs "the incrementalist turn" (166). This incrementalism is a turn away from making large or definitive claims about what it is that texts do or what the world is or could be. Seltzer puts it this way:

> for thousands of years and thousands of miles, each occasioned by a different tie and varying with that tie, and each loosening up the chronology and geography of the nation" (4). Caroline Levine makes a similar point when she argues that "our field has by and large inherited a dominant definition of literary form as spatially unifying, which has often distracted us from the specificity of temporally unfolding terms" (52). I will turn to how temporality becomes a particular fixation for Anthropocene criticism in the next section of this Introduction.

21. As Moretti argues, it is the "very small, and the very large," after all, that "are the forces that shape literary history" (76).

[With] respect to the novel, minor characters; with respect to affect, minor feelings; with respect to political forms, little resistances, infantile subjects [. . .] These forms of one-downmanship – a turn from large events to small (non)events – are the reverse side of one-upmanship of recent academic acclimatizations to globalization. (166)

Seltzer's point is that the expanded scale of both political and literary critique has caused a reciprocal reaction that turns towards the "minor." We see "minor characters" in a book like Jeremy Rosen's *Minor Characters Have Their Day* and "minor feelings" in the minimalism of Sianne Ngai's critique of the zany, the interesting, and the cute. We can even see the "little resistances" of politics in Wai Chee Dimock's "weak theory."

We can add to Seltzer's taxonomy a specifically literary category that we might call "minor readings" or "minor critique" that resists making grand or definitive claims about texts. This is the critical paradigm of critics like Elaine Freedgood and Cannon Schmitt's "denotative reading," Thom Dancer's "critical modesty," or the so-called "descriptive turn" which seeks out "the world's messy profusion of stray details that cannot be assimilated to an already existing theory" (Marcus et al., 11). In fact, the epistemological and critical humility subtending Seltzer's incrementalism runs throughout the critical genre now collected under the banner of postcritique. Postcritical readers and writers are no longer in the business of making large claims on behalf of text.[22] Postcritique is firmly rooted in the minutiae and the micro-scales of the word, of the surface, of the text.

This scaling down is not just true of literary criticism but is equally present in the more expansive world of critical theory. Whether that has been in the realm of biopolitics, new materialism, or object-oriented ontology, the small, just as much as the large, has received a number of diverse and vocal champions. While I will come to the ways in which this turn to matter and material runs the risk of reproducing

---

22. Although not a postcritical or a literary critic, Graham Harman perhaps represents the apotheosis (or, less generously, the nadir) of this mode of "minor reading." In his manifesto for an object-oriented literary criticism, he proposes that instead of analyzing texts, we actually change them to figure out "how each text resists internal holism by attempting various *modifications* of these texts and seeing what happens" (201–202). He wonders, that is, how many words you need to change in *Moby Dick* for it to stop being *Moby Dick*. For Harman, the operative scale is the word.

specifically racist logics in Chapters 3 through 5, I gloss these critical standpoints now as a way to limn how, in opposition to the scalar breadth opened up by the transnational, the planetary, and the world, there is a cleaving to a smaller and more manageable scales of what Seltzer calls the "political minimalism" that counters "the maximalist claims of transnational and transchronological turns, which seems at times to assume the literalism of a direct political, or emancipatory impact on the world or even past worlds" (166). Seltzer's critique is clearly against this incrementalism, but his tone is equally apprehensive of the "transnational and transchronological turns." This suspicion of both the large and the small is what I find telling in Seltzer's work. My overview of these varying scales of critical discourse is not meant to pass judgment on any single analytic. My point is less analytic and more descriptive. What all of these modes of thinking have in common is a central problematic of scale. At their core, each of these critics and critical schools is looking for the right unit of analysis to contextualize, describe, and criticize the world. But, if quantum mechanics, the scalar discourse *par excellence*, has anything to teach literary critics, it is that even our smallest unit of analysis is insufficient for accurately capturing what it is that we think we are analyzing.[23] That said, the inverse is also true: our largest analytics are equally incapable of capturing the complexity, interdependency, and co-constitutionality of both our world and our representations and critiques of it. This Sophie's choice that runs through contemporary criticism – the big or the small, the descriptive or the analytic, the ontological or the epistemic – does not, however, need to be so binaric or limiting.[24] Indeed, as Dimock writes so pointedly in her account of literary scales, contemporary critique is, in fact, "energized by the feedback loops between the very large and the very small," and, I should add, everything in between (*Through*, 77).

23. I am cribbing this idea from Timothy Morton, who argues, "Quantum theory specifies that quanta withdraw from one another, including the quanta with which we measure them. In other words, quanta really are discrete, and one mark of this discreteness is the constant translation or mistranslation of one quantum by another" (*Hyperobjects*, 40).
24. Heather Love captures this impasse in an institutional context: "Given the insecure footing of institutional life in the present, critics have responded to the crisis in the humanities by going big (in data mining, the turn to systems and network theory, and accounts of globalization and world literature) and by going small (in the turn to ethics and new formalism)" (420).

Scaling the Anthropocene

Although this broad swath of critical material points to how scale is a key critical term predating the rise of the Anthropocene in the humanities imaginary, scale as an explicit critical concern has become a, if not the, central term for understanding the Anthropocene. As Bruno Latour puts it,

> [In] the era known as the Anthropocene, such issues [of scale] have become increasingly urgent, since we poor humans – or rather earthlings – remain perplexed as to how to find our place among phenomena, which are at once immensely vaster than we are, and yet subject to our affect. (*Gaia*, 93)

While there are many ways to read this scalar provocation, I want to pause to think about what the Anthropocene means for literary scholarship. In particular, I want to quickly highlight how the Anthropocene, when it is imported from the realm of geological and physical sciences into literary studies, is articulated specifically as an "issue of scale."[25]

At first pass, thinking the Anthropocene appears to be analogous to thinking the transnational on steroids. Instead of questions of nationality, we are now asking questions of stratigraphy and autecology. This would make thinking the Anthropocene appear as simple as zooming further and further out. As Jennifer Wenzel sees it, it has been telling how "suddenly the humanities have embraced thinking at the totalizing scale of the world, globe, or planet" (*Disposition*, 2). A logic of zooming out, in part, underpins Dipesh Chakrabarty's equal parts canonized and cannibalized essay, "The Climate of History: Four Theses." In describing a dual temporal scaling of the human across both the time of capital and climate, he argues

---

25. Zach Horton is particularly concise in making this point about the Anthropocene's scalar distortion: "The 'Anthropocene' is commonly understood to signify a crisis of scale, bringing into focus the temporal, spatial, and causal extent of the human. In this sense, the Anthropocene is less about the discovery of new scales than it is a form of self-reflexive knowledge: it marks humanity's confrontation with itself as a trans-scalar entity" ("Composing," 35). While I agree with Horton's scale of the human, our paths diverge somewhat when it comes to "humanity's confrontation with itself." The Anthropocene is about more than this: it is also about a confrontation with nonhuman agencies and actants across divergent scales.

that the problem of scale remains one of expansion, a thinking that aspires to interweave humans with "a force on the same scale as that released at other times when there has been a mass extinction of species" ("Four," 207). Salient within Chakrabarty's reasoning is the assumption that these scales are fungible – that we can somehow imagine the human at the "same scale" as the planet. Like the thinkers of the transnational and so on, then, the problem is one of zooming out, focusing an analytic lens on a larger moving target. The question of finding a wider vantage remains at the center of a number of renderings of the Anthropocene, at both the critical and the literary level. Derek Woods has pointed to how this has been salient in literary representations and critiques of the Anthropocene. Woods is critical of this gesture, highlighting the way in which aesthetic representations operating at the planetary level remain "invariant," as "[writers] and artists often imagine changes of scale as a smooth and continuous zoom" ("Scale Variance," 201). This type of invariant zooming out or in, in turn, has become a determinant mode for representing the world at the scale of the planet or species.[26] What is lost here is any account of the different valences that actually make up the humans of that humanity.

We see this in a scene in Colson Whitehead's *Zone One*, a text that has become canonical in Anthropocene fiction, Anthropocene literary criticism, and contemporary Black literature. Towards the end of the novel, a zombie survivor known to us as Quiet Storm arranges abandoned cars on the freeway. The narrator cannot make sense of her pattern as he remains on the ground. He is too close to the shapes that Quiet Storm is forming and "doesn't know how to read [the pattern] yet" (233). It is not until later in the novel, when the narrator is in a helicopter flying over the abandoned freeway, that he can discern the pattern. You need to zoom back out to realize that Quiet Storm has been "engaged in their own strategic reconstructions" in her placement of the cars (233). This scene has been taken by critics as emblematic of a new mode of writing in the Anthropocene.[27] While it certainly does offer a new mode of representing the Anthropocene

---

26. Stacy Alaimo sees this as particularly true in the realm of the visual arts: "Prevalent visual depictions of the anthropocene emphasize the colossal scale of anthropogenic impact by zooming out – up and away from the planet" (145).
27. Kate Marshall, for example, describes this moment as one in which "The Quiet Storm finds an appropriate scale to write for a kind of geological time that is more indifferent to the finite time in which her body is embedded, leaving a final message for a viewpoint into which she can only project herself" ("What," 533).

where a human perspective might not be able to interpret what is in front of us, there is a salient logic of zooming out. Although Whitehead is indeed modeling a new grammar in this scene, the syntax of this grammar is tethered to an invariant scale that attempts to just zoom further and further out.

As much as this is an aesthetic issue, it is equally a critical one. Zooming out has also become a preeminent critical register for discussing questions about how we read in the Anthropocene. Across a series of essays, Mark McGurl has emerged as one of the most prominent voices highlighting the relationship between literary form and scale in the Anthropocene. In these essays, McGurl theorizes various generic modes that might "crack open the carapace of human self-concern" ("New," 380). This opening would offer a counterbalance to the ways in which literature has historically tried "to scale down the world to make it comprehensible, meaningful, and manageable to them" ("Posthuman," 540).[28] The Anthropocene, however, tilts this dialectic in the other direction, welcoming the return of the large and the gigantic that had previously been exiled and scrubbed from the literary record. Although McGurl is attuned to the ways in which both the large and the small inform one another, his writing is indicative of a certain strand of thinking that has begun to reify larger and vaster scales of thinking within literary criticism.[29]

If McGurl represents the spatial axis of this equation, there is an equally prevalent temporal rescaling. Benjamin Morgan has catalogued how scale has become stretched along increasingly elongated temporal axes in the era of anthropogenic climate change:

> Scale has recently become a topic of lively debate in two thriving but seemingly unrelated fields: critical reflection about the significance of anthropogenic climate change for historical disciplines, on one hand, and proposed renovations of historicist literary interpretations on the other. In the first instance, reflection about the planetary impacts of humanity or of capitalism has fostered a lively historiographical

---

28. Amitav Ghosh has made a similar point about how the history of realism is a history of scaling down: "Here, then, is another form of resistance, a scalar one, that the Anthropocene presents to the techniques that are most closely identified with the novel: its essence consists of phenomena that were long ago expelled from the territory of the novel – forces of unthinkable magnitude that create unbearably intimate connections over vast gaps in time and space" (63).
29. "And yet it is worth remembering," McGurl writes, "that the scale of the posthuman resides both on the small side of the human and on the large" ("Posthuman," 551).

debate about "deep history" extending beyond the written record and about the possibility of reconciling the timescale of human history with that of planetary systems [...] In the second instance, literary scholars have outlined alternatives to familiar historicist methods: longer durées and nonlinear temporalities that aim to capture the strange time within which literary forms move (44)

Although Morgan is highlighting two seemingly disparate discursive modes, his writing is instructive for the ways in which it moves the Anthropocene across not just space, but also time. But, as Morgan continues, it is not enough to continually expand our scale of critique, taking the Holocene at the expense of the Victorian, for example. Instead, we need to think "in terms of the *coexistence* of scales" (57; emphasis in original). What I am getting at is that as the immensity of the Anthropocene enters literary scholarship, it can often feel as if it is a question of merely tacking further and further out. Matthew Taylor offers a word of caution on this point: we must be aware of "the danger of meeting ever-larger problems with ever-larger solutions" ("At," 116). As should be clear by now, I believe we need a different way to think about crisis that operates at a transscalar level. That is, it cannot be a choice between whether we are encountering a domestic or a planetary novel or adopting a larger or smaller critical lens. Rather, we need a new way to conceive of both aesthetic and critical scales simultaneously.[30]

In response to McGurl, Dimock anticipates the necessity of the transscalar. "This is a moment in the history of the planet, and the history of the institution of literature," she writes, "when a plurality of scale might turn out to be a matter of necessity rather than a matter of indifference" ("Low," 614). This is an insight that I will return to throughout the course of *Transscalar Critique*. Dimock links together literary history and planetary history, moving between political and literary scales to suggest that thinking transscalarly is "a matter of necessity." To imagine this "plurality of scale" is to think about new literary and critical forms not as an importation of vastness from the geologic sciences, but as nuanced and fluid modes of reading the contemporary that embrace contradictory scales and layers simultaneously.

30. Implicit in this zooming out is the way in which contemporary capitalism reimagines all relationality as exchangeable. This is a point that Anna Tsing makes in her critique of scalability. For Tsing, scalability names a logic that seeks "the ability of a project to change scales smoothly without any change in project frames" (38). This is precisely the sort of scalar imaginary of continuity and seamless transition that I want to push against and will trace in Chapter 1.

We can already see this transscalar revision to Anthropocene critique in Chakrabarty's companion piece to "Four Theses," "Postcolonial Studies and the Challenge of Climate Change." Written a few years after "Four Theses," Chakrabarty returns to the question of scale as a disciplinary problem. Chakrabarty realizes that the massiveness of the Anthropocene risks (or, indeed, necessitates) an abstraction of humanity to a level that does not allow for the asymmetries of lived experience. As a committed postcolonial scholar, however, this presents a difficulty for Chakrabarty: the scale of the geologic effaces the violent colonial and anti-Black history upon which it is grounded. Chakrabarty sees this as a methodological issue: how can we, then, think the geological at the same time that we attend to the discursive? Or, more broadly, how do we account for the micro and the macro when we are thinking at such a warped level of abstraction? This is where Chakrabarty moves into the mode of the transscalar. We need to account for the current moment of climate crisis as constituted by this colonial history, thinking

> simultaneously on contradictory registers: as a geophysical force and as a political agent, as a bearer of rights and as authors of actions; subject to both the stochastic forces of nature and open to the contingency of individual human experience; belonging at once to differently-scaled histories of the planet, of life and species, and of human societies. ("Postcolonial," 14)

As he moves through the striated layers of human existence in both the individual and the collective, Chakrabarty is arguing that any account of the Anthropocene needs to revise the lexicons and imaginaries inherited from climate scientists. What is crucial is the simultaneity of "contradictory registers." This is the cornerstone of transscalar thinking: the ability to embrace the contradictory that does not choose between the geologic, on the one hand, and race, on the other. In fact, it is to realize that these myriad scales are not contradictory but rather complementary and co-constitutional. In moving from the life and physical sciences into the humanities, Chakrabarty is acutely aware of the way in which a transscalar genre of the Anthropocene is a necessity.[31]

---

31. This is something he revisits explicitly in his first monograph on the topic, *The Climate of History in a Planetary Age*, where he argues that "Having big and complex brains may very well mean that our big and deep histories can exist alongside and through our small and shallow pasts, that our internal sense of time [. . .] will not always align itself with evolutionary or geological chronologies" (8).

Race in the Anthropocene

What Chakrabarty is driving home is that these macro-scales of thinking – the environment, the Anthropocene, the climate – do not supplant or sublate the violent histories of racism upon which they are grounded. As I will argue throughout this book, we need to understand the Anthropocene alongside the ongoing crisis of anti-Black racism and vice versa. A narrative of the Anthropocene, whether political, literary, or critical, needs to contend with the asymmetrical ground upon which it is written. As Françoise Vergès eloquently phrases it, we need to ask how to "write a history of the environment that includes slavery, colonialism, imperialism and racial capitalism, from the standpoint of those who were made into 'cheap' objects of commerce, their bodies as objects renewable through wars, capture, and enslavement, fabricated as disposable people, whose lives do not matter" (162-3). A central scale to any account of the Anthropocene, in other words, is the scale of Blackness and the ways in which it bisects, intersects, and complicates the geological scale at which human life has now been imagined.

In this thinking, I am certainly not alone. From Simon Lewis and Mark Maslin's groundbreaking *Nature* paper dating the emergence of the Anthropocene to the moment of colonial contact to Nicholas Mirzoeff's provocatively titled "It's Not the Anthropocene, It's the White Supremacy Scene" to the growing work of Black ecology, it seems that just as quickly as the Anthropocene appeared on the critical horizon, its imminent constellations were contested for their obfuscations of race, class, sexuality, and gender. David Farrier offers a particularly pointed diagnosis of the ways that much contemporary ecological theory glosses over the Anthropocene's inequities:

> Anthropocentrism is a pitfall of the Anthropocene [. . .] In particular, the danger is that real lives are subsumed by humanity thought in the abstract, a flattened worldview that disregards the fact that the "we" of the Anthropocene is profoundly conflicted, composed of extremely mismatched orders of culpability and exposure. (16)

This is to say that the scale of the Anthropocene runs the risk of interpellating human subjects into a universal "we" at the expense of the "real lives" and violence that are lost in this flattening of scale. Surveying the field, Elizabeth M. DeLoughrey offers a history of how the Anthropocene as critical and geological category has been questioned:

> Thus, a decade after the coining of the term "Anthropocene" we begin to see the start of a robust dialogue about the origins of our environmental crisis – variously attributed to the dominance of capitalism (Capitalocene, Econocene, Necrocene), transatlantic empire (Plantationocene), patriarchy (Manthropocene), European/white settler colonialism (Eurocene), twentieth-century globalization and its regimes of disposability (Plasticene), or all of the above and their engagements with a frightening alterity (Chthulucene). (22)

While I do not want to throw my weight behind any one of these names in particular, their sheer multiplication and proliferation shake the Anthropocene's temporal start date, its narration, and geology. This requires us to take pause and think about how the granularity of human history impacts the scale at which we are understanding or narrating the Anthropocene. Diana Leong is precise in what the stakes at play are: "Blackness is the specter that haunts the Anthropocene and its possible futures" (15). Put another way, a transscalar mode of critique needs to account for how certain members of the *Anthropos* of the Anthropocene do not fit into a monolithic stratigraphic signature.

No one has made this critique more forcefully or influentially than Kathryn Yusoff:

> The Anthropocene might seem to offer a dystopic future that laments the end of the world, but imperialism and ongoing (settler) colonialisms have been ending worlds for as long as they have been in existence. The Anthropocene as a politically infused geology and scientific/popular discourse is just now noticing the extinction it has chosen to continually overlook in the making of its modernity and freedom. (11-12)

Yusoff rescales the Anthropocene, disputing its "universalist geologic commons" by looking at how alternative Anthropocenes are not just exercises in nomenclature but are, in fact, "intensely political in how they draw the world of the present into being" (14, 34). Underlying Yusoff's argument is a more radical claim about what it means to think at the scale of the Anthropocene. She writes: "The end of the world has already happened for some subjects" (22). To extrapolate, what Yusoff is articulating is a counterhistory of scale, a counterhistory in which the scalar distortion and dysphoria premised by the Anthropocene's threat of imminent extinction for humanity writ large are already felt by Black peoples.

Part of the claim of *Transscalar Critique*, however, is not just that the "end of the world has already happened for some subjects," but that questions of scale have occupied Black Studies for the better part of a few decades. Achille Mbembe describes the Anthropocene as ushering in a "new fungibility [. . .] institutionalized as a new norm of existence and expanded to the entire planet" (6). For Mbembe, the existential threat of the Anthropocene has always been the condition of Blackness. Our era of planetary precarity, he writes, "is what I call the *Becoming black of the world*" (6; emphasis in original). In this sense, our current moment of environmental violence can learn from the scholarship laid out in Black Studies more generally. From the work of Sylvia Wynter, Hortense Spillers, Édouard Glissant, and M. Jacqui Alexander to the contemporary work of Tiffany Lethabo King, Christina Sharpe, Joshua Bennett, and others, a multiply scaled sense of the world – incorporating ontology, politics, geology, epistemology, and literary form – is foundational. And while I certainly agree with Mbembe's characterization, I think that there is also the risk of a certain homogenization that can occur: an erasure of actual Black experience as everyone clamors to reclaim their own fragility (a sort of blackwashing that stands as the counterpoint to the Anthropocene's whitewashing).[32] What I will argue in this book, instead, is that Black literature provides us with the tools to see the co-constitutional inflection points of Blackness and the environment, identifying multiple scales that exist at the same time.

If Chakrabarty is quick to realize how the Anthropocene cannot be imagined without race, we can trace a similar argument in *Zone One*. Throughout the majority of the novel, the race of the narrator is never discussed. But, as the text progresses and the narrator eventually reveals that he is indeed Black, he seems to parrot the Anthropocene logic Chakrabarty critiques above. The zombie apocalypse of the text, which acts as the surrogate for our imminent climate crisis, has created "a single US now" (231). But, as the book finishes, this "US" slowly dissolves. Whitehead gives us a knowing wink. What the Anthropocene does not name, in other words, is a postracial fantasy that we can all hang onto in the face of environmental crisis. That is, scaling up to the planetary and forgoing the racial does not account for what

---

32. Wenzel makes an analogous argument: "To focus on the universality of vulnerability at the expense of the unevenness – to move too quickly to ideas of the human as species, or community as planetary – is not so much a quarantine as a gentrification of the imagination, a gesture towards new forms of community that is blind to the displacements it causes" (*Disposition*, 33).

Chakrabarty describes as the "contingency" of the Anthropocene. But as I argue in the second half of this book, Black Studies provides us with another way to approach that very same contingency.

This is the approach that I take beginning in Chapter 3 of *Transscalar Critique*. The second half of this book follows an alternative genealogy of scale, highlighting the ways in which we can understand the transscalar through a rich critical orthodoxy in Black Studies and in the writing of N. K. Jemisin, Jesmyn Ward, and Paul Beatty. This counternarrative to the primarily white archive that makes up the first half of this book is a way to argue that the transscalar builds upon an intimate understanding of the entanglement of anti-Black violence and environmental crises. These Black writers, in many ways, anticipate the scalar problems of the Anthropocene that I outline in the first half of the book when sketching out the scalar shortcomings of crisis realism in capturing the complexities of crisis. There is a critical shift in the second half of the book as well. If my first two chapters read against the grain, remaining critical of a fledgling strand of contemporary American writing, the remainder of the book reads with the grain, elucidating work that is already transscalar. In this methodological shift, I therefore make the claim that transscalar critique is not just something done to novels but something that they do.

Transscalar Critique

Transscalar critique is not just about representing the world, it is also about what Woods describes as "scalar variance," the general discontinuity and disjuncture of the world that girds "a pluralist ontology that distinguishes scale domains without incorporating them into a more general substance" ("Scale Variance," 218). Woods's use of terms and ideas like "general substance" and "pluralist ontology" signals how literary scholars have started to interrogate the ontological and material scalings of the world, rather than just representations of that world.[33] This is making the case for the ways in which works

---

33. A critical turn towards ontological inquiry, I should add, is not without its critics. Again, this is a place where race complicates the type of broad brushstrokes attending what Mitchum Huehls has described as the "ontological turn." Jordy Rosenberg, for example, describes this ontological turn as a new mode of primitivism that finds its "limit in politics" as it seeks out objects as they appear "unmediated by social order" (n.p.). Cristin Ellis has also taken this ontological turn to task via antebellum literature. She is more generous than Rosenberg but

of art, by drawing attention to scale, actually intervene in the world. Although this is certainly an important aspect of thinking about how literature works in the Anthropocene, it is still only one aspect of the transscalar. Stacy Alaimo, in a turn of phrase that will constantly be echoed across this book, advocates for a mode of critique that is invested in "scale-shifting," wherein "complex epistemological, ontological, ethical, and political perspectives" are brought together in such a way that "the human can no longer retreat to an asylum of separation and denial" (10, 178). Alaimo's claim is that to attend to just the ontological cutting of the literary is to miss an equally important aspect of what texts are and how we read them. That is, an ontological scaling is equally limited in its critical purchase if it does not also attend to other scales.

Concurrent with these Anthropocenic and Black understandings of scale, another iteration of scale is equally important to transscalar critique. In an introduction to a special issue of *MLQ* dedicated to "Scale and Value" in literary history, James English and Ted Underwood offer a brief history of the dominant critical scales of criticism over the past century. They describe a "contraction" that existed during the first half of the twentieth century (reaching its apex with New Criticism) before reversing course into a "crisis of largeness" in the later twentieth century and the beginning of the twenty-first (278, 281). For English and Underwood, literary history is circumscribed by the twin arrivals of scale and crisis that has created a "more concerted effort [. . .] to recalibrate the entire analytic apparatus of literary study, bringing into view matters of concern both smaller and larger than those whose value we have been accustomed to recognize" (282). English and Underwood suggest another way in which methodological questions about scale are percolating across literary studies. In their history of literary criticism, English and Underwood are not concerned with the racial, ontological, or geological scales I have been mapping thus far. Their point is about textual scales. They are asking: what are the units of analysis that we take into account when performing

---

is clear that the type of mappings made by those looking for the ontological comportment of the literary is only seeing half the picture: "But this powerfully expanded map of the entanglements of being and knowing does not tell us what we ought to do with its information" (165). Like Rosenberg, then, Ellis makes the claim that we still need a level of normativity and antiracist activism to buttress these ontological inquiries.

literary criticism? It is between these registers, between these scales, that the transscalar emerges. A properly transscalar mode of critique does not prioritize the ontic at the expense of the epistemic. In my reading, the transscalar is attuned to the vagaries of syntax just as much as it is to questions of Blackness. The point is that these scales, the material, the discursive, and the political, are all entwined; it is scales all the way down.[34]

Key to the transscalar is the claim that there is no one critical scale that is adequate in capturing the complexity of the contemporary. The transscalar is defined in and through its contrapuntal movements. Mariam Thalos makes a similar point in relation to the mathematical and physical sciences. Thalos argues against what she sees as the tendency in the sciences to claim that physics is the only scale that matters for causality and being. For Thalos, the idea that causal interaction only happens at the "microscopic" scale prioritized by physics is to fall into a trap of a "one-scale model of the universe" (83). What Thalos is critiquing is how physics as a discipline dominates all models of causality, assuming the role of a "Master Science," wherein "the macroscopic is always and everywhere slave" to the microscopic (8, 83). Thalos's point is meta-discursive and methodological: there are always other scales at which we can read the world and those scales are just as rich and variegated as any other.

As I will show over the course of *Transscalar Critique*, the stranglehold that physics exerts over the physical sciences is replicated by other discourses across literary criticism.[35] In Chapter 1, for example, I provide readings of the 2008 financial crisis that push back against a nascent Marxist orthodoxy in the literary criticism surrounding that crisis. For many critics of the 2008 financial crisis,

---

34. The transscalar, in this way, channels Karen Barad's work on "intra-action." For Barad, matter and meaning are co-constituted and neither is granted ontological priority. This is what she calls her "ethico-onto-epistem-ology" (185). In her cosmology, the world is constituted by "material-discursive practices through which (ontic and semantic) boundaries are constituted" (141). What I borrow from Barad is the way in which there is no top layer of being. Rather, there is an "ongoing [reconfiguring] of the world" (141) that takes place through the transscalar interplay between divergent materials, discourses, and so on.
35. As a further point of connection, it is worth noting that Thalos's model is reliant upon the work of Black writing. Thalos borrows liberally from literary metaphors and even starts a discussion of what she calls the "play" of scales by giving a close reading to a section of Ntozake Shange's *For Colored Girls Who Have Considered Suicide When the Rainbow is Enuf* (81).

to understand that crisis we need only to account for the economic fallout of the subprime mortgage meltdown. What I argue in this first chapter is that this misses how crisis itself is predicated on an imbrication between the nonhuman/human within the market itself. What is needed, I argue, is a Marxism supplemented by an ecological politics. Similarly, in Chapter 5 I look at the work of Paul Beatty to argue that the scale of Blackness is constantly erased by other scales that attempt to undercut the political purchase of race. Whether that is the economic, the biologic, or the national, different critical scales (however benign their intentions) end up erasing Blackness through a monoscalar appropriation. What is needed, I contend, is a transscalar reading of Blackness that attends to the economic, the national, the environmental, and the biological simultaneously, moving between these scales while also acknowledging their points of departure and friction. This ethos of the transscalar is perhaps best captured by Latour towards the end of *Pandora's Hope*. "I am always slightly surprised by what I do," he writes. "That which acts through me is also surprised by what I do, by the chance to mutate, to change, and to bifurcate [. . .] We are surprised by what we make even when we have, even when we believe we have, complete mastery" (283). Transscalar critique, I argue, is about locating that surprise, being open to the provisional and fleeting assemblages and coalitions that come into being in a transscalar Anthropocene.

Chapter Outlines

McGurl describes how contemporary novels seem to be growing "more and more sophisticated, in fact more realistic, about scale, breaking its crude association with spatial magnitude alone" ("Gigantic," 408). The sophistication that McGurl sounds out is about breaking an understanding of scale that is tethered to "spatial magnitude alone." McGurl wants an understanding of scale that is capacious and multifaceted, not bound by sheer volume and spatiality. *Transscalar Critique* takes this further by applying this fluid definition of scale not just to contemporary novels but to governmental and nongovernmental reports and policies alongside critical theory. It is not enough that fiction can become "more and more sophisticated" about questions of scale. The same needs to be true for all modes of narrative. Part of the push for the transscalar is a way of thinking interdependently across forms and mediums. I model this by bringing texts like the United Nation's Intergovernmental Panel on Climate Change reports and Michael Lewis's nonfictional account of the financial crisis into conversation with literary texts.[36] My reasoning here is that crisis is not contained by the literary sphere, and there is, in fact, a symbiotic transference of the logics and scales that we can trace in both fiction and other cultural and political spheres. Scale does not merely refer to the ontological layerings of the world but is also an epistemic description of our critical modes for encountering that world. This linking of the epistemological and ontological is an interface of the Anthropocene. Timothy Clark writes, "Perhaps too big to see or even to think straight, the Anthropocene challenges us to think counterintuitive relations of scale, effect, perception, knowledge, representation, and calculability" (13). This means that we cannot be enmeshed only in the material, on the one hand, and in the discursive on the other. To live in the Anthropocene is to be constantly oscillating between these points, scaling through their different layerings.

To make this type of reading of contemporary crisis literature has a downside. Throughout this book, a transscalar approach means that I use terms in slippery ways, pushing scale to the very limit of intelligibility.[37] But, as Tobias Menely and Jesse Oak Taylor argue, this is precisely the point for Anthropocene criticism. "It turns out," they write, "that when your object of concern is something like the Anthropocene – multiform, multiscalar, multicausal, multitemporal – a commitment to methodological consistency may be exactly the wrong approach" (13). The same is true, I argue, of understanding contemporary depictions of Blackness. To prioritize "methodological consistency" is to miss out on the richness that is inherent in the contradictory. It is to make a mistake that Michel Chaouli describes as a reductive mode of reading that prioritizes "the outcome of what

---

36. This is also a generic point. As Rosen has pointed out, "If one is interested in a genre as a historically existing cultural phenomenon, then it is desirable to consider related forms of production in different media" (20). This is, as Rosen argues, the necessarily "comparative and heterodox" nature of genre studies as such (20).
37. Scale etymologically lends itself to this type of adaptive understanding. As English and Underwood argue, we often focus on only one half of scale's etymology. Scale, they point out, which is "from the Latin *scala* (ladder) via Old French *escalar* (climb), refers to valuation ('a graduated range of values forming a standard system for measuring or grading') as well as to dimensionality ('the relative size or extent of something')" (277). What this two-prong definition elucidates is the way in which scale is about both size and value. It is in this sense that I use scale to discuss the "dimensionality" of ontology alongside literary methodologies.

is in truth a complex process" (334). That is, instead of the teleological prioritization of the finished product of an analysis, we must attend to the divergence of the process that inflects and informs any one reading. With this as my starting point, I follow literature that also tries to think crises in multivalent ways.

Most of my texts in the first two chapters are realist novels, many of which I derisively christen "crisis realist" novels. Crisis realism describes texts that attempt to mediate crisis at a monoscalar level – this is the logic that I outlined in the domestic rescaling prevalent in 9/11 fiction. Other novels in this book change forms constantly, eliding any sort of definitive taxonomy. This lack of consistency is a literary way of sounding out new forms for thinking crisis in the contemporary. The critical writing that I trace is analogous. Some theorists are fixated on pinning crisis down to a specific causal origin, while other critics are speculative, never willing to fix critique to a definitive object. These speculative critics are primarily the concern of Chapters 3 through 5 and share a background in Black Studies as well as literary critique and ecological theory. By adopting this chameleon-like approach to the literature I cover in this book, I am joining a growing list of contemporary critics that are seeking out new vocabularies and methodologies for mapping the Anthropocene contemporary.[38]

There is no tidy way to wrap up these texts in a single mode of reading. Indeed, if there is any singular point that can be made definitively about the texts in this book it is something that approaches the tautological: each text requires its own transscalar critique. Our contemporary is defined by crises that are continually in excess of our scalar imaginaries. We need to start thinking, therefore, in "experimental and tentative" ways about how we approach these crises. This is a book, then, about crisis and scale. But it is not about any one crisis or about any one scale. Just as 9/11 was quickly displaced by Hurricane Katrina and the financial crisis (Henry Paulson, after all, described the collapse of Lehmann Brothers as "economic 9/11"

---

38. In this search for fluid forms, I take Juliana Chow as a methodological predecessor. For Chow, reading in the Anthropocene is defined by "[coming] to terms with how an approach may be critical at the same time that it is experimental and tentative" (118). Alongside Chow's embrace of "critical partiality," I also find Julietta Singh's nonmasterful critical praxis informative for the ways that it envisages criticism as "vital to this process of imagining otherwise and dwelling elsewhere, to the relentless exercise of unearthing and envisioning new human forms and conceptualizations of agency" (6).

(Tooze, 324)), so too have our scales for representing the world continually been offset by one another. This is particularly true of realism which has lost its stranglehold on the contemporary, morphing into new shapes and forms. This is a book, then, about a number of crises and the different scales that we have used to think those crises across a wide variety of textual sources. Crisis, like the Anthropocene, is an asymmetrical concept. What appears as a crisis for some is not a crisis for others. With this in mind, *Transscalar Critique* maps out these asymmetries as they manifest in aesthetic, critical, and political forms.[39] This is what I mean by an ecology of crises. My literary and critical archives are seeking out a mapping of crisis that is ecological in both its political orientation and its methodology, looking at the ways in which crisis signals a moment wherein we might understand the world in more interdependent and co-constitutional terms.

One of the central gambits of this book is that as the Anthropocene migrates across disciplines, the field of literary criticism is, perhaps more than any other field, capable of addressing its myriad and divergent levels and scales. As literary scholars, we are trained to think about the contrastive viewpoints, scales, and differentials that inflect any one given reading. *Transscalar Critique* follows texts that take this as an imperative. It is, I will contend, literature and literary criticism, particularly a certain strand of contemporary Black critics and writers, that time and time again allow for the granularities of human history to be integrated into a thinking that can also scale the planet. This is not to say that literary scholars are better at doing the work that geologists and climate scientists do. Rather, the point is that a training in attending to the diverse and often contradictory registers of texts is always already transscalar; it is just a matter of foregrounding scalar disjuncture in a way that does not attempt to gloss over them in terms of theoretical homogeneity or continuity.

Chapter 1, "Crisis Realism: Writing Economically, Thinking Ecologically," is emblematic of the type of crisis reading I outlined at the start

---

39. Crucial here is the conceit that even if a crisis is not a crisis for everybody, a pervasive sense of crisis more generally constitutes the contemporary. This is a point that Michael Dango's *Crisis Style* makes eloquently: "Everyone may not agree on what the crises are, or whether a certain event qualifies as a crisis, but the sense of crisis itself is shared across the social and political spectrum. An urgent question for historicizing the present is, in turn, not so much how to itemize all the problems of the world but how to theorize the form of crisis itself: what it means when people sense its pervasiveness – and also its perverseness" (17).

of this Introduction. Following the 2008 subprime mortgage crisis, I look at how this crisis demanded to be imagined across multiple scales at the same time that there was a critical, political, and literary impulse to imagine crisis as occurring on only one scale. Starting with the *Financial Crisis Inquiry Commission Report to Congress*, I develop a thesis about how politicians read the 2008 subprime mortgage crisis as the result of a few bad apples in our banking system. I argue that the formal narrative strategies that developed in response to 9/11 evolved to rescale financial crisis down to the level of the individual. What this did was negate any possibility of systemic critique in lieu of a moral scapegoating of specific individuals. This is what I call "crisis realism," and I trace what begins as a political narrative across literary works by Michael Lewis, Dave Eggers, and Martha McPhee. I also make clear, however, that crisis realism is a critical strategy perpetuated by critics looking for simple, causal explanations to respond to the economic precarity of the contemporary. The issue with crisis realism, for novelists, critics, and politicians, is that it is limited to a monoscalar analytic of contemporary finance: an account, moreover, that is yoked to the hegemony of white, male subjects. What is missing from this account, I contend, is a reading of the economy that acknowledges what William Connolly calls "its imbrication with nonhuman force fields" (*Fragility*, 67).

In the second half of the chapter, I examine how an account of the way in which the market itself is constituted by both human and nonhuman interdependence is largely absent from critical and literary readings of the financial crisis. A transscalar account of financial crisis, I argue, follows the lead of Diane Coole and Samantha Frost in tracing the market through "a multimodal methodology, one congruent with the multitiered ontologies, the complex systems and the stratified reality" (32). Chapter 1, in this sense, is most resonant with my reading of 9/11. Also predating the rise of the Anthropocene-as-critical-category, the financial crisis discloses a moment in which we need to attend to the nonhuman at the same time that we open up our sense of scale. This is implicit in even the most crisis realists of these texts. The Financial Crisis Inquiry Commission, for example, finds itself in the impossible position of trying to find a narrative frame to capture what it describes as the "terrifying animation of household appliances" (656). This is why I argue in Chapter 1 that writing economically requires thinking ecologically.

After my readings of crisis realist fiction, I finish with a look at Joshua Ferris's strange novel, *The Unnamed*. The book follows a successful lawyer as he descends into uncontrollable and unstoppable bouts of walking. As innocuous as this may sound, he has no control over where he is going and finds himself void of agency and autonomy from within his own body. The text's realism begins to fray, devolving into a semi-lucid stream-of-conscious narrative that mirrors the autoimmune toxicity of contemporary capitalism. For Ferris, I argue, it is impossible to extricate financial crisis from environmental crisis. By reading his work as transscalar, my first chapter demonstrates a way of capturing the rhythms of economy in ecology as well as the ecology of the economy.

Using financial crisis as a starting point to discuss ecological politics, my second chapter, "Global Weirding: Climate Crisis and the Anthropocene Imaginary," looks at how climate crisis weirds crisis realism. Using the same methodology as the first chapter, I look at the ways in which both literary authors and the United Nation's Intergovernmental Panel on Climate Change (IPCC) attempt to scale climate crisis down to manageable and solvable units of mitigation. This is the scalar incongruity of politics in the era of climate crisis. Latour is cutting in his diagnosis of the type of political logic we see in the IPCC: "At the very moment when we should be remaking politics, we have at our disposal only the pathetic resources of 'management' and 'governance'" (*Gaia*, 215–216). That is, like 9/11 and the 2008 financial crisis, there is a tendency in political and literary representations of climate crisis to attempt to rescale the crisis as something that can be solved and worked through. For the IPCC, this means that global warming can be stopped (and even reversed) through combinations of economic incentives and technological adaptations.[40] For novelists, this means ascribing a fixed causal genesis to climate crisis and attempting to formalize that through the domestic tropes of crisis realism.

To push back against this rescaling, I borrow the term "weird" from its recent resurgence in literary criticism as a way to describe how, as Mark Fisher puts it, "the background furniture of literary realism" is pulled "into the foreground" (*Weird*, 76). I develop a weird account of realism across Jonathan Franzen's *Freedom*, Barbara Kingsolver's *Flight Behavior*, and Nell Zink's *The Wallcreeper*. Concentrically moving out from realism proper in that respective order, I examine

---

40. This is what someone like Hamilton would call the narrative of the "Good Anthropocene," wherein "the whole, the order of things, a goodness that in the end transcends and defeats the structural obstacles, sufferings, and moral lapses that seem to threaten it" ("Theodicy," 234).

how anthropogenic climate change frays the scale of realism for each of these authors as climate crisis begins to impact the form of their texts. For Franzen, even his domestic marriage plot is complicated by the intrusion of ecological imagery as his protagonist Walter finds himself confronting the "long-term toxicity" and "coal-sludge ponds in Appalachian valleys" of his marriage (333). Kingsolver's novel also struggles to capture climate crisis through its realist techniques. As a climate scientist in the novel puts it, climate crisis remains an "intangible thing [. . .] outside your range" and this remains an incongruent literary problem (367). The scale of realism, in short, does not capture the diffuse and disparate conditions of being in the Anthropocene, and these texts become weirder in their cartography of contemporary crisis.

Whereas both Franzen's and Kingsolver's novels have been widely recognized (and, in many cases, celebrated) for their participation in the emergence of more "conventional and realist" novels dealing with climate crisis (Johns-Putra, 269), Zink's enigmatic *The Wallcreeper* has not been acknowledged to the same extent (either critically or commercially). Her book demands what I describe, following Jesse Oak Taylor, as an "atmospheric" mode of reading. For Taylor, atmospheric reading is a mode of reading "adjacency" that attempts to map the inverted relationship between the background/foreground of life in the Anthropocene (7). The plot of the book moves elliptically, rather than linearly. As readers, we are immersed in the process of uncovering the text's meanings, exposed to its own extemporaneous logics of creation and meaning making. More than any of the texts in the first half of *Transscalar Critique*, Zink's book models a transscalar approach to climate crisis as she uses an atmospheric literary form that relies upon "suspended and associative thinking," rather than definitive, causal chains (Taylor, 14).

The third chapter, "Transscalar Blackness: Race and the Long Anthropocene" takes a step back from the specific crises of the first two chapters to offer a meta-narrative about the ongoing crisis of anti-Black racism, a crisis that has only been amplified in the contemporary, from the 2014 Flint, Michigan, water crisis to the Black Lives Matter protests following the deaths of George Floyd and Breonna Taylor. The quotidian but pervasive nature of anti-Black violence mirrors, in many ways, the perennial crisis of life in the Anthropocene. Christina Sharpe has taken this a step further, arguing that anti-Black racism becomes "pervasive *as* climate" (106; emphasis in original). Sharpe pointedly links all three terms of this book's subtitle – climate, Blackness, crisis – as inextricably bound to one another. I argue that the work of thinking across, to return to my phrasing from Chakrabarty, seemingly "incommensurable scales," has an alternate lineage within a growing archive of Black Studies that understands the ongoing crisis of antiblackness through the lens of environmental destruction. This chapter looks at how Black writing and ecological theory animate one another by examining not just scale, but also the figure of the human.

To trace this counterhistory, I build a miniature genealogy of both scale and the Anthropocene through Black Studies, focusing on writers like Sharpe, Sylvia Wynter, Tiffany Lethabo King, Joshua Bennett, and Zakkiyah Iman Jackson to locate alternative modes of thinking that use, as King phrases it, "Black thought, [as] a place where momentum and velocity as normal vectors are impeded" and, in doing so, "arrests the normative epistemic flow and the violence of the narrativity of humanist thought" (16). In this way, this chapter offers a pause to the narrative arc of the book thinking about how the problematics of scale that feel eminently contemporary have a longer genealogy within Black Studies. Part of the paradox of thinking the Anthropocene is that although the Anthropocene strikes us as very contemporary, the Anthropocene is also geologically long. I seek to renarrate the Anthropocene by looking at how, as early as the 1970s, Wynter is writing about the ways in which any one moment of crisis is distributed across "race, class, gender, sexual orientation, ethnicity, struggles over the environment, global warming, severe climate change, the sharply unequal distribution of the earth resources" ("Unsettling" 260). For Wynter and the other writers in this chapter, there is a sense that the *Anthropos* of the Anthropocene is a limited category. Each of these writers, in different ways, looks to literary form to reimagine both human and literary genres, highlighting the always multiple and operative scales of the contemporary. There is not the fetishization of species-level thinking that plagues much ecological theory nor the prioritization of another scale of critique, like the economic. Indeed, these writers provide us with what I describe as a critically long Anthropocene to locate a dual movement that oscillates between "environmental history sedimented in ongoing unequal exposure but also reveals insurgent visions of an environmental future" (Roane and Hobsey). This transscalar mode requires an interrogation of form. Wynter herself is invested in critiquing the specific "genre of the human" that has been circumscribed by a white, hegemonic form of humanity ("Unsettled," 288). Her usage of genre further underlines the intimacy between both human and literary genres, tying together the questions of scale, race, and crisis pointedly. All of the authors in this chapter, that is, are equally invested in the heuristic and material possibilities of the novel in imagining a more equitable world.

Dispersed throughout this chapter is a reading of N. K. Jemisin's 2020 novel, *The City We Became*. Moving away from realism entirely, I take up Jemisin's speculative fiction as a way to demonstrate that Black literature, particularly Afrofuturist literature, provides us with a vantage from which to see the transscalar at play. *The City We Became* is a book that is defined by crisis – from 9/11 to climate change to Indigenous genocide to an imagined alien invasion – but it also understands how these crises do not act as individual puncta, but rather are contrapuntal, drawing attention to the deeply engrained and symbiotic histories of anti-Black violence and anthropogenic climate change. Wenzel argues that part of the issue with understanding the uneven distribution of climate change and subtending climate injustice has to do with how particular literary forms exert a stranglehold on our critical imaginaries. Even unbounded by realism, she argues, genre fiction often ends up reproducing "predominant narratives" that remain "inadequate for apprehending the challenges of the present" (*Disposition*, 33). One of the key arguments of *Transscalar Critique* is that this is indeed correct, but starting in Chapter 3, I look at how there are existent forms that challenge this inadequacy. This is not to say that Jemisin necessarily offers a paradigm for thinking through the joint histories of racialized and climatic violence that can be replicated by other writers, but I do argue that we can catch glimmers of new imaginaries that take form when detached from the gravities of crisis realism.

Building upon the formal interrogation of this chapter, the fourth chapter, "Improbable Metaphor: Jesmyn Ward and the Asymmetries of the Anthropocene," turns to Jesmyn Ward to look at how Anthropocene criticism scales up, imagining humanity as an undifferentiated geologic force at the expense of an accounting with the ways in which ecological crisis is inseparable from the current crisis of anti-blackness. Beginning with a short critique of Dave Eggers's *Zeitoun*, I look at how Ward's fiction which centers around Hurricane Katrina demonstrates the inextricability of geology, climate, and Blackness, while critiquing the scalar abstraction performed in much ecological theory. Eggers's novel remains limited in its scale, focusing solely on the redemptive narrative of an individual family and replicating the logic of crisis realism. The work of Ward, however, provides a counterpoint to this model of crisis mediation. Set in the Faulkner-esque town of Bois Sauvage, her novels are an interrogation of the way that crisis operates across scales.

Moreover, for Ward, thinking about the crisis of scale requires an interrogation of literary form. After living through Katrina's simultaneous environmental and racial violence, Ward describes how she felt like the storm "unmade the world, tree by water by house by person [. . .] Even in language, it had reduced us to improbable metaphor" (163). For Ward, to think in the mode of "improbable metaphor" is to recognize the violence that exists at the nexus of race and the environment while also articulating a new futural tense that moves across scales. I trace this across Ward's three novels, blending all three together to provide a kaleidoscopic perspective on how climate and race are forever entwined in the long history of environmental destruction and anti-Black violence that is embedded in the Mississippi Delta. This is, of course, most readily true in her Hurricane Katrina novel, *Salvage the Bones*, which incorporates myth alongside its realist structure to think through the ongoing crisis of anti-Black violence and Hurricane Katrina. But it is also true of her other works, from the FEMA-inflected landscape of *Sing, Unburied, Sing*, where the Deepwater Horizon explosion exasperates the environmental inequities wrought by Katrina, to her debut novel, *Where the Line Bleeds*, set in the summer doldrums before Katrina. In all of Ward's work, I argue, temporal, spatial, and ontological scales begin to collide with one another as the structure of the novel begins to fray. In particular, I look at how, in *Sing, Unburied, Sing*, this intentional blurring of the line between fantasy and realism creates an alternative ecology, an intimacy and textual closeness between these disparate hermeneutic scales so that the form of her work imagines a provisional ecology of readership.

The final chapter of *Transscalar Critique*, "Unmitigated Blackness: Paul Beatty's Transscalar Satire," continues to turn away from realism by looking at an alternate literary tradition, satire. Julian Murphet argues that satire is, in fact, "the time-honored genre" for thinking outside "the ideological current of humanism and the inhumanity of the industrializing marketplace" and is, therefore, primed for Anthropocene narratives (654). Outside of both capital and anthropocentrism, then, Murphet argues that satire is able to simultaneously think the Anthropocene and maintain its mode of political critique. Like Ward's fiction dissolving into fantasy, Beatty produces a new mode of Anthropocene literature that responds to the continual crisis of anti-Black violence, specifically the continual police killing of unarmed Black men in America. Although his most recent novel is most clearly written under the shadow of the deaths of Trayvon Martin and Michael Brown (among others), Beatty's work, starting with his 1996 debut, *The White Boy Shuffle*, has long been concerned with the crisis of Blackness in post-Civil Rights America. At the same time, he is also very invested in questions of environmentalism, economics, and nationhood. Satire, I argue, allows Beatty to think at the scale of Blackness at the same time that he is thinking about what it means to exist in the Anthropocene. Although Beatty's work certainly is not traditionally read as part of an environmental canon, his writing makes it clear that he is invested in the way in which a transscalar approach is necessary to understand race. As the protagonist of *The Sellout* asks a friend basking in the ecstasy of Obama's election, "'And what about the Native Americans? What about the Chinese, the Japanese, the Mexicans, the poor, the forests, the water, the air, the fucking California condor?'" (289). For Beatty, to think the crisis of Blackness in the contemporary is also to think about "the fucking California condor." We cannot leave behind any of these metrics to prioritize any one mode of reading.

Beatty's satire rejects any stable ground beneath its object of critique; it is perpetually turning in on itself. In this way, Beatty's work begins to anticipate its own readings, creating not just a transscalar mode of literary fiction, but also a transscalar mode of critique. A book like his novel *Tuff*, for example, is aware of how it is too easy to override race politics with a prioritization of the economic, thus preempting any type of conclusive Marxist reading. His debut novel, *The White Boy Shuffle*, satirizes the cosmetic multiculturalism of corporate America while also maintaining the necessary thrust of identity politics. *Slumberland* complicates what we mean by a species, thus making difficult an extractive new materialist or even Anthropocentric reading. Beginning with the Rodney King beatings in *The White Boy Shuffle* and the shooting and killing of the narrator's unnamed father in *The Sellout*, Beatty's novels ask what it means to be Black in America today. Beatty doesn't offer any type of definitive answer, but rather uses the transscalar possibilities of satire to continually think what it means to exist in an Anthropocene present where racism is climatic. Beatty produces transscalar fiction that is able to create what *The Sellout*'s narrator calls "Unmitigated Blackness": "the acceptance of contradiction not being a sin" (277). And this, to me, is what is at the heart of a transscalar approach to fiction. It is a way to accept contradiction not as shortcoming or pitfall, but as a necessary outgrowth of literary criticism. Transscalar critique, in the case of Beatty, is what Sharpe calls the possibility of "seeing and reading otherwise" (117), in a present that is defined by the claustrophobia of continual crisis.

Chapter 1

Crisis Realism: Writing Economically, Thinking Ecologically

Senator, you asked me my opinion as an economist, but unfortunately this is a matter for psychology.

Benjamin Bernanke, testifying to Congress on the subprime mortgage crisis

We establish tribunals to judge offenses and crimes; we seek to say who the culprit is. Who? A question in the singular. It's precisely that one I'm abandoning for another, rarer, that we never pose, in the plural.

Michel Serres, Biogea

In January 2011, the Financial Crisis Inquiry Commission (FCIC), headed by Phil Angelides and made up of four Republican appointees and six Democrats, submitted *The Financial Crisis Inquiry Report* to Congress. The report begins with a brief outline of its aims: "This report endeavors to expose the facts, identify responsibility, unravel myths, and help us understand how the crisis could have been avoided. It is an attempt to record history, not to rewrite, nor allow it to be rewritten" (xv). Although this passage scans as standard introductory fare, there is a generic logic that underpins it. In its prefatory material, the FCIC is laying out a very clear understanding of the 2008 subprime mortgage crisis. The 2008 global financial meltdown that brought the world economy to its knees, it argues, has been shrouded in "myths," and it is now, with the 20/20 vantage of hindsight, time to "identify responsibility." The FCIC continues: "The crisis was the result of human action and inaction, not of Mother Nature or computer models gone haywire [. . .] To paraphrase Shakespeare, the fault lies not in the stars, but in us" (xvii). What becomes increasingly clear, as this preface continues, is the scale of crisis. At the root cause of the 2008 financial crisis, the FCIC argues, are individuals that can be held responsible. Tethered to this mode of reading is a formal conceit. The report seeks to "explain in *clear, understandable* terms how our complex financial system worked, how the pieces fit together, and how the crisis occurred" (xii; emphasis added). The FCIC wants to leverage "clear, understandable" diction to get to the heart of the subprime mortgage crisis.

What is suggested by the FCIC in these opening pages is a twofold understanding of crisis. First, there is the scale at which it wants to read the crisis. There are individuals who are responsible, not, as the Shakespeare citation suggests, cosmic forces. Second, there is a formal premise. The FCIC seeks to claw back the diffuse technical jargon of finance (not to mention the equally diffuse literary language of Shakespeare), to sound out a genre for reading crisis. This is what I describe throughout this chapter as "crisis realism." Crisis realism relies upon a mappable and representable logic of cause and effect, moving from system to subject, replicating the same genre of thinking that Michel Serres pinpoints in the above epigraph: thinking of "the singular," rather than the "plural." What is left out in the rescaling, as this chapter will argue, is an investigation into both the mechanics of neoliberalism and the ecological dimensions of economic crisis. The FCIC misses the transscalar force of crisis as it seeks to "record history" and to assign blame to individuals.

Annie McClanahan begins her study of behavioral economics and realist literary form with a similar understanding of the missed opportunity in the wake of the 2008 financial crisis. "Why, at the same time we frequently described the global financial system as impossibly complex, massive, and impenetrable," she asks, "did we also want to insist on the causal power of personal ailing or individual folly?" (22) McClanahan is articulating a paradox inherent in representations of the 2008 financial crisis. On the one hand, there is the sense that the market itself is "complex, massive, and impenetrable." The market, in this rendering, remains ontologically discrete and "impenetrable" from analysis, a scale too large to critique. On the other hand, at this moment of crisis, our hermeneutic modes of reading return to the "causal power of personal ailing or individual folly." In this reversion to "individual folly," crisis is rescaled from the impenetrability of the market to the psychology of the individual. Just like Ben Bernanke, we start asking psychological questions when we should be asking economic ones.

These two scales of financial crisis, the impenetrability of the market and the culpability of the individual, suggest that our understanding of financial crisis is forced to shuttle between two vastly different poles in order to make itself legible. This is what McClanahan describes as an economic "problem of scale" (29). By reverting to this human measurement, we end up focusing our analytic crosshairs on the micro, missing the way larger (and the more insidious) mechanics of neoliberalism are responsible for that very crisis. McClanahan traces this throughout a large body of 2008 literature and film, arguing that there is a fixation on thinking of the financial crisis in terms of human psychology.[1] This is a logic of scalar invariance where, as McClanahan writes, "the difference between individuals and the market [. . .] is merely a matter of scale," which rests on a presupposition of fungibility where we can just as easily jump from one to another (31).[2] That is, there is a belief that we can move seamlessly between scales, allowing the individual to take the place of the system and vice versa.

This is what crisis realism describes: a generic form that forecloses on systemic critique in order to reify individual culpability. The scale of the individual is taken as the defining metric of and for financial crisis. By focusing on the individual, crisis realism short-circuits systemic critique by remaining mired in the doldrums of individual culpability. Consequently, the market remains conspicuously absent

---

1. McClanahan is not alone in this reading but enters a rich and varied conversation. Alison Shonkwiler's history of financial fiction also describes the "generic tendency of the novel to reframe structural conflicts as personal ones" (102). Jeff Kinkle and Alberto Toscano plot this onto a domestic topography, describing the post-2008 impulse to resolve "widespread anxiety and hardship either into the simplistic identification of culprits or into the backdrop for the trials and tribulations of the nuclear family and the aspirational individual" ("Filming," 39). Indeed, in a special issue of *Novel* dedicated to neoliberalism and contemporary fiction, Nancy Armstrong and John Marx argue, "It can seem as if the contemporary novel is more like a diagnostic tool than a fount of actionable information or a repository of instructions for conduct" (164). Anna Kornbluh weighs in through her longer history of the realist novel, writing in near polemical terms: "In our epoch of global financial turmoil, we have not only to reckon with collateralized debt obligations, toxic assets, and zombie banks, but also with the obfuscating din of economic discourses that explain away the contradictions of capital as merely psychological phenomena" (*Realizing*, 156).
2. This is a problem that Anna Tsing describes as one wherein we have begun to believe "that everything on earth – and beyond – might be scalable, and thus exchangeable at market values. This was utilitarianism, which eventually congealed as modern economics and contributed to forging more scalability – or at least its appearance" (40).

from crisis realist texts as the individual is continually reproduced as the barometer of and for crisis.³ In this chapter, I take crisis realism as my starting point to argue that this is an ineffective way to map financial crisis. I argue that we need a transscalar approach to financial crisis. Financial crisis, like the way I read 9/11 in my Introduction, extends beyond human scales and forces a reckoning with a world in excess of those humans. The monoscalar imaginary of crisis realism leaves the conditions that produce crisis outside the frame of analysis. This chapter, then, starts as a critique of crisis realism, but then turns to a transscalar reading of the 2008 financial crisis that responds to the immediacy of financial crisis, while also situating it within the larger crisis of life in the Anthropocene.⁴

To make this argument, I first outline how crisis realism has become the dominant genre for writing and critiquing the 2008 financial crisis. I trace this through Dave Eggers's *A Hologram for the King* (2012), Martha McPhee's novel *Dear Money* (2010), and Michael Lewis's nonfictional account *The Big Short* (2010). These texts are emblematic of some of the dominant tropes of crisis realism but are also self-conscious in pointing to how their ostensible realist frames are not wholly successful in mediating financial crisis. I focus on both literary fiction and nonfiction to make the case that this generic mode has subsumed both the literary and the popular imaginary in the wake of the financial crisis. At the same time, I turn to these books to find moments that are productive in their failure to capture the immensity of financial crisis. By inhabiting their formal failures, I point to how these texts produce a mode of reading that is pedagogical by gesturing towards a type of ecological thinking that they are ultimately unable to fully inhabit.⁵

---

3. I should add that it is not just in crisis realist texts that the market remains absent. Arjun Appadurai begins his account of the 2008 financial crisis "by noting the enormous and still under-theorized role of the market as a cultural fact in our world today in the United States" (56).
4. This rereading of financial crisis has also started to percolate within the cultural mainstream. See in particular the *New Yorker*'s podcast series of conversations between Adam Davidson, Henry Paulson, and David Remnick, "The Financial Crisis and Climate Crisis."
5. My language of *failure* is meant to evoke critics like Julietta Singh who have taken the queer politics of failure from thinkers like Jack Halberstam and José Muñoz and brought it to bear on ecological politics. "In failing to master, in confronting our own desires for mastery where we least expect or recognize those desires," Singh writes, "we become vulnerable to other possibilities for living, for being together in common, for *feeling* injustice and refusing it without the need to engage it through forms of conquest" (21; emphasis in original).

This is where my work departs from that of critics like McClanahan. McClanahan is content to critique these financial crisis novels. "The credit-crisis novel reminds us of the difficulty of representing the individual as an autonomous market actor endowed with infinite consumer freedom," she writes, "while also burdening that individual with full responsibility for his own reproduction in an economy fueled by consumer debt" (54). For McClanahan, it is enough to filter these texts through a Marxist framework and formulate a larger point about "an economy fueled by consumer debt." Although this is an important starting point, it misses the more generative aspects of these works. The "difficulty" of this rescaling produces an opening into how we read financial crisis. It is not a failure in a pejorative sense, but a productive one. That is, financial crisis models the impossibility for mediating smoothly between one scale and another, suggesting the limit point of an invariant scalar paradigm. To make this final point, I finish this chapter with a reading of Joshua Ferris's *The Unnamed* (2010). This novel is transscalar in the way the economic and the environmental become co-constitutional inflection points. This is indexed not just by the content of the book where the environmental is imbricated within the logics of financial crisis, but by Ferris's foray into formal experimentation. As I made clear in the Introduction, it is not just nonhuman scales that the transscalar accounts for, but literary ones. This formal experimentation is a transscalar approach to what it means to think of the specifics of financial crisis against the backdrop of the Anthropocene. In this twinned mode of critique, I arrive at the subtitle of this chapter: writing economically requires a mode of thinking ecologically.

Framing Crisis

In many ways, crisis realism makes sense as a genre of neoliberalism. Just as crisis realism relies upon the individual, so too does neoliberalism reify the individual. Under neoliberalism, the individual subject is taken as the be-all-end-all, what Michel Foucault calls *homo economicus*, or man as "entrepreneur of himself" (226). For Foucault, neoliberalism differentiates itself from classic liberalism by understanding that power works through the individual as "the surface of contact between the individual and the power exercised on him, and so the principle of the regulation of power over the individual will be only this kind of grid of homo economicus" (252). Using the individual as its interface is an intentional trick of scale-shifting built into the DNA of neoliberalism. Neoliberalism purposely obfuscates its own scalar working by presenting us with a smokescreen of the individual. We see only the forest, whether that forest is filled with greedy bankers or imaginary welfare queens, and thus avoid critiquing the larger machinery of neoliberalism by turning to the individual.

We can trace this crisis realist rescaling across the post-2008 crisis narrative archive. Andrew Lawson describes how the individual has been instrumental in "constructing links between cause and effect, identifying villains, and laying blame" in narratives that attempt to mediate the "subprime storm" (50). In other words, once the dust and debt settled, the impulse was to craft a narrative that revealed specific human actors responsible for the crisis. We see this in *The Big Short*, as Lewis ends his Preface by cataloguing the specific individuals (and hedge funds) who had the "nerve" to peer into the "black box of modern finance" in order to "[grasp] the flaws of its machinery" (xviii). Even though Lewis is critiquing the larger structural conditions that resulted in the subprime meltdown, he can do so only by thinking in generic terms of villains and heroes. This is equally true of *A Hologram for the King*, where Eggers plots the post-2008 crisis through his protagonist, Alan. The novel follows Alan, an underemployed, middle-aged salesman sent to Saudi Arabia to secure an audience with King Abdullah at the fictionalized King Abdullah Economic City and eventually sell him IT software for holographic meetings. From the outset, the text alerts us to its status as post-2008 artifact. We can see this as Alan reflects on his inability to pay for his daughter Kit's college tuition:

> He could not pay [Kit's] tuition because he had made a series of foolish decisions in his life. He had not planned well. He had not had courage when he needed it. His decisions had been short sighted. The decisions of his peers had been short sighted. These decisions had been foolish and expedient. (4)

In this opening monologue, Eggers offers a hermeneutic framework: Alan is representative of the individuals who stand on the other side of the looking glass to Lewis's flawed machinery. The text pivots from a rumination about Alan's inability to pay for his daughter's college to the "decisions of his peers," thus reading Alan as representative of the individual motivations that produced this moment of global financial destitution. This passage points to the scalable invariance outlined above: Alan is at once responsible for this moment, but in his metonymical rendering, he becomes fungible, easily substituted for any one of his "peers."

Daniel Mattingly doubles down on this, reading *A Hologram for the King* as steeped in this mode of financial crisis metonymy: "Alan himself is emblematic of America's suddenly vulnerable middle class fearing further financial upheaval. Alan embodies an older, more personal, industrial and manufacturing-based America seeking redemption" (106). Mattingly uses metonymy to pinpoint Eggers's economic critique as hinged to the tension and differences between industrial and financial capital. This is voiced by Alan's father, Ron, in a phone call. "But the bridges I did not see coming," Ron tells Alan.

> By God, we're having other people make our *bridges*. And now you're in Saudi Arabia, selling a hologram to the pharaohs. That takes the cake [. . .] These are actual *things*. They're making actual *things* over there, and we're making websites and holograms. (84; emphasis in original)

Here, the scale of Eggers's critique is brought to the fore: he is offering a criticism of the abstraction performed by financialization.[6] The crisis of financial crisis is the loss of the individual from the process of production. This reading of crisis is an inversion of the FCIC. Instead of looking for the individuals at the center of financial crisis, Eggers is making the reciprocal claim that financial crisis is precisely about the lack of individuals within financial markets. What is telling here is that Eggers's diagnostic mode is not all that different from the FCIC. Both the FCIC and Alan, from different ends of the spectrum, are attempting to humanize the economic. The FCIC wants the individuals responsible for the crisis to be held accountable; Eggers thinks that the reason there was a crisis in the first place is that there weren't any individuals acting responsibly. Although the politics behind these impulses may be different, both the FCIC and Eggers are looking for the individual at the heart of the crisis.

Both of these texts, in short, are trying to find a way to lay the blame at someone else's feet by rescaling financial crisis back to the individual. This understanding backbones Eggers's continual critique

---

6. This particular literary impulse is what Leigh Claire La Berge and Alison Shonkwiler describe as an aspiration in financial crisis fiction to "expose and make legible the conditions that have been produced by so-called illegible abstractions of finance capital" (8).

of abstraction mouthed by Alan. In a climactic moment, Alan reflects on his former career working for Schwinn Bicycles:

> Alan's people had come to America from Ireland during the famine [. . .] They started manufacturing brass buttons, and the buttons had led to a foundry in South Boston [. . .] Their names were all over buildings in Boston. Churches and hospital wings. Then there was the Depression, and everyone started over. Alan's father had no second home in Chatham. He was a foreman at the Stride Rite factory in Roxbury. He did fine and saved enough for his son, Alan, to go to college. But Alan dropped out of college to sell Fuller Brush products, and then sold bicycles, and did fine, extremely well for a while there, until he and others decided to have others, ten thousand miles away, build the things they sold, and soon left himself with nothing to sell. (64)

This passage functions metonymically to produce a swansong in miniature for the American manufacturing industry. At the heart of this passage is an account of the collapse of American manufacturing and white masculinity that relies upon the key term "decision." This is a central motif through the text. As indexed in the earlier scene, the word is central to the dissipated agency that Eggers imagines as the transition into neoliberalism. This word points out from the text to an alternative history, a history wherein Alan and his cohort did not decide to outsource manufacturing and, therefore, did not lose their job and the world did not end with Alan becoming "irrelevant" (189).[7] Put simply, *A Hologram for the King* tries to diagnose the current crisis as the shift from bicycles to holograms. In this sense, it becomes a crisis of materiality, a crisis of abstraction wherein Alan can no longer "return to one's origin, build something lasting" (234).[8] Eggers takes this search for "something lasting" to its limit, satirizing it through Alan's attempt to sell a hologram. Implicit within this critique is the suggestion that

---

7. Interestingly, Serres read a conjoined etymology of the terms "crisis" and "decision": "The word crisis thus reveals its legal origin. It involves a decision made by a jury and their foreman. The word de-cision, of Latin origins, means to cut in two, as with scissors" (*Times*, xi). This perhaps explains why critics remain continually invested in trying to locate the moment of decision that ends up producing crisis.
8. Sianne Ngai critiques this as the "impulse to triumphantly uncover a thingly substance [. . .] as the hidden truth of abstraction" that runs rampant in personalized accounts of neoliberalism ("Visceral Abstractions," 52). Roitman puts this in terms specific to the 2008 financial crisis, describing a narrative impulse "to document a differential between the 'real economy,' on the one hand, and

if different decisions had been made, crisis would have been averted. Alan's point is commonplace across the political spectrum and plays right into the hands of white grievance, just as easily lifted from the rhetoric of Bernie Sanders as from Donald Trump. These agents of financial doom, the story goes, made a decision to outsource jobs and thus, if only they could return to their "origins," crisis would be rectified and nullified; America would still be great.[9] Crisis is the result of the outsourcing of American manufacturing and blame should be taken by the individuals responsible for it.

What I want to make clear is that Eggers's individual scaling of financial crisis is not so much a critique of neoliberalism as it is a critique of the individuals operating under neoliberalism. Eggers's nostalgic pining for a world of "origins" and manufacturing, moreover, is also bound up with the reproduction of a particularly troubling gendered and racial paradigm. The text acts as an effigy for an eclipsed mode of production that underwrote white American masculinity and, by extension, American hegemony. It is the end of an era when, as Alan reminisces, it was "easy on guys like me" (134). This white masculinity-in-crisis is a dominant trope of post-2008 texts, recycling some of the post-9/11 literary forms that I critiqued in my Introduction by neutralizing systemic critique through recourse to pre-existing literary and critical forms. Instead of co-opting the planetary dimensions of crisis smuggled into the fringes of the *9/11 Commission Report*, many post-2008 narratives miss the way in which financial crisis exists on a transscalar horizon by borrowing the worst tropes of 9/11 fiction.[10]

Diana Negra and Yvonne Tasker take to task the specific recycling of these motifs: "In an era in which accounts of economic decline frequently privilege male subjectivity, it is instructive to consider the

---

a 'fictive' or 'overvalued' state of affairs, which is seemingly immaterial, on the other" (43). That said, this very idea of abstraction has a vexed status in our current moment. "[Abstraction] is itself one of the greatest abstractions of modern critical thought," Timothy Bewes writes, "a term whose endlessly recursive quality is liable to induce a sense of vertigo" (1200).

9. This is an aesthetic rescaling of crisis that Kinkle and Toscano have identified as "an immensely oversimplified narrativization of amorphous or anonymous global power dynamics" (*Cartographies*, 69).
10. Laura Finch describes how the 2008 financial crisis activated a very specific formal framing: "[In] response to this amorphous event, the desire for a narrative frame is an integral part of the experience of the event itself" (734). Roitman takes this further, arguing this is symptomatic of crisis itself: "Crisis is taken to be the basis for a method, permitting and justifying narration in terms of analogous historical events and logical recurrences" (69). This is remarkably true of

renewal of long-established tropes of masculinity in 'crisis'" (2). This is problematic for financial crisis narratives. The falling man narrative of post-9/11 literature morphs into what Negra and Tasker describe as the "failing man" (9).[11] The hedge fund manager protagonist, Adam, of Jonathan Dee's Pulitzer Prize-nominated 2008-crisis novel, concisely phrases it: "[What] people didn't appreciate was how fragile a state it was. You had to work so hard just to maintain it: let up even for a moment and that was where time took over" ("'Stuck between Meanings,'" 243). Another way to describe this is that the scale of white masculinity is redeployed in this moment of crisis, but this scale is even more restricted in its analytic and descriptive capacity.

This is to say that reactivating this gendered and racial logic of 9/11 is another place wherein the monoscalar imaginary of crisis realist form returns to an exhausted mode of critique. In a particularly revealing passage in *A Hologram for the King*, we are confronted with the limits of this critical paradigm:

> Some days he could encompass the world. Some days he could see for miles. Some days he climbed over the foothills of indifference to see the landscape of his life and future for what it was: mappable, traversable, achievable. Everything he wanted to do had been done before, so why couldn't he do it again? He could. If only he could engage on a continual basis. If only he could draw up a plan and execute it. (16)

post-2008 fiction. Suman Gupta reads this as a recycling of literary forms related to "more or less sensationalist accounts of insider-experiences and exposés and formulaic 'genre fiction,' and their modernist and Victorian predecessors" (462). Kirk Boyle and Daniel Morzowski also take up this historical framing: "Analyses proliferate as the frame of historical analogue slipped further into the past, from the Savings and Loan scandal of the 1980s to the fuel crisis of the 1970s and onwards of the dark days of the 1930s" (xii).

11. This is to say that the very bodies that were supposed to secure the perpetuation and post-9/11 restitution of American hegemony begin to collapse on themselves post-2008. Hamilton Carroll describes the double-edge of this "failing man" paradigm of white masculinity: "If the phenomenon of masculinity in crisis that is a constitutive feature of cultural discourse in the contemporary United States serves primarily as a ruse or a lure through which (predominantly white) masculinity has been able to secure and maintain its privilege, the global recession has put pressure on the typical narrative tropes of masculine empowerment enabled by such crisis discourse" (203). That is, this discourse of masculinity is no longer taken *a priori* as it was in post-9/11 novels. Rather, there is an increase in the "pressure" that is exerted by "global recession" on this gendered and racialized paradigm.

This scene highlights the limits of crisis realism. Alan is imagining a cartography of totality, the fantasy of a fully realized realism of capital that allows him to see everything and, therefore, formulate a "plan," a decision on how to remedy crisis. Instead of looking at how crisis might be imagined as an opening into something else, Alan only wants to "do it again," to return to a pre-crisis equilibrium. But, of course, this desire to "encompass the world" is impossible. Frederic Jameson is precise here: "[No] one [has] ever seen that totality, nor is capitalism ever visible as such, but only in its symptoms [. . .] Every representation is partial" (*Representing*, 6). This partiality is what Eggers is using Alan to rail against. Partiality is what makes it impossible to use the individual (whether that be a person or novel) to mediate crisis as it exists across scales. Partiality, however, is generative if we start thinking about crisis in different terms.

The Time of Crisis

When Alan aspires to find totality but is left traversing the "foothills of indifference," there is something instructive in how the novel suggests thinking financial crisis might also be like thinking the Anthropocene. Against a landscape of "indifference," this impossibility of totality suggests a way that we can rethink Alan's aspiration of totality transscalarly. Describing how the Anthropocene is also a confrontation with an excess beyond any type of totalizable representation, Juliana Chow picks up on this idea of partiality as critical practice. Critiquing "metonymic comprehensiveness," Chow argues that this partiality is not a shortcoming, but rather a productive formal feature of life in the Anthropocene (129). What we need to do, Chow argues, is come to terms with that partiality and give up our fantasies of totality and mastery. Capital and the Anthropocene, in their scalar vastness, both remain outside of our grasp, and this means that we have to think differently about how mediate them.[12] And it is here, in the dissonance of totality mapped across an arid, apocalyptic, and oil-built topography,

---

12. Although not explicitly engaging with the Anthropocene, this also resonates with Shonkwiler's reading of financial crisis novels that "[confront] the problem of totality new ways" through "an aesthetic mode that seeks to undo, or at least to disturb, the corporate drive toward a unified totality, calling attention to these projected coherences" (72). Shonkwiler is looking for the gaps and failures of texts that interrupt narratives of "unified totality."

that we glean the ways in which ecological thinking begins to percolate through financial crisis writing.

Alan, stuck within the "landscape of his life" in the petro-vista of Saudi Arabia, is trying to sound out a new form of reading. If he cannot formulate a "plan," he needs to figure out new ways of reading the world. By the end of the novel, we see him coming to terms with what this means. After becoming involved with a Saudi Arabian doctor, Zahara, the temporal structure of the text begins to shift. Instead of returning to a pre-crisis equilibrium to "do it again," Alan begins to think about crisis as non-teleological, not so much an interruption, but a new way of being: "Then maybe I'll stay, Alan said. He wasn't being sent away, after all, and he couldn't go home yet, not empty handed like this. So he would stay. He had to. Otherwise who would be here when the King came again?" (312). This moment is about staking out repetition as a new formal vocabulary. It is no longer the teleology of crisis realism that attempts to work through crisis, but an inhabitation with the moment of crisis, what Alan calls a mode of "amnesia" (312). If crisis isn't something that can be rectified, if Alan can't merely return home and start over, then perhaps our terms of critique need to become what Chow calls "experimental and tentative" in the face of this ongoing crisis (118).

Part of the problem is that financial crisis, like the Anthropocene (but unlike, say, 9/11), is not a singular event and, therefore, as Pieter Vermeulen claims, "lacks the readability and narratability of 9/11, and [requires] different strategies of engagement for which no narrative templates [are] available" (14–15). In fact, both financial crisis and the Anthropocene are recalcitrant to the very possibility of a singular "narrative template" as these are not events in the way we tend to think of crises. Jameson summarizes how this works for financial crisis. Financial crises "are not self-explanatory," he argues, as their "very nature as 'events' in the first place is not secured in advance" and must "be explained in order to come into visible existence as temporal phenomenon" (*Antinomies*, 211). The temporality of financial crisis is belated, becoming intelligible only retroactively.[13] This is also what it means to live in the Anthropocene where we did not know we

---

13. Part of this belatedness is due to the way neoliberalism is hinged to a necessary repetition of crisis. Eva Cherniavsky and Tom Foster argue that crisis "seems no longer cyclical but a permanent feature of life in late capitalist society" (712). This is a way of saying that a financial crisis is particularly asymmetrical, and what is a crisis for one set of people is not a crisis for others.

had been writing ourselves into the geologic record for the past few centuries. A mortgage, a house, a car payment that had looked benign or like the bedrock of securing financial futurity turn out to be malignant, slowly causing a financial cancer. Indeed, even the language of "toxic assets" suggests this type of eerie cohabitation and proximity to environmental crisis. Unlike other forms of crisis that pockmark our contemporary – from 9/11 to COVID-19 – and that allow for the fantasy of a pre-crisis past, financial crisis and the Anthropocene make it increasingly difficult to mark the space of crisis/non-crisis. Crisis seems to insinuate itself more and more into the banality of the everyday.[14]

The banality of crisis also impacts narrative form. If crisis is no longer an interruption but an ongoing condition, what sort of stories do we tell about crisis? This is a problem at the heart of *Transscalar Critique*. As crisis becomes the conditions of life, what sort of formal structures might we use to narrate this crisis? Eric Cazdyn takes this question up as he thinks through financial crisis. Financial crisis, he argues, is no longer "defined by its short-termness – requiring a decision on the spot," but rather a constitutive temporality "with no possibility of deferral, evasion, or repression" (3). We return here to the key idea of "decision." This new mode of crisis does not allow for this type of agentive account of subjectivity. With "no possibility of deferral," Cazdyn continues, "[Crisis] is extended, rolled out flat all the way to the indefinite 'long term.' And there is the meantime, now permanent, thus permitting the present to fully colonize the future" (46–47). Like Alan realizing that he cannot return to his pre-crisis world, financial crisis is a confrontation with a perennial "meantime," a consumptive and insidious "present," "[colonizing] the future" and foreclosing on a crisis-free world. This *longue durée*

---

14. Critics like David Harvey are part of a rich history theorizing this nexus between what we might call the non-crisis of financial crisis: "[Crises] are, in effect, not only inevitable but also necessary, since this is the only way in which balance can be restored and the internal contradictions of capital accumulation can be at least temporarily resolved. Crises are, as it were, the irrational rationalizers of an always unstable capitalism" (71). This is a similar line of thought that is increasingly being taken up in Anthropocene theory. Stephanie LeMenager, for example, has coined the term "everyday Anthropocene" to describe how life in the Anthropocene is a continual transscalar confrontation with crisis: "By 'everyday Anthropocene' I imply the present tense, lived time of the Anthropocene, and I recommend paying attention to what it means to live, day by day, through climate shift and the economic and sociological injuries that underwrite it" ("Climate Change and the Struggle," 225).

of crisis, the "meantime" of the amnesiac in *A Hologram for the King*, understands crisis as repetition, a condition of being.

This is where we might see an opening in the novel beyond neoliberalism's individualized terms of critique. By the end of the book, Eggers has modeled a crisis that is always present. The critical impulse of unmasking and attempting to reveal the causal or agentive origin of crisis, therefore, is misguided. One of the issues that continually plagues crisis realist narratives is a fixation on human subjects. One way of approaching financial crisis at the transscalar level, then, is not just to start thinking about the individuals of the market, but to start thinking how the market itself exists on a scale in excess of those humans.

Scales of the Market

Scaling out from individual people, however, is harder than it sounds. Towards the end of McPhee's *Dear Money*, for example, the novelist-turned-stock-broker India Palmer takes a moment of respite from her daily grind as a Wall Street power broker. She pauses and thinks about what we mean when we say "the market":

> It was something beyond logic or reckoning. Something firm beneath our feet. Something that kept us warm at night and the rain from falling on our heads. Something to look upon. Some landscape to survey and assess and regard. Something real. Real estate. (338).

This passage is filled with contradictions as McPhee uses India to ponder an ontological dissection of the market. She moves between scales, starting out with something ineffable "beyond logic or reckoning," only to move in the next sentence into the more manageable scale of an entity "beneath our feet." "It's fascinating," India tells her boss after her first day of work, "like a machine" (184).[15] While machine-like metaphors may be commonplace in financial novels dating back to Frank Norris, McPhee uses India to try out another scale of description a few pages later. As India and her colleagues discuss "Frannie, Freddie, Ginnie," India again circuits the market through a machinic metaphor before she stops and realizes that this

---

15. I should add that the FCIC report also features a section called "The CDO Machine."

does not quite work: "What best described them as a group, was a perfect rationality and unambiguous self-interest. Or that is what I recall believing at that moment, before I came to know them, before they became human to me" (189). Here, we have two different images working at two different scales. On the one hand, the market appears as it did earlier, "beyond logic or reckoning," as "a perfect rationality." On the other hand, the market is rescaled as it slowly "became human" to India. The market is both machine and human, somehow able to move between these positions fluidly and simultaneously. By continually switching metaphors, McPhee gives us insight into the ways in which we need to approach the market as a transscalar entity, somehow both human and nonhuman.[16]

On the one hand, McPhee uses India to join the naturalist tradition of those like Norris and Theodore Dreiser, who have aligned the market itself with nonhuman forces, what McClanahan describes as the "wildly mixed metaphor of a natural catastrophe" that often saturates post-2008 texts (41).[17] But, on the other hand, the market is also something human, wherein even India herself becomes "part of the organism" (211). This slipperiness between machinic and organic, human and nonhuman metaphors underlines how the market needs to be approached at a transscalar level. This is a generic issue: thinking through this multiply scaled representation of the market stretches the realist novel to the limit. We again return to the two paths of realism that I outlined in my Introduction. An acknowledgment of the more-than-human market means that the realist novel transitions into what Carroll and McClanahan see as the post-2008 "complex ontology"

---

16. As a point of contrast, we can take Philip Mirowski's insightful reading of the 2008 crisis. He provides insight into the ways in which classic neoliberal theory has always relied on the market "as a monolithic entity" that appears as a "static conception" (104, 62). However, as McPhee makes clear, this "monolithic" facade belies a salient ontological plurality. Latour is helpful in unpacking this contrast, writing that anytime we look for the market, we find "nothing solid or durable [. . .] only new phantoms, just as invisible" (*Modes*, 388). For Andrew Hoberek, this becomes a specifically literary problem: "[Following] the subprime mortgage crisis the novel – straining like the news media to think the crisis in the absence of a robust critique of capitalism – figures the gulf between capitalist theory and capitalist reality as a crisis in realistic representation as such" ("Post-recession realism," 48–49).
17. The naturalist references are a dime a dozen in McPhee's novel, particularly as India makes the decision to be swept up in the Pygmalion plot and joins a stock brokerage. India thinks, "I want to be a poor girl in a Dreiser novel and hear the rich man claim me: 'You're my girl now. Come with me. You're mine'" (125).

where realism starts to look a lot like science fiction (658). That is, thinking through the scales of the market starts to fray the scalar invariance of crisis realism.

As much as this is a novelistic problem, it is also a political one. The FCIC also struggles to find a genre to describe the market. When the FCIC tells the origin story of the subprime mortgage crisis, the Committee writes, "Like a science fiction movie in which ordinary household objects turn hostile, familiar market mechanisms were being transformed" (6). Here, objects assume the role of subjects. It is not the human that the FCIC wants to blame, but "household objects" that seem to be doing the acting. The FCIC is introducing a generic multiplicity into its text; this is not the "clear, understandable" language that they staked out initially, but a "science fiction movie." Carroll and McClanahan summarize the FCIC's generic interplay: "Even in the opening pages of this most realist of text, then, we are swept from the documentary impulse of interviews and expert analysis to alien events and the terrifying animation of household appliances" (656). As the FCIC attempts to unmask the individual subjects of financial crisis, it is confronted with the "complex machinery" of neoliberalism that resists reduction to the scale of crisis realism (xxiii). There is an inhuman scale that enters the text, a destabilization enacted by the market in this moment of crisis. As India describes it in *Dear Money*, "I felt possessed by an alien force – the capital markets of the world" (284).[18]

The "alien force" that complicates our genres of reading financial crisis reaches a fever pitch in *The Big Short*. Like McPhee, Lewis toys with naturalized metaphors. We see this when he describes the trader Danny Moses on September 18 waiting for Lehmann Brothers to collapse. "Danny's trading life was man versus man," writes Lewis, "but this felt more like man versus nature: The synthetic CDO had become a synthetic natural disaster" (239). Collateralized Debt Obligations (CDOs), the synthetic trading products that brought the world economy to its knees, have, like household appliances, turned into Frankenstein's monster, displacing human mastery. Even "natural disaster" is supplanted by the "synthetic" crisis. At the very level of image, then, Lewis has to describe the market transscalarly.

18. These "alien" slippages are also prescient for their dovetailing with the new materialist reading of the post-2008 financial topography. Diane Coole and Samantha Frost describe this as a "recognition that particular effects are the outcome of intricate interlocking systems whose interactions and dynamic processes are variable and, for the most part, unpredictable" (29).

Although Lewis promises a glimpse inside the "black box" of the "doomsday machine" (228), he seems to wrestle with a form that continually exceeds itself, pointing to a failure to place humans at the center of his causal schematic.[19]

On the one hand, these texts gesture towards scaling financial crisis through crisis realism's human metrics. Lewis writes, "The catastrophe was foreseeable, yet only a handful noticed" (105). On the other, this does not do justice to the complex narrative that Lewis produces. When Lewis tells the story of Greg Lippmann, an early subprime crisis sage, explaining to American International Group (AIG) that they were insuring worthless bonds, Lewis at first describes a monoscalar account of crisis:

> For a brief moment, Lippmann thought he'd changed the world, all by himself. He had walked into AIG [Financial Products] and had shown them how Deutsche Bank, along with every other Wall Street firm, was playing them for fools, and they'd understood. (84)

However, this account of causality and agency is quickly revoked as Lewis begins the next chapter, rewriting Lippmann's meeting: "[AIG] hadn't. Not really" (85). In this way, *The Big Short* slowly shifts from being a realist account of the crisis into something different. When Lewis describes the financial crisis as a "postmodern literary puzzle," he could just as easily be describing his own book (92).

This postmodern twist seeps through Lewis's footnotes, which begin to resemble those in Vladimir Nabokov's *Pale Fire*.[20] They become a supplement that keeps undercutting the text's realist aspirations. Quite often, these footnotes are aware of their meta-discursive role, offering meditations on the inadequacy of form to capture the scale of the market. For example, as Lewis narrates the history of the short market

---

19. We see an analogous moment when India describes her boss reflecting on the crash in *Dear Money*: "He'd be quoted later as saying that he hadn't understood the fine points, the entire structure, the complexity, but he'd had the gut feel that Wall Street, the financial world, had created a doomsday machine – a machine that people around the globe were oblivious of because they believed we knew what we were doing over here" (312).
20. There is a similar circumlocution in *Dear Money*. In India's attempts to demystify credit default swaps and mortgage tranches, she is constantly using other commodities as analogy. As in Eggers, this is a longing for a solidity to the market by using Toyotas and other manufactured products. This never seems to work; India is always doubling backing on herself, wanting to, as she phrases it, "put it another way" (270).

for CDOs envisaged by its founder, Michael Burry, a footnote breaks the narrative's fourth wall and addresses the reader directly: "Dear Reader: If you have followed the story this far, you deserve not only a gold star, but an answer to a complicated question" (77).[21] This "complicated question," how the market reshaped itself to subsume a huge amount of synthetic risks, is not answered, as Lewis describes a foundational "lack of transparency" at its heart (77).

It is not that the market remains resistant just to reading, but also the way we talk about the market. "Bond market terminology," Lewis writes, "was designed less to convey meaning than to bewilder outsiders" (126). It is not just that we cannot understand the market, but that we have developed vocabularies unable to do the necessary analytic work. Lewis returns to this later, writing, "It's too much to expect the people who run big Wall Street firms to speak plain English, since so much of their livelihood depends on people believing that what they do cannot be translated into plain English" (218). We have now returned to where we started. The "clear, understandable" prose of the FCIC is put into opposition with the belief that Wall Street's logic and workings "cannot be translated into plain English." Even the scale of the language of the market is multiple. It is both above and beyond "plain English." It is, then, a matter of thinking about the market across these scales, not content with the realism that the FCIC fantasizes about, but also not settling with the technical obfuscation performed by financiers.

What Lewis's footnotes do is allow him to inhabit a middle ground between these positions, rethinking his book's generic status. It is as if financial markets exceed realism's ability to, as Steve Eisman, one of the book's protagonists, puts it, "[explain] the world in stories" (153). The footnotes, however, allow Lewis to move between scales. He is, at once, able to develop a plot while also addressing the

---

21. Interestingly, this breakage of form and direct address to the reader is a defining feature of Adam McKay's cinematic adaptation of *The Big Short* (2015), where celebrities, like the late Anthony Bourdain, are brought in to help explain facets of the crisis. We see a similar move in McPhee's novel when India thinks: "And the fact that I cannot tell you, that nobody can tell you – that you had to be there – is the very purpose of all such ceremony" (218). This formal encroachment on the reader/text boundary is symptomatic of post-2008 art. In Rebecca Colesworthy's reading of Martin Scorsese's post-2008 film *The Wolf of Wall Street* (2013), she describes a similar maneuver. "In addressing the camera [. . .] [the protagonist] makes a show of talking to us straight," she writes, "[yet], he makes a pitch [. . .] for the impossibility of understanding his misdeeds" (1170).

reader, inhabiting a dual mode of address that responds to the ways that financial crisis exists along two temporal axes. Throughout the text, Lewis locates temporal disjuncture as a site of crisis. The crisis, Lewis suggests, brings into relief a temporal incongruity: "The model used by Wall Street to price trillions of dollars' worth of derivatives thought of the financial world as an orderly, continuous process" (116). The neoliberal market requires a temporal continuity wherein "the distant future would look more like the present," produced by "the foreshortened, statistically meaningless past to predict the future" (121, 141). Ultimately, this limited temporal imaginary allowed "[the] entire modern world [. . .] to buy now and pay later" (222). But, as Eisman explains, "The models don't have any idea of what this world has become" (161).[22] We no longer live in a time where we have the chance to "pay later." Like living in the Anthropocene, we have moved onto a horizon where we have no idea "what this world has become." Lewis's language anticipates the Anthropocene as a world that has gone beyond the scale and temporal structure of the present. This is a particular problem for realism. As Jameson argues, it is the present that is always at stake in the realist novel: "[The] realistic novelist has a vested interest, an ontological stake, in the solidity of social reality" (*Antinomies*, 5). This "vested interest" continually reproduces "a perpetual present," which "requires a conviction to the massive weight and persistence of the present as such" (*Antinomies*, 28, 145). This mode of realism, like the older financial models used to predict the market, is no longer an accurate picture of "what this world has become." To think the market, then, is to think transscalarly. To understand this new crisis-defined present, we have to start thinking at a level that can account for the Frankensteinian logic of a world of "synthetic natural disaster" and "household objects [turned] hostile."[23] Part of a transscalar approach to economic crisis means writing economically and thinking ecologically.

---

22. McPhee doubles down on this in *Dear Money*, describing India's "abstract sense of how the market reacts" outside of "prescription [. . .] since none exists" (266).
23. My claim here about the shaky ontology of the market troubling realist form is in some respects a rehashing of Kornbluh's reading of the Victorian novel. Kornbluh argues that this idea of a *real* economy is always fantastical, raising "the specter that any valorized exchange is ontologically unstable, logically ungrounded" (*Realizing Capital*, 6).

Economic Ecologies

What I am arguing is that the 2008 financial crisis produces a moment of reckoning for humans, particularly white male humans, who are no longer a tenable metric for mediating crisis. And, as such, the 2008 financial crisis is a limit point for crisis realism that seeks to restore a pre-crisis equilibrium via those very humans. Diane Coole and Samantha Frost, in an essay articulating a new mode of both economic and ecological politics, describe how this failure can lead to something generative: "[If] there is a lesson to be learned from recent events associated with subprime lending [. . .] it is how few people any longer grasp the complexities of the deregulated financial system, and yet how many are affected" (31). The complexity and interdependency of "the deregulated financial system," Coole and Frost argue, means that it is not just people that are at risk. Their understanding is of an ecological "many." Part of living in the Anthropocene means that we have to start thinking about nonhumans' claims to crisis with as much seriousness as we do human ones. To think through this contemporary crisis, then, requires a genre of thinking that Coole and Frost describe as "a multimodal methodology" that is "congruent with the multitiered ontologies, the complex systems, and the stratified reality" of the Anthropocene (32). Transscalar critique is just such "a multimodal methodology" that wants to think about economic crisis differently. It is not just human subjects that we need to be cognizant of, but the "multitiered ontologies" and "complex systems" of our interdependent world. New forms of representation, therefore, are required to think through this "stratified reality."

This line of thinking has becoming increasingly prevalent in certain corners of financial crisis critique. Paul Crosthwaithe, for example, argues that although the market may, at some point, have been a "human creation," we are no longer the puppet-masters (46). Crosthwaithe is claiming that encounters with financial crisis inaugurate a mode of nonhuman thinking as we come to terms with an economic relationality that is not solely composed of human, or even sentient, beings:

> Financial crises reveal this inhuman dimension of capital, a capital that is composed at once of abundant, diverse content and pure, formal structure; that is both subjective and objective; organic and mechanical; affective and impassive; libidinal and anhedonic; human

and alien; living and dead; Symbolic and Real. In a crisis, the inner workings of capital are exposed to view: the churning of meaningless numbers regulated by a remorseless machinic logic. (46–47)

Crosthwaithe is pointing to an "inhuman" excess of the market. Financial crisis is a moment that forces a reckoning with a causality of "machinic logic" wherein the human is effaced by "meaningless numbers." At the same time, this "multitiered" encounter with the market means that we cannot just leave the human dimension out; we have to account for the "organic and mechanical." Indeed, we cannot leave the ghosts out of their machines as we take stock of both the "living and dead." Like the FCIC and India in *Dear Money*, Crosthwaite argues that it is not just the human crisis we are witnessing but also an "alien" crisis. What we see here is the way in which thinking through the ontology of the market results in a cross-pollination between the ecological and the economic.

This is not to say that we should think of the market in terms that naturalize it. In many ways, this is the smoke-and-mirror show that neoliberalism tries to perform. By naturalizing the market, neoliberal discourse keeps the market outside of analysis and critique. Latour even goes so far as to deride the fact that the economy has been reproduced in neoliberal discourse as a "second Nature" (*Modes*, 383). Latour develops a Janus-faced account of the economic to combat this. We cannot slip into complacent modes of thinking or representation, Latour argues, as this type of discourse ends up glossing over the "hot, violent, rhythmic, contradictory, rapid, discontinuous, pounded out" logics of the market and instead reproduces "these immense boiling cauldrons [. . .] described to you as ice-cold, rational, coherent, and continuous manifestation of the calculation of interest alone" (*Modes*, 385). This is to say that thinking through the market requires a transscalar mode of reading. It is not that there are no rational modes of "interest," but these interests cohabit and contend with the "boiling cauldrons" of contradiction. William Connolly hammers home this point, arguing, "[Neoliberalism] act as if the models [of the market] would work if only the world did not contain so many 'outside' factors that are, in fact, imbricated and entangled in a thousand ways" (*Fragility*, 26). Instead, we need to maintain an interdependent and multifaceted account of the market.

To articulate this, Connolly goes on to argue that we need to think the ecology of economics and the economics of ecology. For him, life in the Anthropocene means that we cannot have the economic, on the one hand, and the ecological, on the other.[24] We need, in effect, to move between these scales simultaneously and constantly. He writes,

> To encounter the Anthropocene is to keep in mind that there were rather rapid changes in several of these force fields even before capitalism and the others became geological forces. The combination of capitalist processes and the amplifiers in nonhuman geological forces must be encountered together. (*Facing*, 4)

This passage gets to the center of Connolly's transscalar approach. First, he is quick to differentiate between "capitalism" and other "force fields" before they "became geological forces." That is, he is careful not to collapse or overdetermine one or the other, making an easy causal diagram that moves from industrial capitalism to the Anthropocene unilaterally and linearly. At the same time, he argues we must think through these scales "together," and that you cannot read one without the other.[25] "Today, as capitalism becomes more global, intensive, and fast-moving," he writes, "its imbrication with nonhuman force fields of multiple types increases" (*Fragility*, 67). The market is both beyond the human and produced by the human,

---

24. This is not, in and of itself, a new claim. As early as *Specters of Marx*, Jacques Derrida anticipates how thinking economically requires thinking ecologically. Derrida reads Marx's commodity as a more-than-human suture revealed in the heart of the market. Exchange-value, for Derrida, is a site of encounter with the nonhuman as "[the table] stands up and addresses itself to others [. . .] before the others, its fellows, here then is the apparition of a strange creature: at the same time Life, Thing, Beast, Object, Commodity, Automaton – in a word specter" (190). Jason Moore develops this strand of contemporary Marxism to argue that this inextricable layering and intersection of human and nonhumans is the condition of living in the Anthropocene. This is what he calls the "Capitalocene," a neologism that blends these two modes of thinking. He argues that it is no longer possible to separate the human from the nonhuman when looking at the economy. Theorizing the economic demands a confrontation with "the irreducibly dialectical relation between human and extra-human in the web of life" (5).
25. Margaret Ronda puts this in a historical framework, arguing that it begins to occur on a larger scale after World War II: "The terminology of the Great Acceleration attunes us to the particular entwining of the economic and the ecological in this period, a distinctive phase within the longer history of the production of nature in capitalism wherein the contradiction immanent to this system became increasingly pronounced" (3).

and we need to envisage a critical and literary form that attends to this "imbrication" of scales.[26]

We can see glimmers of this in the FCIC's report. In their Introduction, they briefly discuss how the 2008 subprime crisis was the result of a much larger "systemic breakdown" (xxii). However, they downplay these implications by quickly reducing the crisis to "a result of human mistakes" due to "human nature and individual and societal responsibility" (xxiii, xxii). The market in this rendering remains what Latour calls the "continuous manifestation of the calculation of interest alone" (*Modes*, 386), and it is the human error that caused the slip. But there is still something prescient in their acknowledgment of the disjuncture between system and individual. In fact, it is this transscalar nature that, as Connolly puts it, precipitates crisis: "As wider bands of culture and nature are incorporated into economic processes the limits, fractures, and contingencies of economic assemblages multiply" (*Fragility*, 191). That is, the fact that the market is not solely the human market means that it is more prone to crisis.[27]

Every time we attempt to think the economy, Latour argues, we are confronted with "vast sets of people and things that form organizations of astounding complexity and influence, covering the planet with their reticulations" (*Modes*, 387). Economics, as a discourse and

---

26. Connolly writes elsewhere that this does not mean giving up the individual as a scale of critique, but rather realizing how the individual is one scale entangled within others: "We affirm care for the human estate in its worldly entanglements, as that care stretches into regional asymmetries that haunt the world and toward other species with which we are entangled" ("Extinction," 19). Tsing makes a similar point in the way in which she is quick to point out the transscalar productivity of maintaining myriad scales simultaneously. "While I refuse to reduce either economy or ecology to the other," she writes, "there is one connection between economy and environment that seems important to introduce up front: the history of the human concentration of wealth through making both humans and nonhumans into resources for investment. This history has inspired investors to imbue both people and things with alienation, that is, the ability to stand alone, as if the entanglements of living did not matter" (5).
27. Moore also argues that it is this co-production that shifts from "the *signal* crisis of 2008" into "the unpredictable but inevitable onset of terminal crisis" (1; emphasis in original). For Moore, the elasticity of a "terminal crisis" "suggests we may be seeing something very different from the familiar pattern [. . .] This indicates we may be experiencing not merely a transition from one phase of capitalism to another, but something more epochal: the breakdown of the strategies and relations that have sustained capital accumulation over the past five centuries" (1).

description of the world, does not capture the complexity and interdependency of a transscalar world. Neoliberalism's greatest trick has been reducing everything to economic relationality. Dierdra Reber is eloquent on this point: "To put it another way, we cannot think our way out of a discourse that conflates the free-market narrative with that of the human condition itself" (190). Concomitantly, this means that, as literary critics, we are often guilty of a similar sin. Whether it is the marriage plot that stands in for 9/11 or the disgruntled, laid-off white man that stands in for the subprime mortgage crisis, all the complexities and valences of being are filtered through an economic lens and read as an interface of the market. Anna Kornbluh critiques McClanahan for perpetuating this mode of criticism. Kornbluh argues that we also need a transscalar mode of performing critique, thinking of texts as "more than evidence, more than information, more than data" points on a graph of economic stratification. ("We," 400"). We need, simply, to undo the stranglehold that the economic places on our critical imaginaries. Mark McGurl puts this succinctly: We need to "[let] go of the primacy of the economic sphere in its account of that change, heavily supplementing Marxian contradictions with ecological ones" ("New," 386).[28] To reiterate, it is not that we need to do away with Marxist readings; we should, however, be wary of how these critical apparatuses overdetermine our critical vocabulary.[29] It isn't just, as Latour argues, that we need to move "from *eco*nomy to *eco*logy," but that we also move back from ecology to economy (*Modes*, 23; emphasis in original).

Consider here the final pages of Jess Walter's post-2008 novel, *The Financial Lives of the Poets*. Towards the end of the book, the main character, Matt, a laid-off financial reporter who has begun to dabble in both poetry and weed dealing, tries to think through what has happened to him:

---

28. Coole and Frost make a similar argument: "But coming after poststructuralism and its criticisms, no workable version of Marxism can advance a historical metanarrative, aspire to the identification of determining economic laws, valorize an originary, pristine nature, or envisage communism as history's idealized material destiny" (30). Again, this is not to say that we throw Marxism out with the bathwater, but that we retain Marxist analytics while also acknowledging its limits and understanding how it intersects with other critical scales.
29. Serres puts this eloquently in his reading of the 2008 crisis: "I am not saying that the economy is marginal; it remains central – but to believe that [it is everything], embellished by the cosmetic aura of democracy, it is the only power that will lead us to extinction" (*Times*, 23).

> It's as if the whole country believes we've done something to deserve this collapse, this global warming and endless war, this pile of shit we're in. We've lived beyond our means, spent the future, sapped resources, lived on the bubble. Economists pretend they're studying a social science, and while the economy *is* a machine of hugely complex systems, it's also organic, the whole a reflection of the cells that make it up, a god made in *our* image. (154–155; emphasis in original)

Matt is thinking in an ecological and economic mode, moving between "cells" and "hugely complex systems" shifting between "endless war" and "global warming," just as easily he is able to think through "spent resources" and the housing "bubble." In fact, it is only once we start thinking all these things together that we realize the way they are folding in on one another constantly, animating each other. This is a moment of using the ecological to think the economic across myriad scales. Tellingly, in the shift from "in" to "is" and the shift from the first-person singular to the plural, financial crisis is imagined as a condition of being, not an interruption. Walter uses this formal experimentation to develop a reading of the economy that begins to gesture towards an ecological mode of interdependence, interconnection, and immanence: an economic critique, that is, that is also an ecological critique and an ecological critique that is an economic one.

At the very end of the book, Matt returns to this reading:

> It's all connected, these crises – marriage, finances, weed dealing – they are interrelated [. . .] like the housing market and the stock market and the credit market. We can try to separate them, but these are interrelated systems, reliant upon one another, broken, fucked-up, ruined systems. (212)

There is no ability to parse out, separate, purify, or analyze different modes of crisis. Walters is approaching something akin to what Coole and Frost call "a detotalized totality" of ecological thinking that acknowledges capital's "multitude of interconnected and unexpected crises, as well as its productivity and reproduction" (29). This "productivity and reproduction" is how crisis inaugurates an encounter with an immanent ecological being that is interdependent and more than human. Matt phrases this precisely: "And my epiphany is this: there are no such things as epiphanies – no moments of revelation, no great reveals of motives and fortunes" (251). There isn't a man behind the mask and there may not be anything outside of crisis.

Ferris's View from Nowhere

Joshua Ferris's *The Unnamed* continues to confront the relationship between the economic and the ecological head-on. At first pass, the book is very much in line with other post-2008 fiction – particularly in his focus on the dissolution of a white, middle-class family – but Ferris avoids the narrative baggage of crisis realism, focusing in on a larger landscape of crisis:

> It was the cruelest winter. The winds were rabid off the rivers. Ice came down like poisoned darts [. . .] The long-term debate about changing weather was put aside for immediate concern for the elderly and the shut-ins, while the children went weeks without school [. . .] The cold was mother of invention, a vengeful mother whose lessons were delivered at the end of a lash. (3)

This opening paragraph begins not with economic ruminations, but with an ecological meditation. Our attention is drawn not to any one character but rather to a landscape and world in crisis, afflicted and ravaged by anthropogenic climate change. The weather is the main character here: personified, sure, but also nebulous and multifaceted. It isn't just any one thing. Rather, like McPhee's articulation of the market, we see both "poisoned darts" and a "vengeful mother." Ferris experiments with different metaphorical scalings to try to capture the violence of a New York winter. This inaugural scene instructs us in a new way to approach a nominal financial crisis novel. To read this text, to understand this narrativization of crisis, we have to be attuned to a much broader swath and distribution of agency. This focus on the environment and the landscape, an interrogation into the agency of weather, becomes a dominant motif throughout *The Unnamed*. Rabid winds, this is to say, are just as important as any character in the novel.

This opening scene sets the stage for a novel that highlights how myriad scales of crisis intersect in the Anthropocene. The narrator, Tim Farnsworth, is a successful lawyer in Manhattan, consumed by work until he is consumed by the titular unnamed disease that forces him to start walking. He walks until his body collapses, at the whim and mercy of his feet. The book begins *in media res* with a second onset of the disease, and Tim's wife and daughter, Jane and Becka, have their lives upended as they drive around New York retrieving him from wherever he has been deposited. As the book progresses, we slowly learn that the first time Tim suffered from this malady, he had gone to a number of specialists across the country seeking out, but ultimately failing to receive, a diagnosis.

I should be clear that although *The Unnamed* is a book about weather and a disease, it is also very a post-2008 financial crisis novel. Tim's walking trips take him through landscapes of "half-finished Tudor-style homes on acre plots with dumpsters in the streets full of broken Sheetrock and mounds of rose-hued stone gravel in the driveways that with their air of thwarted expectancy accentuated the abandonment of the stillborn development" (218). It is against the salient backdrop of financial crisis, then, that the novel unfolds and, in some respects, one reading of the book props up crisis realist tendencies. Consider this passage from the novel's opening pages:

> He was going to lose the house and everything in it. The rare pleasure of a bath, the copper pots hanging above the kitchen island, his family – again he would lose his family. He stood just inside the door and took stock. Everything in it had been taken for granted. How had that happened again? (4)

This could be lifted directly from Eggers. By starting with an inventory of loss, beginning with the house and ending with his family, we see in miniature the domestic landscape of the post-2008 world.[30] The world that had been "taken for granted" starts to crumble, and we are left to sift through the ruins.

What this does is present the crisis of the white male as a rescaled version of the housing crisis, Tim's body acting as a metonym and a way to contain and mediate the crisis through the metric of the human. This plays out via Tim, who becomes obsessed with a causal inquiry into his disease. Tim wants to know how the disease "happened again." Indeed, it is this attempted inquiry into causality that seems to plague him. Tim's taxonomic impulse and inability to classify his disease as a specific thing is what keeps him up at night (when he is not walking): "'There is no laboratory examination to confirm the presence or absence of the condition,' he was told by a doctor named Regis, 'so there is no reason to believe the disease has a definite physical cause or, I suppose, even exists at all'" (41). This indeterminacy haunts him to the point where he walks around with

---

30. Doubling down on this, Jane is also a high-end real estate broker who spends her days traveling between various upmarket subdivisions of the sort that remain unbuilt in the suburban countryside of post-2008 America.

the snippet of an article from *The New England Medical Journal* as proof that he has been diagnosed as "[he] just wanted something to show people" (85).

Throughout the novel, then, Tim, with his law-oriented mind, clings to a theology of evidence, a way to understand the world in ways that we saw in *The Big Short*.[31] But this reliance on a picture of an old world that does not resemble the new world makes locating this type of evidence challenging:

> Yet there was no precedent for what he suffered, and no proof of what qualified as a disease among the physicians and clinical investigators: a toxin, a pathogen, a genetic disorder. No evidence of any physical cause. No evidence, no precedent – and the experts could give no positive testimony. That only left his mind. (54)

Almost lending itself as a microcosm for living in the Anthropocene, the disease puts Tim in uncharted territories. As Tim takes inventory of the shifted contours of his daily life, he is quick to realize he is up against a scalar distortion: "They were up against a specter that dwarfed the daily vexings" (20). Cause and effect are diffuse and myriad, spread across various scales. Tim remains resistant to the possibility of pathologizing the disease, though, and continues to try to seek out physical answers. Even the body, then, is forced to shift between scales. His mind laboriously tries to piece together some sort of rational understanding of the disease, while his body continues walking, drained of all agency, as it remains "at the mercy of an unknown world" (62).

Being at "the mercy of an unknown world" marks a generic shift in the text, as the causal and human-centric scales of crisis realism start to fray. Returning to the scale of language, the disease that afflicts Tim causes him to rethink the basic mechanics of narrative. Tim's internal narrative voice shifts into the first-person plural as he tries to contend with a self that is multiple. After a particularly miserable and long walking bout, Tim calls Jane to tell her that he no longer wants her to come and pick him up from his ambulatory nightmares. Instead, he tells her: "'Jane, you don't have to worry about us. We're going to be just fine'" (200). The text slowly dissolves into a whirl of internal

---

31. As he says to himself at another moment in the novel, "But what evidence was there? You had been chiseled by reason to a diamond point. You were deferential to logic and evidence, skeptical of specious oratory, an enemy of hearsay" (232).

monologues that, like the opening depiction of weather, play with our expectations about the relationship between plot, character, and form. "You, on the other hand, you hum," Tim tells his quickly fracturing self, "You vibrate with cold pain. You moan dumbly of want and complaint. Your steady low register, it would have driven them mad" (207). Tim has to start looking to a "low register" to understand his body. It is a way for Tim to start opening up the scales of narrative. Tim's initial drive to locate "empirical evidence [...] to exonerate" himself, becomes subservient to his inhabitation by the perennial crisis of his disease (65). In this way, Tim begins to think of his self as more than just his self, allowing the vibrational intensities of the disease to bring him into contact with a larger ecology of being. Although this relationship between Tim and his disease is often antagonistic (it is only in moments of complete exhaustion that Tim claims that "they were at peace" (215)), this is still about trying to reform the world in a way that allows for a centrifugal ecology to scale Tim outwards. As he makes his way through the post-financial crisis landscape, he is providing an alternative to the sort of cognitive mapping we saw in Eggers. He is trying to inhabit an environment that "proved itself to be indifferent on the mildest days, dependably vicious or antagonist on all others" (233). This opening up and thinking outside of the boundaries of the human is also, as Ferris makes clear, a question of narrative form. "You want the old comforts and narratives," Tim imagines the voice of the disease saying to him, "the great words repeated in the dark and over the head of newborns and the bodies of the dead" (233). But these "old comforts and narratives" do not capture what it means to live now. This is the fantasy of a pre-crisis past.

This rethinking of narrative is what makes Ferris's novel able to think simultaneously about ecology and economy. When Tim and his family realize that the disease is "Not finite. Chronic," the text begins to gesture towards other modes of reading (32). Indeed, as Jane thinks later on, "If he was just wasting from cancer or old age, she'd sit with him. If he just had an expiration date, of course she'd sit with him [...] But this thing, this could go on forever" (116). We are not dealing with a momentary interruption in a larger non-crisis-inflected narrative, but a new "forever." For Tim, this understanding of his disease becomes about formulating a new way of reading the world, as he tells his doctor he is contending with "a point of view'" (227). This new "point of view" is a way of confronting a continual condition of crisis:

> His condition never went into remission again, the walking never ceased. The nature of how he walked and his relationship to it as that

thing which hijacked his body and led him into the wilderness (for everywhere was a wilderness to him who had known only the interiors of homes and offices and school buildings and restaurants and courthouses and hotels) changed over time, over a long adjustment and many misfortunes. (247)

Tim has been exposed to a "wilderness" that has become "everywhere." This is what crisis looks like in the Anthropocene. There is no before or after. What needs to change, Ferris makes clear, is the "relationship" to this crisis, our narrative handling of the subject matter. We cannot seek out some sort of equilibrium that rescales crisis into manageable terms. No, this is a book that models what it looks like to encounter the myriad scales of the Anthropocene at all levels. The self, the marker and receptacle for realist signification, is hollowed. Instead, we have to look for new modes of apprehension that read within the margins, looking "everywhere, in the wildflowers, the wheat fields, the collapsed barns, the passing trains, the church spires, the stilled ponds, the rising suns" (279).

By looking at the "collapsed barns" and "stilled ponds" of his new world, Tim learns how to read the world in a different way. Instead of seeking out the closure of "an explanation, that his paperwork listed the causes and unlocked the mechanics and offered a justification" (284), Tim begins, "[for] the first time he began to pay attention to the things he saw on his walks" (287). This is a way of thinking about new modes of narratives: "They were fleeting, they were middles without beginnings or ends" (287). This is crisis in the Anthropocene present where crisis has become the condition of being. We cannot just fill out new "paperwork," but have to be okay with the partial, looking at the "fleeting" that happens in fits and starts. It is up to us to figure out how to read these new narrative landscapes. *The Unnamed* rehearses the partial reading of the Anthropocene by postponing attempts at critical mastery. As more and more tests are done on Tim, it is always "more of the same [. . .] greater inconclusiveness, additional absence of evidence, the final barrier removed from boundless interpretation" (107). At every turn, we are forced to contend with the myriad scales of crisis. Whether it is Tim's sickness or the skies that "were all drumspit and fury" that make Jane "feel a child's awe at the natural world" (190), the novel is instructive for how it maintains these scales simultaneously.

This is formalized in the novel's third act. After a brief period of remission, the disease returns in full force, dissolving any residues of a realist narrative. The book becomes impressionistic as Tim's "world had constricted to exclude everything but himself, and then was riven in two [. . .] 'You and me,' he cried, 'you son of a bitch!'" (197). As Tim dies in a blizzard at the end of the novel, the text models what it means to read without mastery or for identificatory closure. The text shifts into a mode of listening, a way of being attuned to the world: "Instead [Tim] chose to do as he had done the night before: settle deep inside himself and listen to the strange and subtle operations going on inside his body. He listened for his heart to whisper its soft word" (310).[32] Tim does not try to escape his imminent death; he dissolves into the immanence of a new rhythm.

This agentless sense of being is what makes *The Unnamed* such an interesting example of literary form and the post-2008 financial crisis novel. What *The Unnamed* models is a type of crisis reading that does not reproduce a mode of inquiry bent on definitive causes or closure. In broader terms, Tim's new way of reading the world does not search for what Latour derides as a "rear world of the beyond" that "may debunk, reveal, unveil, but only as long as you establish, through this process of creative destruction, a privileged access to the world of reality behind the veils of appearances" ("Attempt," 475). This is where I run into a limit with McClanahan's critique of financial crisis narratives. The critical genre McClanahan puts forward is content in debunking the ways in which the cultural ends up reproducing the economic. This is an interesting place to start, but, as I argued earlier, this ultimately reproduces the idea that the economic is the only vocabulary with which we can describe the world. The goal of transscalar critique is to think beyond these economic diagrams of cause and effect, labor and surplus, blame and culpability, autonomy and agency. As *The Unnamed* unshackles itself from the symptoms of crisis realism, it outlines an ecological mode of thinking.

Rebecca Colesworthy argues that the 2008 financial crisis is particularly instructive in how it requires a recalibration of symptomatic reading. As she sifts through the academic accounts of the crisis, she

---

32. Julietta Singh also turns to the aural as a countermodel to hegemonic modes of mastery, another mode of nonmastery reading. She writes: "I dwell on listening as a critical mode of becoming vulnerable to the voices – human and nonhuman, audible and muted – that are always sounding even when we have not been trained or allowed ourselves to listen: Listening, as opposed to voicing that which we 'know.' Listening, as an act that might let each other in – psychically, physically – to another's way of inhabiting the world; to being entities that are always touching and being touched by others, even when we are not aware of this touching, even when this touching is entirely unpredictable" (27).

wonders, "Is demystification the most appropriate trope for the theoretical and political work of critique today? Is it the solution or part of the problem?" (1174). It is not enough just to say, as McClanahan might, that Eggers offers us a bad representation of financial crisis and that Ferris offers us a good one. Although I agree with Colesworthy's diagnosis and impulse to push past this epistemology of dissimulation, I want to take this further into ecological terrain to argue that a transscalar mode of reading financial crisis allows us to come to terms with the ecology of economy and vice versa. Financial crisis is an opening, a way of thinking through the interdependence of being. Serres writes:

> Like lightning, the financial crisis [. . .] strikes back at us. Indeed, facing reality as it is, facing the things of the world, we confront the same situation as in the economy where we depend on what actually depends on us, money, the market, work, and commerce. (*Times*, 28)

In this lexicon of interdependence, Serres moves crisis into an explicitly ecological register by claiming that crisis exceeds both the epistemic mastery of the realist novel and the economic critique of Marxism that often attend those novels.

Like the Anthropocene, the crisis of financial crisis may be a misnomer as it describes a perennial and constituent condition of being. What a moment like 2008 does is bring our attention to the underlying structural conditions that preceded this crisis. Laura Finch is apt in her description of this logic: "In a moment of crisis when the commonly agreed map for the economy suddenly shows the uncharted waters at its edges, the impulse is to delegitimate these unmapped areas and return to the solid grounds of business as usual" (734). Here are the two paths charted by financial crisis narratives. The formal retreats into crisis realism are attempts to return to "business as usual." The other path is to follow Finch's terrestrial metaphors into thinking how the larger world is caught in a moment of flux. This second path does not rely upon a critical mode of reading agency and causality as hinged to the human. What happens in a crisis is that we are called to rethink our modes of understanding the world. This is also the heart of ecological politics. Timothy Morton argues that ecological hermeneutics produce a "sense of being close, even too close, to other lifeforms, of having them under one's skin" (*Hyperobjects*, 139). Financial crisis is one such moment of contact that produces the possibility for ecological thinking in the sense that thinking through the constitution of the market forces us to recognize the imbrication of the human within more-than-human force fields. This requires new forms of reading that leave behind agentive narratives buttressing the workings of realism.

What Ferris's novel does is produce the sketches of a mode of thinking without offering any grand narrative. Like the partial reading that disavows mastery over texts, Shonkwiler would describe this mode of rethinking crisis as the "modest" ambition of the contemporary financial novel: "Even where the literary text successfully interferes with capital's representational process, such effort may remain at the level of minor disruption" (xxx). This "minor disruption" models a realism that momentarily opens itself up and suspends teleological and representational logic, before returning to more traditional forms. Ferris realizes that attempting to capture the myriad scales of crisis in the Anthropocene is not a one-size-fits-all solution. It is the momentary opening and rifts in narrative form that might provide better blueprints. It is not so much a cartography of crisis that we should strive for but, to prelude my next chapter, an atmosphere of crisis. This gesture outwards towards the transscalar, towards the way in which realism requires a polyvocality, is what I will trace in Chapter 2, which deals with a crisis that, perhaps even more than financial crisis, requires recalibrated scales of reading: anthropogenic climate change.

Chapter 2

Global Weirding: Climate Crisis and the Anthropocene Imaginary

> At the very moment when we should be remaking politics, we have at our disposal only the pathetic resources of "management" and "governance."
>
> Bruno Latour, *Facing Gaia*

> One need not choose a particular scale at which to read; stories can be read at multiple scales simultaneously.
>
> Christine Marran, *Ecology Without Culture*

Halfway through Barbara Kingsolver's 2012 novel, *Flight Behavior*, the protagonist, Dellarobia Turnbow, tries to explain the threat of anthropogenic climate change to her climate change-sceptic husband, Cub. Dellarobia wants to convince him that the monarch butterflies that unexpectedly landed on their property in rural Tennessee and the increasingly drastic fluxes in temperature are both symptoms of climate change. "The weather's turned weird," she tells him (260). It is a telling word choice: for Dellarobia, "weird" is the only adjective she can think of that maps these two seemingly disparate entities. But Cub pounces, twisting her language into the all-too-familiar tone of right-wing punditry, scoffing, "They don't call it global weirding" (261). Dellarobia, used to the reticence of her husband, thinks about this for a second and realizes that he may have a point, conceding, "I know. But I think that's actually the idea" (261). Dellarobia and Cub, repurposing the term briefly popularized by *New York Times* columnist Thomas Friedman, rehearse in miniature the difficulties we encounter when talking about climate crisis: it is not just changes in temperature that constitute our moment of anthropogenic climate crisis, it is something far weirder.[1]

In this sense, Kingsolver is using Dellarobia to respond to a much larger renegotiation of what we mean by the "crisis" of climate crisis. This is a renegotiation that has plagued policy makers since the 1998 inception of the Intergovernmental Panel on Climate Change (IPCC). The international bellwether for climate change science and policy recommendations, the IPCC's semi-regular Assessment Reports remain the benchmark for international consensus on anthropogenic climate change. But it was not until 2007 that the IPCC started thinking about global warming outside of temperature metrics. In 2007's *Fourth Assessment Report on Climate Change*, the IPCC revises its 2001 *Third Assessment Report*, explaining, "Advances since the [*Third Assessment Report*] show that discernible human influences extend beyond average temperatures to other aspects of climate" (40). This is a crucial intervention into the stakes of crisis: climate crisis is no longer measurable as merely a rise in temperature.[2] However, even while acknowledging the nebulous nature of climate crisis, there is another type of logic that emerges in the IPCC's *Fourth Assessment Report*. The IPCC claims that "mitigation and adaptation, taking into account actual and avoided climate change damages, co-benefits, sustainability, equity and attitudes to risk," coupled with technological innovation and solutions, offer "high agreement and much evidence that all stabilization levels assessed can be achieved" (64, 68; emphasis removed). The IPCC, in other words, slips into the mode of crisis realism, arguing that climate crisis is a rupture, a momentary interruption in the terrestrial

---

1. In an introduction to a special issue of *Paradoxa* dedicated to the relationship between science fiction, climate, and the weird, Gerry Canavan and Andrew Hageman argue that weirdness, and its capaciousness as a term, should be considered the trope *par excellence* for climate crisis. "Both *climate change* and *global warming*, as terms, seem to produce a kind of tactical denialism from opponents," they write. "*Global weirding* tried to short-circuit this kind of denialist wordplay by focusing instead on the unpredictable disruptions that have been caused and will continue to be caused by the coming years of anthropogenic global warming" (n.p.; emphasis in original).
2. A global warming level of 4°C was the then common metonym for crisis. This is best outlined in the World Bank's ongoing series of publications, *Turn Down the Heat*. See, in particular, Schnellnhuber's 2012 *Turn Down the Heat: Why a 4°C Warmer World Must be Avoided*.

narrative of the earth.³ The IPCC cannot think past "mitigation and adaptation" in diagnosing climate crisis.⁴

Just as Dellarobia warns her husband not to be overly zealous in his attempts to taxonomize climate change, the IPCC acknowledges how climate crisis has become even weirder by 2014's *Fifth Assessment Report*:

> Uncertainties in the past and present are the limits of available measurements, especially for rare events, and the challenges of evaluating causation in complex or multi-component process that can span physical, biological and human systems. For the future, climate change involves changing likelihoods of diverse outcomes. (37)

This is where the Anthropocene enters the world envisaged by the IPCC. Climate crisis is no longer solvable through a combination of technology, economics, and human cooperation. We are now dealing with a scalar distortion that moves across the "physical, biological" planes of the world simultaneously in "complex" and unprecedented ways. What occurs sometime between 2007 and 2014 is the realization that the IPCC needs to develop a vocabulary that thinks through the geological scale of the terrestrial world at the same time that it accounts for the scale of human biology.

---

3. Equally problematic is the economic tenor of the *Fourth Assessment Report*. There is a focus on "substantial economic potential for the mitigation of global [Greenhouse Gas] Emissions over the coming decades that could offset the projected growth of global emissions or reduce emissions below current levels" (58). It is not that climate crisis does not or cannot have an economic component, but the claim here is that we should take climate change seriously only for the potential lost to "economic benefits."
4. Lindsay Thomas provides an excellent reading of how "mitigation and adaptation" calcify into the neoliberal logic of management that Bruno Latour derides in my epigraph. She argues that the management rhetoric implicit within the IPCC (and other policy organizations) offers a "formalization and codification of living in the present" that facilitates not change but merely a bleak acceptance of "scientific methods or protocols for getting on with things, even – or perhaps especially – amid disaster" (160). This idea of climate management is, at its core, a scalar issue. Zach Horton writes: "The dominant scale technique of the Anthropocene is one in which technoscience is conjoined with a universal overview of all scales. The human returns as villain and savior – in fact, as the entire cast of an apocalyptic theater that subsumes all scales and collapses the difference between them" ("Cosmic," 55). This is to say, entities like the IPCC keep zooming out, hoping that they will find a monoscalar plane for climate crisis.

Moving between the planetary and the biological, the IPCC begins to implicitly model a transscalar understanding of climate crisis. The crisis of climate crisis has moved onto a diffuse horizon where "no single option is sufficient by itself," and, therefore, "effective mitigation will not be achieved if individual agents advance their own interests independently" (94, 102).[5] Even more so than financial crisis, climate crisis presents a crisis in excess of individual subjects, human and nonhuman alike. In fact, the very crisis is one situated at the collision of human and nonhuman worlds. To come to terms with this scale of crisis, the IPCC is moving from imagining the singularity of climate crisis as event into a mode of crisis as a condition of being. Crisis is no longer a singular moment that can be solved or worked through. This again returns us to familiar territory. If climate crisis becomes an ambient condition of being, what literary forms are capable of responding to climate crisis when the narrative cushions of "individual agents" may not be enough? Or, simply, how can we capture the weirdness and violence of anthropogenic climate crisis through the novel?

In this chapter, I read two novels alongside *Flight Behavior* to look at how a cross-section of contemporary novels have attempted to mediate climate crisis in its nascent weirdness: Jonathan Franzen's 2010 *Freedom* and Nell Zink's 2014 *The Wallcreeper*. These novels have been chosen to reflect two things. First, these authors take climate crisis as one of their main plot points. Each book has a plot that is driven by myriad and multiple iterations of climate crisis. Second, this archive traces a condensed history of the realist novel in the contemporary. If the crisis realism I described in my last chapter names financial crisis literature's failure to rescale crisis through familiar tropes and forms, there is a contiguous formal incongruity between climate crisis and realism. Franzen, Kingsolver, and Zink all use realist form to mediate climate crisis while simultaneously confronting the generic limits of realism for representing what cannot be scaled back down to the level of the individual.

I should be clear from the jump that the question of literary form and scale has a rich history in environmental writing and ecocriticism

---

5. The *Fourth Assessment Report*, on the other hand, entertains the possibility that individual "changes in lifestyle and behavior patterns" may move the needle (59). It continues, "The rate and magnitude of human-induced climate change and its associated impacts are determined by human choices defining alternative socio-economic futures and mitigation actions that influence emissions pathways" (70).

more generally. As early as 1995, Laurence Buell was highlighting this formal problem in his seminal *The Environmental Imagination*. "[Environmental] crisis involves a crisis of the imagination," he writes, "the amelioration of which depends on finding better ways of imaging nature and humanity's relation to it" (2). Buell reads climate crisis as an aporia to narrativization, arguing that "even if human perception could register environmental stimuli, literature could not" (84). The scalar incommensurability between "human perception" and "environmental stimuli," Buell claims, is too vast to be contained by a genre like realism. It is easy to see, therefore, why climate crisis has long been the fodder of genre fiction. As Mark McGurl puts it, science fiction and other genre fiction are "literary forms willing to risk artistic ludicrousness in their representation of the inhumanly large and long" ("Posthuman," 539). At the risk of literary seriousness, genre fiction, McGurl argues, is willing to incorporate scales that exceed the human.[6] However, as the Anthropocene ascends in our scientific and cultural imaginaries, climate crisis has begun to increasingly migrate from this ostracization in genre back into works of realist fiction.[7] That said, there remains a formal problem. Rob Nixon describes how climate crisis makes it difficult to "plot and give figurative shape to formless threats" (10). The challenge for environmental fiction, then, has been to "intervene representationally" by "[devising] iconic symbols that embody amorphous calamities as well as narrative forms that infuse those symbols with dramatic urgency" (10). This is a central concern of this chapter, where I look at how these narratives try to give immediacy and form to the "amorphous calamities" of climate crisis.

This chapter begins with an extended reading of Franzen's *Freedom*. Franzen's novel, the most commercially successful of all three books, is an attempt to distance his work from the postmodernist

---

6. This is even more true of what is now referred to as "Cli-Fi." For more on this, see J. K. Ullrich and Sarah Stankorb. I will also return to genre fiction in the following chapter.
7. Franzen and Kingsolver, in particular, are part of this nascent boom in realist fiction attempting to grapple with climate crisis. Adam Trexler describes this "rise of realist fiction" as a way of understanding how climate crisis has become "widespread, and various," as well as, I would add, salient in contemporary fiction (233). This has only increased in volume in the intervening years since Trexler published his study of "Anthropocene Fiction." Climate crisis, simply, is everywhere we look, not just in the apocalyptic images of genre fiction.

"difficulty" of his 2001 opus, *The Corrections* (*How*, 239).[8] As such, his approach remains most concentrically within the crisis realist tradition and ostensibly uses a mode of scalar fungibility moving between climate and domestic crises interchangeably, critiquing individual culpability rather than the systemic conditions that have led to climate change. Kingsolver's text also employs the symbiotic registers of crisis realism by moving between the domestic and the environmental. That said, both Kingsolver and Franzen are suspicious of the efficacy of mapping climate crisis through domestic scales. Both texts begin to rehearse the failure of realism to capture the scalar distortion of climate crisis by short-circuiting this scalar invariance. I end this chapter with a reading of Zink. Her difficult and winding novel is the furthest from realism proper but still maintains some of its most identifiable markers: namely, the marriage plot. Zink's book takes Dellarobia's injunction for global weirding as a formal challenge and begins to sketch what I describe as a "weird realism" that offers a literary model of encountering the continual crisis of the Anthropocene. The text moves between scales in quick-fire succession, challenging readers to find stable ground and markers for what we are accustomed to in the realist novel. Zink slowly dissolves the possibility of maintaining the realist distance between narrative background and foreground.

This dissolution of background/foreground is not just a literary conceit, but a critical one. Just as my last chapter attended to the ways in which writing economically required a mode of reading ecologically, this is also a chapter about what it means to read climate crisis critically. As the increasing number of critical monographs and special collections on the Anthropocene contend, reading in the Anthropocene requires new critical vocabularies and methodologies.[9] Borrowing the terms from Jesse Oak Taylor, I argue that reading climate crisis requires a transscalar mode of "atmospheric" reading. For Taylor, atmospheric reading names a way to read outside the

---

8. This is an outgrowth of what Paul Dawson describes as "Franzen's lament for the novel's loss of authority since the nineteenth century and its increasing obsolescence in contemporary society" (151).
9. In their introduction, to the (aptly named) collection *Anthropocene Readings*, Tobias Menely and Jesse Oak Taylor outline how reading in the Anthropocene requires a "multiform, *multiscalar*, multitemporal" critical mode resistant to "methodological consistency" (13; emphasis in original). They describe this mode as an "invariably polyglot, salvage practice in which we employ all of our tools to discover meaning amid the ruins" (13).

monoscalar imaginary by opening into a constellation of "new meanings and [. . .] unanticipated effects" generated from the realization that "we don't live *on* that swirling blue marble known as earth; we live in it" (8; emphasis in original). This immanent critical mode of thinking is a way to read texts for pulsations, textures, and movements outside "the human individual as the key locus of agency, ethics, and subjectivity" (14). It is a mode of "adjacency," a type of reading that forecloses on critical mastery by developing new lexicons of cohabitation, immanence, and ecological interdependence (7).[10] To put it simply, if weird realism names the literary form of the climate crisis novel, atmospheric reading names the critical form best suited to read climate crisis transscalarly.[11] Scale-shifting between these two forms, weird realism and atmospheric reading, this chapter outlines what it means to both imagine and critique climate crisis in the Anthropocene epoch.

Jonathan Franzen's Climate Realism

Part of the issue of narrating climate crisis is that, like financial crisis, it forecloses on the type of before-and-after narratives that saturate accounts of crises in the crisis realist tradition. David Farrier puts this pointedly: "Thinking about the time of environmental disaster involves negotiating the tension between the dehistoricizing and narrowly linear effect of thinking disaster in terms of a 'ruptural' catastrophe and the normalization of an enduring disaster which lacks a specific moment" (451). Climate crisis negates the "specific moment" of crisis and, therefore, resists preexisting temporal forms as it becomes an "enduring disaster" with no end point.[12] For Dipesh Chakrabarty, the Anthropocene throws the temporal phenomenology

10. Taylor describes how he is not concerned with what is "either on the surface or concealed in the depth" and instead wants reading to "[extend] outward to envelop the interpenetrating contexts of composition, production, and reception" (8).
11. I am not the first to make this connection between the weird and the atmospheric. Eileen Joy has described how a mode of "weird reading" seeks a hermeneutics "like the weather, an atmospheric medium with an unpredictable life of its own that nevertheless drenches us" (32).
12. Christophe Bonneuil and Jean-Baptiste Fressoz are direct in their reading of crisis in and of the Anthropocene: "The term 'crisis' denotes a transitory state, while the Anthropocene is a point of no return. It indicates a geological bifurcation with no foreseeable return to the normality of the Holocene" (48).

of the human into contact with timespans and scales that "are normally assumed to be working at such different and distinct paces that they are treated as processes separate from one another for all practical purposes" ("Anthropocene," 44). What this does, in effect, is rework human temporality and spatiality across scales. There are no more "different and distinct places" for reading the world, just the immanence of competing, contradictory, and complementary trajectories. As Chakrabarty writes, "[The] current crisis can precipitate a sense of the present that disconnects the future from the past by putting such a future beyond the grasp of historical sensibility" ("Four," 197). Chakrabarty claims that the Anthropocene's temporal disjuncture erodes the present into a multiply scaled entanglement. "Climate change is not a one-event problem," he writes. "Nor is it amenable to a single rational solution" ("Postcolonial," 13). Chakrabarty is describing the way that climate crisis is distributed outside the "single rational solution" of mitigation and adaptation, governance and management. Indeed, no attempt to think through climate crisis can remain monoscalar as ecological forces cause "us to move back and forth between thinking on [. . .] different scales at once" (Chakrabarty, "Anthropocene," 49). The scale of the human, in effect, has gotten much weirder. We are a stratigraphic force at the same moment we realize that, as individuals, we no longer have much agency at all. In an inversion to the master narratives that accompany human beings becoming geological agents, we are actually both smaller and larger than we thought we were.[13]

In a collection of essays published shortly after *Freedom*, Franzen circles around climate crisis, trying to capture both how large and how small human beings are in the world. His love of birding, for example, brings him into a type of ecological contact with the nonhuman world: "Because now not merely liking nature but loving a specific and vital part of it, I had no choice but to start worrying about the environment again" (*Farther*, 12). His love of birds opens him to a world above and beyond the human. This scaling outwards, however, is also a scaling inward as "a portal to an important, less-centered part of myself"

---

13. It is, as Timothy Morton describes, "the gradual realization by humans that they are not running the show, at the very moment of their most powerful technical mastery on a planetary scale" (*Hyperobjects*, 164). In this reading, I differ from critics like Donna Haraway. It is not that the "species Man as the agent of the Anthropocene" has returned as geologic hegemon (47). It is the opposite: the Anthropocene signals a threshold that dissolves these bounded scales.

(*Farther*, 13). This appreciation of both the centrifugal and centripetal scalings of the environment are very much tied to Franzen's literary and critical aspirations. He writes:

> It can be very pretty nature. And since I'd been fired up by critical theory, and was looking for things to find wrong with the world and reasons to hate the people who ran it, I naturally gravitated to environmentalism, because there were certainly plenty of things wrong with the environment. (*Farther*, 11)

Criticism, signaled here by "critical theory," and environmentalism are entwined for Franzen; both modes pull him further inwards while alerting him to a world that is infinitely in excess of itself. He finishes this essay by noting,

> When you stay in your room and rage or sneer or shrug your shoulders, as I did for many years, the world and its problems are impossibly daunting. But when you go out and put yourself in real relation to real people, or even just real animals, there's a very real danger that you might end up loving them. (*Farther*, 13)

There is a shift in the disposition and tone that he takes as a critic. He does not want to merely "shrug" his shoulders and sneer with the ironic apathy of the critic. Instead of the narcissistic reflexivity he identifies with a critical culture of "technoconsumerism" and high theory (*Farther*, 6), Franzen realizes that being invested in ecology brings his critical praxis into a space of interdependency; it is not just "rage" that he has to contend with but "love" as the "real danger" of environmental immanence.

Just as much as this is about a critical mode, Franzen also thinks through the literary implications of environmentalism. In an essay about birding in the South Pacific, Franzen quickly changes course to write a history-in-miniature of the realist novel. Franzen begins by offering an analogy: his encounter with rare birds mirrors how readers encounter fictional characters in stories. Whether it is seeing a rare bird or the appearance of Friday in *Robinson Crusoe*, "[no] matter how carefully we defend ourselves, all it takes is one footprint of another real person to recall us to the endlessly interesting hazards of living relationships" (*Farther*, 52). This is another moment when a reshaped critical rendering of the world opens into the "hazards of living relationships." This literary ecology brings him not only into contact with a world outside the self, but also into an unknown interiority. Both reading *Robinson Crusoe* and Franzen's experience birding on the South Pacific Island of Masfuera become a rich "microcosm of human possibilities that you contain within yourself" (*Farther*, 127). Taken as an aesthetic and critical treatise, then, these essays work transscalarly, invested equally in the web of "living relationships" and the "microcosm of human possibilities," simultaneously. Moreover, by tracing this through *Robinson Crusoe* and, by extension, the novel, Franzen suggests that the realist novel should be able to capture this transscalar complexity, moving between scales fluidly.

This is what *Freedom* tries to tackle: the paradox that the novel should plot environmental politics while at the same time querying individual interiority and the "endlessly interesting hazards of living relationships." *Freedom* is, after all, a domestic drama about the decline of the Berglund family in the storied tradition of the Victorian social realist novel.[14] We follow Walter and Patty Berglund's courtship, marriage, divorce, and eventual reconciliation across some twenty years and two generations. The book traces Walter and Patty and their two children, Joey and Jessica, from Minnesota through varying states of domestic chaos in New York, Washington D.C., Argentina, and a variety of other locales, before resolving itself in the idyllic holiday surround of Nameless Lake in Northern Minnesota. Like its nineteenth-century predecessors, the novel is ambitious in its scope and range, cutting across diverse cross-sections of time and space (if not socio-economic or racial lines), while also representing Franzen's first foray into making climate crisis part of his plot through the "greener than Greenpeace" character of Walter (3).[15]

Our introduction to Walter offers him as both the paragon and the foil of environmentalism. Patty's section of the narrative, a memoir titled "Mistakes Were Made: Autobiography of Patty Berglund by Patty Berglund (Composed at Her Therapist's Suggestion)," builds on this duality. There is no substantive environmental critique in Patty's section, but her brief mentions of the environment are used as a narrative device to give depth to Walter's character. In certain ways, Patty actually blocks Walter's aspirational environmentalism. We see this when she describes how Walter's leftist politics dissipate next to Patty's hope of "[living] in a beautiful old house and [having]

---

14. *The Guardian*'s review compared the novel to *Bleak House*, describing its "old-fashioned solidity and social realism" (n.p.).
15. A theme which he carries on in the follow-up, *Purity*.

two children" (102): "And Walter, despite being an avowed feminist and committed to the student activist, Zero Population Growth, embraced her entire domestic program without reservation, because she really *was* exactly what he wanted in a woman" (119; emphasis in original). In this scene that introduces Franzen's metonymy for climate crisis, population growth, Patty mentions Walter's ecological politics only as an aside. The environmental appears here, but it is only a trope to bring into relief the differences between Walter and Patty.[16] As Adam Trexler's reading of the novel contends: "Instead of circulating through the characters of the novel, the environment is merely a psychological preoccupation [. . .] *Freedom*'s aesthetics ultimately treat political organization as a symptom of poor character, pathologizing attempts to address environmental issue" (226). This is just another way of saying that it is a scalar misreading of the environment as "pathologizing" the individual. The environment, in these early sections of the novels, only travels in one direction, giving us access to Walter, without the reciprocal gesture of doing any type of environmental thinking.

In this sense, Franzen seems to prioritize a centripetal scaling of climate crisis that only moves inward, revealing the friction between the two protagonists. This is a reversion to crisis realism: Franzen does not allow climate crisis to rewrite generic conventions, but instead uses generic conventions to rewrite climate crisis. But just as Franzen is aware of how his birding habit actually puts him into contact with a much larger world, *Freedom* is also telling because of how the environmental exerts a certain pressure on the structure of the text, introducing a scale beyond the usual ken of a realist novel. We see this when ecological politics enter the plot. In the novel's midsection, "2004," environmental crisis interrupts the narrative flow, stopping plot development and veering into the territory of polemic. At this point, Richard Katz, Patty's former and future lover and Walter's former and future best friend, has become a famous musician, and Walter and Patty have left Minneapolis for D.C. to work for the oil evangelical Vin Haven at the Cerulean Warbler Trust. The Trust is a pet project of the billionaire and combines energy extraction with long-term environmental reclamation. Walter is poached from his environmental law firm in Minnesota to provide green currency

---

16. This is repeated when Walter meets Patty's parents and "He asked Joyce if she was familiar with the Club of Rome [. . .] Walter explained that the Club of Rome was devoted to exploring the limits of growth" (121). Walter is then immediately made fun of for his earnestness by both of Patty's parents.

to Haven's controversial mountaintop removal scheme in exchange for the land being preserved as cerulean warbler migration ground. Walter and his assistant (and soon-to-be lover), Lalitha, have recently gone "rogue" after learning about Haven's dodgy coal contracts (217). Instead of focusing on the cerulean warbler, Lalitha and Walter decide to funnel money from the trust into summer internships and a music festival dedicated to educating people about the dangers of population growth. To give the veneer of cool to a definitively uncool topic, they ask Katz and his A-list roster of musician friends to play at the festival. Talking with Katz, Walter is able to give voice to his own narrative of climate crisis:

> You remember Aristotle and the different kind of causes? Efficient and formal and final? Well, nest-predation by crows and feral cats is an efficient cause of the warbler's decline. And fragmentation of the habit is a formal cause of *that*. But what's the final cause? The final cause is the root of pretty much every problem we have. The final cause is too many damn people on the planet [. . .] Yes, per capita consumption is rising. Yes, the Chinese are illegally vacuuming up resources down there. But the real problem is population pressure. (219; emphasis in original)

In this passage two things come into focus. At the substantive level, Walter offers a causal reading of climate crisis. He points to diffuse origins, only to reinscribe climate crisis within an Aristotelian paradigm of "final cause": "population pressure."[17] But at the formal level, the text stops the development of plot by reverting to a didactic mode: Walter and Katz's discussion is not developmental for the narrative but appears in an insulated space adjacent to the plot. That is, whereas the rest of the text is plot-driven, anytime the environmental enters the narrative it interrupts the flow of the novel, a scale too big for narrative.

And this might be the point. As Walter drives through West Virginia, a story about John Kerry on the radio sparks a tirade: "[The] world population had increased by 7,000,000 [in two weeks] [. . .] to clear-cut forests and befoul streams and pave over grasslands and throw plastic

---

17. Jeffrey Williams is pessimistic about the efficacy of Walter's ecological politics and what it says about Franzen's politics more generally: "*Freedom* is fatalistic. It is not that Franzen advocates neoliberalism, and in fact he exposes some of its dubious values, but, adhering to the convention of literary realism, he cannot imagine any other possibility. It is a disturbing sign of the times that the most bruited novel of the past decade [. . .] assumes there is little chance for fundamental change through normative democratic channels" (95).

garbage into the Pacific Ocean and burn gasoline and coal [...] and obey the fucking pope and pop out twelve families" (313). How can a novel move between these scales? How can you represent seven million people and "plastic garbage" in the Pacific and "grasslands," while also thinking through Vatican politics? Franzen dramatizes the impossibility of moving between these scales. Margaret Hunt Graham tracks this environmental interruption to narrative in a survey of reviews of *Freedom*:

> If you took it from the reviewers, there was something *weirdly* interruptive about [*Freedom*'s] eco-politics [...] [Somewhere] in this critical mass of complaints is an interesting collective observation, which is that there exists a certain formal incongruity between the parts of *Freedom* that touch upon overpopulation and the parts that touch upon other totalizing political problems. (295; emphasis added)

This is, simply, a problem of scale. Realism may have been able to handle "other totalizing problems,"[18] but it fails when it comes to climate crisis. Tellingly, Graham describes this as weird: climate crisis remains "weirdly interruptive" to the development of narrative.

Climate crisis results in what Graham calls "didactic discourse" that remains outside of the text (296). This didactic discourse "arrives in *Freedom* not as part of the story but via passages or monologues or dialogue or thought, each characterized by a kind of discursive excess or flow" (296). This parallel structure requires us to read this "discursive excess" atmospherically. That is, Walter's tirades against population growth are not the most important feature.[19] What is

---

18. Graham cites "imperial war" as one of these other "totalizing political problems" that Franzen is able to tackle within the parameters of realism in the novel (295). From the first pages of Joey's section of the novel, "Womanland," transnational events and geopolitical conflicts are scaled down to the personal as 9/11 "became the seed of his intensely *personal* resentment of the terrorist attacks" (232; emphasis in original). Aligned with the crisis realist tradition, the realist plot is in fact driven forward by the War on Terror. After getting caught up in the fringes of the wartime economy, Joey goes to Patagonia to fill an order of A10 truck parts for the US military. The War on Terror in these scenes is used as part of Joey's moral bildungsroman.
19. Still stuck in his narrative about final causes, Walter even risks hierarchizing different iterations of climate crises. He says to Patty at one point: "'Global warming is a huge threat,' [...] declining the bait, 'but it's still not as bad as radioactive waste. It turns out that species can adapt a lot faster than we used to think'" (323).

interesting for our purposes, however, is how the text thematizes a mode of reading via this formal excess. Just as Franzen was clear that his understanding of environmentalism changed the way he performed critique, so too does *Freedom* require a critical reorientation. By suggesting that the plot cannot contain climate crisis, Franzen forces us, as critics, to look elsewhere and to consider the way that an atmospheric critical approach allows us to see how the environmental begins to creep into the very form of the novel.

Timothy Morton, in a challenge to outdated modes of ecocriticism and environmentalism, argues that critics have been fixated with archives that recycle the same tired tropes of pastoral and naturalistic writing. Morton advocates for a "[move] beyond the simple mention of 'environmental' content, and toward the idea of environmental form" (*Ecology*, 3).[20] As *Freedom*'s inability to narrate climate crisis makes clear, a "simple mention" of climate crisis does not work. What is more interesting, then, is to think about how form becomes inflected with an ecological mode of thinking. Consider this moment after Lalitha is killed in a car crash and Walter retreats to the house at Nameless Lake. Here, Patty's initial use of environmental metaphors to describe Walter is inverted. No longer do these metaphors just work centripetally; they also work centrifugally. "Walter was frightened by the long-term toxicity they were creating with their fights. He could feel it pooling in their marriage like the coal-sludge ponds in Appalachian valleys" (333). This metaphor moves across plateaus of "long-term toxicity" back into his marriage before ending with "coal-sludge ponds in Appalachian valleys." The text is not using the environment to scale an individual character, but rather using the multiplicity and fungibility of metaphors to inhabit multiple scales at once.

What I am describing in the novel is how climate crisis reshapes the form of *Freedom*. There isn't a way to contain or limit the environmental from the non-environmental as even the domestic becomes a site of carbon toxicity. In this reading of Franzen, I am capturing what Christine Marran describes as the "domestic turn" in environmental writing. For Marran, this is a way to claim that there is no there there when we talk of the environment. Climate crisis, Marran argues, has pervaded even the "household [as] a microcosm of ecological affiliations

---

20. Timothy Clark makes a similar point: "Criticism may not be just a matter of helping the construction of an eco-cosmopolitan identity, or of defending texts that make phenomena such as climate change more forcibly apprehensible" (20).

that have come to link humans to their environment in industrial modernity" (101). This is true throughout *Freedom*. We see this when Joey imagines having sex with his friend's sister through climatic imagery: "Jenna excited him the way large sums of money did, the way the delicious abdication of social responsibility and embrace of excessive resource consumption did" (388). Sex, capital, and the environmental all coalesce, turning in on one another as Joey tries to think of the right metaphor to describe how much he wants to have sex with Jenna. The fact that he has to cycle through these metaphors to find the right scale at which to mediate his desire suggests an inextricable layering of crises.

This mode of reading the domestic through the environmental climaxes when Walter reads Patty's memoir. After he finishes her work, Walter realizes the extent and length of her various infidelities and asks her to move out. Before he sits down and opens her memoir, he feels optimistic, refreshed to finally regain a sense of trust and clarity with his wife. But, as soon as he finishes the memoir, he looks outside to think: "[The] sun on his office windows was a different sun from the one he'd always known" (458). On the one hand, the world outside of Walter is scaled down to his affective mood. But, as he reflects further on this shift in understanding the world, the scale has shifted, leaving Walter behind: "The world was moving ahead, the world was full of winners [. . .] while Walter was left behind with the dead and dying and forgotten, the endangered species of the world, the nonadaptive" (480). Walter is not the final link of the metaphor – he is dispersed across a topography of "the dead and dying and forgotten, the endangered species of the world, the nonadaptive." The human, if we can stretch this further, is not the determinant metric. Although these metaphors are, in part, used to animate the personal crises of the Berglund family, they are also something weirder. They index how crisis is not contained within the family but is constellated across a much larger continuum. This is what Marran describes as "a deep sense of the susceptibility of humans, plants, and animals to the kind of contamination that is hard to trace" (105). Or, to rework the old feminist maxim, the personal becomes the environmental.

This, however, creates a suture in the novel. The form of *Freedom* points to this atmospheric mode of the transscalar while the plot of the novel cannot escape its crisis realist trappings.[21] When Walter

---

21. In fact, as Aine Mahon argues, it is the novel's prioritization of the domestic scale in the plot that neutralizes any political radicalism: "For all Walter and Patty's errancy and despair, however, Franzen finds finally in their marriage the approach of salvation" (101).

tells Katz that "[we're] not trying to overthrow the whole system, we're just trying to mitigate [. . .] We want to do with population the whole thing Gore's doing with climate change," his IPCC-resonant language reveals the limits of the realist plot (362). Climate crisis, Walter argues, is just another crisis, scalable and containable. We see this especially pronounced in the final section of the text after Walter returns to Nameless Lake. Here, the plot's devaluing of ecological politics occurs at the syntactical level: "[Walter had] apparently founded a radical environmental group that had shut down after the death of its co-founder, a strangely named young woman who clearly hadn't been the mother of his children" (544–545). Although the sentence starts by gesturing towards the ecological politics of the novel, this is subsumed by the death of Lalitha after she and Walter have an extramarital affair. Moreover, the sentence separating these two maintains a grammatical and temporal divide. The gesture towards the ecological becomes syntactically subordinated to the larger workings of the plot. These two narratives are proximate but remain apart, crossing only at the occasional site of metaphor. *Freedom*, in effect, cannot sustain its explorative, environmental possibilities. Instead of allowing the formal excess of climate crisis to reshape the novel, the text rescales its political radicalism through a parallelism between the environmental and the domestic: on one side, Walter's environmentalism; on the other, the story of *Freedom*. Moreover, a detached perspective signaled by the "apparently" keeps us at the safe and sanitized distance by the affordance of ironic, narrative closure. But maybe this is the point. These two scales, while not immediately reconcilable in the realist novel, still point towards Franzen's larger understanding that climate crisis itself is transscalar, outside crisis realism's telos of mitigation.

A realism able to map climate crisis teleologically is what Morton describes as "ecomimetic." Ecomimesis is, in effect, the attempt to resituate the boundaries of the foreground and the background – a way to hammer out the weirdness of the climatic. Climate crisis forecloses the maintenance of these positions as it interrupts "the metaphysical illusion of rigid narrow boundaries between inside and outside" (*Ecological*, 39). Ecomimesis, to counter this, tries to restructure this boundary. Morton argues, moreover, that ecomimesis is an effect of a scalar interface:

> Ecomimesis tries to fuse the layer of narrative and the layer of narration, creating a paradoxical loop about whose paradoxical and loopy qualities ecomimesis is perpetually in denial. The denial within

ecomimesis is a symptom of the larger loop of whose machinations ecomimesis is a small, human-scaled, 'lived experience' region. Its job is to flatten out the inherent twists in a chiasmus, to make the twist into a pure circle. (*Dark*, 57)

Morton is describing literary attempts to rescale the excess of climate crisis to manageable sizes, creating hierarchies that miss the "larger loop." But *Freedom*, for all its pitfalls in terms of plot, shows how difficult it is to think climate crisis without these twists. The text only artificially clings to the idea that climate crisis can be taxonomized and captured cartographically when in fact it exists atmospherically. *The Washington Post*'s reviewer, Ron Charles, describes the novel as "[arresting] the story" by interrupting the narrative and "[hectoring] us about the loss of wildlife." What Charles misses is that climate crisis pervades all aspects of the text.

Barbara Kingsolver's Scalar Imaginary

Kingsolver's *Flight Behavior*, like *Freedom*, also uses the building blocks of literary realism to narrate climate crisis. Indeed, both books share a number of formal and substantive similarities. *Flight Behavior*'s plot begins with the trapping of domestic realism, following Dellarobia and her family as their lives are upended by both migrating monarch butterflies and marital strife. The butterflies unexpectedly winter in the Appalachian forest on the Turnbow property instead of their usual breeding grounds in southern Mexico at the exact same time that Dellarobia dreams of an extramarital tryst with her cable guy. The butterflies cause a local and national stir with everyone from lepidopterists to priests to news anchors attempting to explain their sudden appearance.[22] Trexler follows this domestic thread of the novel to identify a tension within the book. He describes it as aestheticizing climate crisis as a "flood of orange wings" that make climate crisis appear "gently, gorgeously palpable without simplifying human characters' inner lives" (227). Trexler is highlighting two components of the novel. First, he points to its constitutive realism. By maintaining

---

22. Like Franzen, Kingsolver's novel was hailed as part of a new wave of climate crisis fiction that, as Adeline Johns-Putra describes it, revises the usual generic expectations of apocalyptic narratives with more "conventional and realist form" (269).

the "inner lives" of its characters and their domestic woes, Kingsolver is attempting to mediate climate through the scale of the human. Second, he is pointing to how this scaling risks making climate crisis "palpable." Extrapolating from Trexler, we might argue that the risk here is that a focus on the interiority of the characters means that climate crisis is relegated to a manageable, micro scale. But it is actually the inverse that occurs. Like Franzen's Anthropocene-inflected metaphors, by focusing on a climate crisis event that is not a tsunami or a 4°C rise in heat, Kingsolver is trying to navigate what Stephanie LeMenager calls the "everyday Anthropocene." Kingsolver's attention to the "inner lives" of Dellarobia and her family seeks out "a more granular and personal account of near catastrophic change" ("Climate Change and the Struggle," 225). By having this seemingly innocuous deviation of migratory patterns of butterflies at the center of her novel, Kingsolver is pointing to the ways in which climate crisis is a perennial part of our everyday experience, whether we realize it or not.

This granular account of climate crisis also means that crisis assumes a more ambient place in the novel. Written against the backdrop of the 2008 financial crisis, Kingsolver attempts to maintain two scales of critique by filtering them through one another. The text grapples with anthropogenic climate change at the same time that it looks at the economic hardships of life in rural Appalachia. Dellarobia's family land has been contracted to a logging company that is scheduled to "clear-cut the whole deal" after Dellarobia's father-in-law, Bear Turnbow, is forced to pay back the large sum of money he borrowed at subprime rates "to expand his machine shop" during the height of the pre-2008 bubble (39, 38). This is the tension at the center of the plot: Cub wants to clear-cut the land and get rid of the butterflies while Dellarobia wants to work with the scientists that descend on the Turnbow property to save both the forests and the butterflies. The novel produces a sort of Sophie's choice: do the Turnbows sacrifice economic comfort for environmental sustainability or give in to the extractive necessity of life in the middle of a global recession?

These competing claims to crisis, Cub's economic one and Dellarobia's environmental one, are brought into tension when Dr. Ovid Byron, a lepidopterist from New Mexico, arrives in Cleary, Tennessee. Dr. Byron has no time for the Turnbows' economic claims on the land and cannot understand why anyone would rush him through his work. Against this backdrop, Dellarobia articulates a contestatory crisis hierarchy: "She resented [Dr. Byron's] new list of cares, wondering how they stacked up against, say, a foreclosure notice or a car breakdown you walked home from without any hope of repair" (220). Climate crisis is a crisis of a privileged class. Dellarobia imagines that people who can spend their time thinking about questions of sustainability are free from issues like "a foreclosure notice or a car breakdown." In fact, Kingsolver goes so far as to speculate that the ecological is subsumed by the economic for certain peoples. Both Dr. Byron and Dellarobia try to segment crises, reading one at a time. Thinking back to when she first found the butterflies, Dellarobia remembers, "Everyone could have missed them, given the tendency for all eyes to remain glued to the road ahead and last month's bills" (75). These accounts of crisis are monoscalar. The novel, however, suggests that the reciprocal logic that I outlined in my last chapter is equally true: we cannot read ecological crisis without accounting for its economic dimensions.

This transscalar understanding of climate crisis is also explored by the IPCC in a 2018 special report on limiting global temperature changes. Like Dellarobia, the IPCC revises its earlier readings of climate crisis to offer a granular exposition of the asymmetries of lived human experience and race. The IPCC describes how crisis arises "from potentially complex interactions between the changing climate and the underlying vulnerability and exposure of people, societies and ecosystems" (58). Here, the IPCC realizes that thinking through the crisis of climate crisis requires a cultural shift. It is not enough to take top-down approaches; policy is effective when it "[combines] public support for research and development with policy mixes that provide incentives for technology diffusion" (*Special*, 30). Although the IPCC remains fixated with technological solutions, there is an opening in its understanding of the narrative frameworks of climate crisis:

> Social justice and equity are core aspects of climate-resilient development pathways that aim to limit global warming to 1.5°C [. . .] The potential for climate resilient development pathways differs between and within regions and nations, due to different development contexts and systemic vulnerabilities. (*Special*, 31)

The IPCC is sounding out ways to integrate climate crisis into discussions of the "different development contexts and systemic vulnerabilities." Climate crisis affects different populations differently. What this means is that there is a political impetus to start building the narrative architecture that can account for this multiply scaled understanding of climate crisis.[23]

This is not to say that there should be a reprioritization of the economic over the ecological. It is, however, to say that there needs to be a transscalar approach that reads these crises simultaneously. We still need to be vigilant in avoiding what Ben Dibley and Brett Neilson describe as the "actuarial imaginary" of climate crisis wherein "the ecological comes to be discursively framed and institutionally managed as the 'terrestrial infrastructure for global capital'" (148). This is another way of saying that the economic and the ecological must exist simultaneously – one scale cannot be given precedence over the other. By creating these tensions between Dellarobia/Cub and Dellarobia/Dr. Byron in *Flight Behavior*, both scales of crises are given weight, filtered through one another to show their inextricability. What is even more crucial is that this attention to the asymmetries of climate crisis claws back the impulse to interpellate humanity *en masse* via what Marran calls the "totalizing language of Anthropocene discourse" (119). By seeking out the "granular and personal," Kingsolver is able to narrate these asymmetries back into the text, accounting for a transscalar Anthropocene. The economic may be the constitutive scale at which residents of rural Tennessee think, but this does not mean that this should come at the expense of the ecological. Rather, Kingsolver is trying to figure out a way to inhabit multiple scales simultaneously, a narrative approach to the transscalar everyday realities of the Anthropocene. This is what Patrick Murphy reads as Kingsolver's critique of "the failure of the educated middle-class professional strata of the population to speak to the lives, needs, and desires of their less educated and lower paid fellow citizens" (160). Unlike Franzen's novel, which is exclusively concerned with these "middle-class professional strata," Kingsolver's is looking at populations that are often glossed over in discussions of climate. Kingsolver uses Dellarobia to mouth a critique of the same people that populate Franzen's novel: "They would never come see what Tennessee was like, any more than she would get a degree in science and figure out the climate things Dr. Byron described. Nobody truly decided for themselves" (166).

23. The IPCC continues: "Populations at disproportionately higher risk of adverse consequences of global warming of 1.5°C and beyond include disadvantaged and vulnerable populations, some indigenous peoples, and local communities dependent on agricultural or coastal livelihoods" (*Special,* 21).

More than just introducing competing discursive scales at which to read climate crisis, Kingsolver also introduces a generic multiplicity into the text as a way of confronting a sense of what Dellarobia describes as that which she had "no name" for (22). Kingsolver turns to what Frederick Buell calls a "thoughtful, even introspective version of the bildungsroman" (282). Although the bildungsroman as literary form is often seen as a scaling down cathexing to the individual's development of consciousness, for Kingsolver it signals a scaling up and out. Dellarobia thinks: "Miracle or not, this thing on the mountain was a gift. To herself in particular, she'd dared to imagine. Not once had she considered that it might have been stolen from someone else" (101). The proprietary sense of religious ownership implied in Dellarobia's miracle-for-one is now rearticulated as a moment of ecological consciousness connecting her farm to the Michoacán region of Mexico. Dellarobia's sense of scale is shaken by her ignorance for "the huge things she didn't know" (103). Before the butterflies, Dellarobia's "world had been the size of a kitchen" (244). After the butterflies, however, her sense of scale drastically revises itself: "The person who'd lit out one day to shed an existence that felt about the size of one of those plastic eggs that pantyhose came in. From that day on, week by week, the size of her life had doubled out" (342). Her encounter with the butterflies has opened her centrifugally, reconfiguring her being across a larger spatio-temporal continuum. As her life "doubled out" and she confronts the "huge things she didn't know," climate crisis begins to further interrupt the feel of her everyday being. Dellarobia, in effect, begins to read the world atmospherically, trying to think about climate across diffuse and competing scales simultaneously.

This atmospheric presence of the Anthropocene means that the plot is driven by climate crisis. That is, the novel does not trade in the "didactic discourse" that interrupts narrative development in Franzen. The ecological, in effect, becomes the constitutive content of Dellarobia's bildung. Kingsolver, therefore, is effective in formalizing how climate crisis is not supplementary to the text, but rather is the text. This is why Kingsolver introduces different forms and scales to create an atmospheric rendering of climate crisis. Kingsolver forces her readers to realize that, as Dellarobia has it, the world is no longer "centered around what they want" as "nature will [no longer] organize itself around what suits them" (256). This is a way of narrating climate crisis outside of the inherited markers and anthropocentric metrics of crisis realism. Like the "nature" Dellarobia is describing,

Kingsolver is reaching for a different representative mode to capture the weirdness of climate crisis.

This formal indeterminacy is underlined when the novel makes another generic pivot into the realm of the ecological thriller. Instead of murders and intrigue, the drama and suspense of the text are imagined through temperature: "January made its way like a high-wire walker, placing one foot, then another, on the freezing line. It wavered, rising to forty, dipping to thirty, but never plunged. A small, nervous audience watched" (247). This signals an important shift in terms of the relationship between form and content. Starting with economic and religious scales to mediate the ecological, the novel then imagines climate crisis as a thriller hinged to a potential shift in degrees Fahrenheit. The drama culminates in mid-March when an unexpected snow arrives: "At some unmeasured moment the temperature fell through the floor and the rain turned crystalline, descending noiselessly in the dark and stunning Dellarobia the following morning" (411). This is a line that could be lifted from a Tana French book: the "crystalline" rain, the silent horror, the psychological unease. The novel, here, has moved into a new mode of what Dellarobia calls "biological treachery" (412).

That said, Kingsolver still retains a strand of crisis realism. Unable to fully jettison the teleology of crisis realism, Kingsolver hangs onto a domestic narrative to resolve Dellarobia's varying crises. This means that the language of the marriage plot risks neutralizing the novel's ecological consciousness. This is most redolent in the relationship between Dr. Byron and Dellarobia. After seeing him naked through the window of his trailer, Dellarobia thinks: "Not again, this losing her mind to a man. She'd thought surely something had changed, for all the strange fortunes those butterflies had brought her. She thought she could be free" (254). Dellarobia lapses into a solipsistic mode of scaling the climate. The butterflies have been inverted, no longer working centrifugally by bringing Dellarobia into contact with the world; instead, they work centripetally to bring Dellarobia into a romance plot. Timothy Clark reads Kingsolver's novel as full of this type of gesture where romance trumps the political. The ecological, according to Clark, is merely a foil for the development of character:

> [The] insects seem to have come almost entirely to symbolize a positive turning point in one character's life, a kind of visual background to symbolize a positive turning point in one character's life, a kind of visual background music for Dellarobia's story. (177)

In Clark's reading, Kingsolver is figuring a return to the world of backgrounds and foregrounds. Although Kingsolver has asked what "a whole new earth [. . .] where you could count on nothing you'd ever known or trusted" might look like (325), Clark is arguing that the text forgoes its speculative possibilities by resituating a background/foreground distinction as romance is given priority over the "background music" of climate crisis. There are certainly grounds to support this reading. The butterflies continue their journey northward (relatively) unharmed. Dellarobia leaves her husband and is set to begin college classes in the fall. Although briefly inseparable, these plots depart from one another before settling back into adjacent textual spaces.[24]

This, however, does not capture what is actually happening in the novel. When Dellarobia imagines her children's response to her and Cub's divorce, she thinks of it as "[a] whole world melting around them [. . .] The loss or rearrangement of everything [they'd] ever known and trusted" (429). Like Franzen, the language of the Anthropocene cohabits with and inflects the domestic. The domestic and the environmental scales are inextricably linked, informing and animating one another. For Dellarobia, it is the realization that "[she] was slowly submitting to [Dr. Byron's] sense of weather as everything" (319).[25] This is the realization that there is no world outside climate crisis; there isn't any possible "evacuation plan" (27). During a fight between her and Cub, they argue over whether or not she can just leave Cleary and start over. In this fight, Dellarobia articulates the immanent crisis of the Anthropocene succinctly. She asks Cub, "And what if there was no other place?" (175). Dellarobia is using Anthropocene diction to dissolve the boundary between the inside/outside, realizing that thinking climate crisis in the Anthropocene means realizing there is "no other place," and that, yes, maybe weather is everything.

Ursula Heise argues that ecological writing requires "[the] creation of a vision of the global that integrates allegory – still a mode that is hard to avoid in representations of the whole planet – into a more complex formal framework able to accommodate social and

---

24. Clark, I should note, is generous in his reading, pointing out that this limns a larger problem of "how a novelist may negotiate a global issue opaque to immediate or empirical understanding" (177).
25. This reading of "weather as everything" runs throughout contemporary environmental thinking. Morton calls it "a thin slice of an image, a caricature of global climate" (*Hyperobjects*, 70).

cultural multiplicity" (21). This shuttling between forms signifies the scalar multiplicity and polyvocality of Anthropocene thinking. This "complex formal framework" comes fully to fruition in the final pages of *Flight Behavior*. The text begins to leave behind its realist strictures and signifiers to become something much closer to allegory. A huge rain descends upon Cleary and the text moves towards full "Noah's Ark" allegory (422). The novel finishes with an embrace of an allegorical mode, pointing to Heise's encompassing sense of scale:

> The sky was too bright and the ground so unreliable, she couldn't look up for very long. Instead her eyes held steady on the fire bursts of wings reflected across water, a merging of flame and flood. Above the lake of the world, flanked by white mountains, they flew out to a new earth. (433)

This final scene is Kingsolver's dismissal of realism. She allows the novel to finish in a surrealist flooding recalcitrant to realist taxonomy: "She comprehended the terms of what she saw, but couldn't turn away from it [. . .] For the moment her fascination transcended ordinary fear and safety" (431). Unlike at the beginning of the book, Dellarobia realizes that she is encountering a crisis in excess of her scalar imaginary, but she also realizes that there is no space outside of crisis. Even though she lacks comprehension, she is stuck in a mode of immanence unable to "turn away from it." Although she uses the language of transcendence, what is being described is a mode of "just swimming," the inability to "turn away." This is an allegory for climate crisis in the Anthropocene – there is no before and after, there is no return to a façade of Holocene equilibrium, there is just the immanence of swimming.

This shift into allegory is a weirding of the novel's ostensible and putative realism, what Heise might describe as a "wary kind of experimentalism" backboning the text's "ecological dynamism" (64). Kingsolver's novelistic insight lies in the movement between realism and other competing genres that places the novel into a precarious site of indecision, unable to fully move past its inherited formal logic, but still invested in attempting to capture the scalar dysphoria of the Anthropocene. When Tina, a CNN news anchor reporting on the butterflies, interviews Dellarobia and Dr. Byron, she wants to read the butterflies as "the beauty of this phenomenon" (364). She tries to imagine the butterflies as offering a glimpse into a benevolent and aesthetically pleasing form of anthropogenic climate change. Dr. Byron turns to her, reminding her that they in fact represent "[pervasive] environmental damage" (365) that "won't fit in a nutshell" (364).[26] The scale of crisis, in other words, exceeds the possibility of realist form. Crisis remains, as Dr. Byron phrases it, an "intangible thing [. . .] outside your range" (367).

Remaining "outside your range" is, simply, the textualization of the problem of representing climate crisis. Thinking climate crisis requires movement beyond our normal range. In a moment that seems to ventriloquize Kingsolver's aesthetic theory, Dellarobia says to Dr. Byron, "People can only see things they already recognize [. . .] They'll see it if they know it" (282). Dellarobia's grappling with the inheritance of form returns to the impossibility of scaling climate crisis. Dr. Byron responds: "And how do you see the end of the world?" (282). This is what is at stake when we try to read and write the Anthropocene. Kingsolver is asking what type of literary forms are suited to address an uncertain world. Through her myriad generic experiments and competing scalar models, Kingsolver attempts to fashion the right form for climate crisis.

This shifting between forms is what I see as the contours of a weird realism. Morton describes the weird as a "twisted, looping form" reminding us that "we live in a universe of finitude and fragility, a world [. . .] surrounded by mysterious hermeneutical codes of unknowing" (*Dark*, 6). For Morton, two things come into focus from and through the weird. The first point is that the weird is about cohabitation with a "universe of finitude and fragility." This is what Dellarobia is trying to tell Cub in the scene I introduced this chapter with: it is not just about a world heating up, but a far more precarious sense of being in the world where we are constantly brushing up against one another, competing at different vibrational intensities. The second point Morton makes is a critical one about reading weirdness. The weird is about "mysterious hermeneutical codes of unknowing." To get to the weirdness of climate crisis, we cannot maintain fantasies of critical mastery. This is where weirdness as literary form dovetails once again with the type of atmospheric reading I have laid out. To exist in this world of "finitude and fragility," we have to read the world in exploratory and experimental ways, searching out atmospheric adjacency.

26. The aesthetic dimension of climate is paradoxical for Dellarobia. As Dellarobia reflects in one passage, "If these butterflies were refugees of a horrible misfortune, there could be no beauty in them" (143). This is a something that Ian Baucom and Matthew Omelsky have critiqued as "[the] simultaneous aesthetic beauty and imminent devastation" that is the hallmark of "climate-changed inflected aesthetics" (6).

The late Mark Fisher's final monograph similarly theorized the resurgence of weirdness as a critical and aesthetic category. For Fisher, the weird as a literary form names a way of thinking "that which lies beyond standard perception, cognition and experience" (*Weird*, 9). Fisher sees the weird as a generic "egress" that opens up "contact between incommensurable worlds" (26, 39). Although he reads this in terms of science fiction and horror, there is the inflection of the transscalar in this definition. The transscalar, like the weird, looks at the "contact between incommensurable worlds," mapping new scalar relations that are brought into being in the Anthropocene. Fisher's transitory trope of the egress is a way to conceptualize the movement between multiple scales. Moreover, the weird places pressure on realism. Fisher writes that the weird illuminates "the background furniture of literary realism" by pulling it "into the foreground" (76). The inanimate "furniture" and objects of realism are brought to the fore, subverting standard subject–object paradigms. This topsy-turvy relationship between background and foreground is where Fisher cites the emergence of a different critical mode of apprehending weirded relationships. Disintegrating the space between the background/foreground means that we have to start reading atmospherically, looking to a literary and critical form that works transscalarly.

Kate Marshall picks up on this atmospheric mode of reading when she approaches weird fiction through an explicitly ecological lens. She argues that reading weird literature means that we need to be "far less interested in deconstructing subjects than thinking otherwise from the beginning about the persons, objects, and landscapes" ("Weird," 646). This is, in the terms of *Transscalar Critique*, a direct rebuttal to the critical project of crisis realism. We are not invested in the types of subject–object relations that map cause and effect. We have to start "thinking otherwise" about the scales and relations of "persons, objects, and landscapes" that account for the interdependency of life in the Anthropocene. This is what I mean when I say that if weird realism names a literary form for mediating climate crisis in the Anthropocene, the critical form that attends to it has to be atmospheric, invested in new modes of reading and critiquing.

Zink's Weird Realism

Where Kingsolver produces a novel that is watermarked with weirdness, before you even start *The Wallcreeper*, the cover of the North

American edition announces weirdness as its defining feature. "Nell Zink is a writer of extraordinary talent and range," none other than Jonathan Franzen writes on the blurb. "Her work insistently raises the possibility that the world is larger and stranger than the world you think you know." Franzen's endorsement registers the weirdness of this short and bristling novel before you have even begun it. But, *The Wallcreeper* is certainly still a realist novel tackling the crisis of anthropogenic climate crisis. Despite its novelistic funhouse mirrors, it has a plot that fits nicely within some of the parameters of crisis realism I have traced across the first half of *Transscalar Critique*. The book follows Stephen and Tiff, newlyweds that move from Philadelphia to Europe after Stephen's pharmaceutical company transfers him abroad. Once in Europe, they settle in Berne (where they briefly adopt the titular wallcreeper), move to Berlin, and, along the way, have a number of jaunts and affairs in southern Germany and the Balkans. Against this domestic drama, Stephen and Tiff slowly become radical environmentalists. As in Kingsolver and Franzen, then, there is a twinned plot: an ecological bildungsroman paired with the marriage plot of the crisis realist novel. Stephen, like Walter Berglund, is an avid bird watcher, but after the death of their pet wallcreeper, he becomes involved with the Global River Alliance with the goal of "[selling] the idea that the Rhine should be looking like the Yukon" (80). Tiff also gets involved in this "riparian passion" through her affair with an environmental lobbyist, Olaf, and later with an environmentalist priest, Genrot, who invites her to live in a small cabin in Breitenhagen (171). Tiff goes so far as to commit an act of environmental terrorism by making a "gap in the cladding" that floods a tree farm on the banks of the Elbe (143). After a brief period of marital estrangement, when Stephen gets hooked on heroin and Tiff enjoys her life as an environmental activist in Breitenhagen, the two reconcile and go hiking in the Balkans, "wowing each village in turn like Christ's entry into Jerusalem," before Stephen suffers a heart attack while swimming and dies (143). Despite this wandering and often tangential plot, Zink, like Kingsolver and Franzen, maintains a realist pole within the novel. There is a symbiotic exchange: domestic dramas are mirrored by environmental ones, while the plot is driven forward by romantic crises as much as it is by environmental ones. Moreover, the book ultimately enacts a certain domestic closure. As with Dellarobia (but unlike Walter and Patty's marital reconciliation), Tiff's encounter with climate crisis gives her life a sense of purpose and allows her to seek out personal validation after separating from her spouse.

However, whereas Franzen and Kingsolver trace linear plots that move from A to B in a fairly straightforward manner, Zink creates a knottier, modular novel that weirds its ostensible realism. The first jarring, staccato sentence of the novel provides an introductory defamiliarization: "I was looking at the map when Stephen swerved, hit the rock, and occasioned the miscarriage" (7). The reader has no foothold, thrown from a car into the narrative, unsure of who Stephen is, where we are, or why a miscarriage is relegated to the margins of a subordinate clause. This is a novel that, from the outset, allows the background noise to disorient the reader, demanding that we pay attention not just to characters, but also to the "landscapes" that Marshall cites as a hallmark of the weird. Stephen's response to Tiff's miscarriage is to celebrate finding the wallcreeper. "It's like the most wonderful bird. But it's a species of least concern and actually they're all over the place except anyplace you would normally go. I identified it before I hit it," he proudly tells the bleeding Tiff (7). The opening scene models a critical paradigm. Stephen is unwilling to distinguish a hierarchy of events. The miscarriage that should occupy the foreground is made contingent and secondary to finding the wallcreeper. The wallcreeper may be a "species of least concern," but that just requires Stephen and Tiff to recalibrate their vision and look at the places that "you [wouldn't] normally go." As the initial scene develops, the miscarriage is displaced not only by Stephen's reading of the wallcreeper or the text's syntactical subordination, but also by Tiff. When she manages to crawl out of the crashed car, there is a vertiginous disassociation of self: "I opened the door and put my feet outside, threw up, and lay down, not in the vomit but near it. The fir tops next to me had their roots at the bottom of a cliff" (7). Tiff moves centrifugally from the self into a larger ecological landscape with the fir trees, their roots offering a more stable grounding than her dislocated sense of self.

Robin Romm captures this formal weirdness in her review for *The New York Times*. The novel defamiliarizes through an "inverted emotional landscape" wherein "that opening miscarriage is pretty forgettable, but a wallcreeper can rock your world." Writing in a nonhuman lexicon, Romm argues that it is the inversion of "landscape" that defines the text. This inverted narrative hierarchy is amplified when Tiff thinks about what she describes as a "preoccupation with my internal monologue" (126). She thinks these monologues are "the sort of thing it is always better to write down than to indulge in at dinner" as they blind her to "competing subtexts" (126). This passage summarizes the formal innovation of *The Wallcreeper*.

Different threads compete at different vibratory frequencies, causing feedback loops that swerve in and out of one another. Trying to capture "competing subtexts" means that *The Wallcreeper* is less about the traditional arrangement of the realist narrative or its subtending mode of reading. Zink trades these forms for atmospheric, *ad hoc* arrangements. The book is, like Stephen's bird watching, an attempt to "[fight] entropy the only way he knew how, with marks in a notebook" (149). This is the scalar limit that Zink is pushing up against. Zink argues that we cannot scale down climate crisis but can only attempt to mediate it momentarily. These "marks in a notebook" may ultimately be futile, but they still represent a fleeting and provisional moment of encounter. Against this "entropy," Zink is looking to find new forms for "an incoherent jumble of meaningless forces that gets rolled in earth's diurnal course like rocks and stones and trees" (179). Narrating an "incoherent jumble of meaningless forces" strikes me as the perfect description of weird realism in the Anthropocene. Against the geologic strata of "rocks and stones," the text is not quite an incoherent jumble, but it hovers on that border, testing the elasticity of realism.

Realism's elasticity is brought to a breaking point in the novel in moments where Tiff tries to form a coherent sense of her self. We see this in a scene that follows the opening car crash. Tiff and Stephen arrive back at their house in Berne, and Tiff crawls into bed to recover from her miscarriage. As she lies in bed, she tries to make sense of what is happening to her body:

> But my – what am I going to call it? My down there plays a minor role in several scenes to come. It appeared to be connected to the underside of my stomach with shock cords stretched too tight. I rolled over on my side and coughed. I wasn't pregnant, I noticed. I clenched my hands into claws and cried like a drift log in heavy surf. Stephen put his hands on my ears. Much later he told me he thought if I couldn't hear myself I might stop. He said it reminded him of feedback mounting in an amplifier. (9)

This scene subordinates what should be the affective *gravitas* of losing a baby to a slow dissection and anatomization of the self. Tiff is no longer Tiff as she starts to become alien entities via a metaphorical imaginary of nonhuman signifiers ("claws," "a drift log in heavy surf"). As Stephen puts his hands on her ears to block out Tiff's crying, he models a different way of reading the world. Tiff's words are turned inside out, hollowed of meaning and signification, turned into the rumbling noise of "feedback," the swell of an atmospheric background.

This proliferation of nonhuman imagery and the swell of "feedback" is a way for Zink to narrate climate crisis. It is not just one of many causal inputs in her text but is integrated into the very form of the novel, swelling in and out in the distorted wash of feedback, pockmarking even Tiff's imaginary as she tries to describe her body. The text flickers on the boundary between the realist novel and an "incoherent jumble." This is best captured in a moment when Tiff looks in a mirror:

> [Everything] in the whole universe is contagious if you look at it long enough. Just opening your eyes puts you in front of a mirror, psychologically speaking. Garbage in, garbage out. Or rather, garbage goes in, but you never get rid of it. It just lies there turning to dust and slowly wafting a thin layer of grime on every other object in your brain. Scraping the gunk off is not only a major challenge, but the chief burden of existence. (33)

Here, again, the realism of the novel is turned inside out. The body becomes a constitutive part of its environment as Tiff realizes it is impossible to think through anything without thinking through "the whole universe." Although she tries to scrape off this "gunk," the ultimate realization is that there is no inside or outside: "you never get rid of it," all that changes is the amplification. At a much higher frequency, then, Zink is looking at how climate crisis distorts metaphor. Tiff starts with one metaphor before she finds it insufficient and revises it. This extemporaneous revision of tropes unfixes the text (like Stephen with the miscarriage/bird) from a determinant hierarchy as the reader is implicated in its very process of forming meaning. We, like Tiff, are reading the world through a warped and distorted mirror. This mirror is not a mirror that reifies the outside as a marker of human subjectivity but a mirror that levels the optic and ontological playing field through a diffractive lens.[27]

---

27. I use the term "diffractive" to capture Karen Barad's equally transscalar hermeneutics: "[Unlike] methods of reading one text or set of ideas against another where one set serves as a fixed frame of reference, diffraction involves reading insights through one another in ways that help illuminate differences as they emerge" (30). This is a transscalar mode of reading that requires a foreclosure of the realist novel's "fixed frame of reference." The world is too close and too multiple – in short, too weird – to make any definitive claims.

Just as metaphor and the scale of language are crucial sites for Franzen and Kingsolver, metaphor is an equally important way for Zink to capture the interdependence of the world. In Tiff's description of Berne, she cannot help but sound out different human and nonhuman metaphors as she describes the city:

> Berne lived inward on itself. But it wasn't self-sufficient; it was more like a tumor with blood vessels to supply everything it needed: capital, expats, immigrants, stone, cement, paper, ink, clay, paint. No, not a tumor. A flower with roots stretching to the horizon, sucking in nutrients, but not just a single flower: a bed of mixed perennials. A flower meadow where butterflies could lay eggs and die in peace, knowing their caterpillars would not be ground to pulp by the mowers. Continuity of an aesthetic that had become an aesthetic of continuity. (25)

Zink cycles through metaphors, alternating between human and nonhuman imagery. Revising and reframing the metaphor of the city – tumor into flower into meadow – is an attempt to give form to that which exceeds form. In effect, the metaphor cannot be anything but a tautology: "Continuity of an aesthetic that had become an aesthetic of continuity." Berne becomes what Morton calls a "strange sticky Möbius strip," wherein Tiff cannot extricate herself from the meditative process or figure out where the boundaries of the human intersect with the nonhuman (*Hyperobjects*, 180). After she runs into an old lover on the streets, an analogical process occurs:

> Knowledge, an allergen. Boredom, the mind's spring flood, the sole conceivable force for good, the sole means – for human awareness – of striving toward complexity. Diversity through flooding. Or something, because the allergy metaphor tended to make the spring flood be tears and snot, which couldn't be right. I felt overwhelmed by a new mystic rationalism. (166)

What Tiff is modeling is an atmospheric criticism of the Anthropocene. This "new mystic rationalism" is one that is in excess of her subjectivity, that clings to two poles of discursive thinking – rational, yet "mystic." Tiff feels overwhelmed, "flooded," by the very process of metaphorical projection as she realizes there is always an ambiguous "or something" that is left out of any one analytic scale.

Atmospheric Readings of the Anthropocene

In short, Zink uses Tiff to describe the limits of critical mastery in the Anthropocene. Atmospheric reading is about the disavowal of mastery, about an awareness that there will always be an "or something" that is beyond critical comprehension. Just as Ferris turns to the aural at the end of *The Unnamed*, Zink seems to wonder if literature may not be the best medium for addressing this "something." Following its publication, Zink described *The Wallcreeper* as "a dubstep novel with a bird in it" ("Henry"). Jenny Turner riffs on this characterization: "The dubstep has a little to do with the narrator's husband who moonlights as a DJ, but is mostly a reference to the novel's method, which is fast, brainy, choppy." What strikes me about Zink and Turner is the way they are thinking through the text sonically. This is another way of describing an atmospheric mode of reading – we are surrounded by the text aurally. This mode of listening is what Julietta Singh has described as the ecological praxis "of being vulnerable to the voices – human and nonhuman, audible and muted – that are always sounding" (27). For Singh, listening describes inhabiting the atmospheric textures of a text that doesn't presuppose a type of critical containment. It is a way to "let each other in" interdependently (27). The sonic scale is one of subterranean pulsations that can easily pass below our radar. Consider a scene where Stephen plays some dubplates in their Berne apartment: "Loose sheets of paper on his desk would rise and fall with the bass. If the house had been newer, the roof tiles would have rattled. But it was soft, with fungi and moss as integral elements in the construction, so nothing really rattled much" (75). Zink moves from a description of the bass in his 12-inch dance records into a description of how the music itself is entwined with the construction of the house's architecture. The fungi and moss become "integral elements" not just in the house, but also in the way the music is heard becoming just as integrated into the music as the bass.

Listening to the text in the critical sense is an atmospheric reading, a way of attempting to grapple with modes of reading that exceed us. As the narrator says of Stephen, "Stephen never had a strategy about anything. He just went ahead and did stuff, then tried retrospectively to figure out why" (119). Or, as Stephen himself says, "All anybody wants to know is little sketchy bits of information, strictly censored" (39). What Zink is grappling for within this text is what Amitav Ghosh has characterized as literature's foundational issue of scale. Ghosh writes that the Anthropocene's "form of resistance" is "a scalar one" that returns as "phenomena that were long ago expelled from the territory of the novel – forces of unthinkable magnitude that create unbearably intimate connections over vast gaps in time and space" (63). If the return of these repressed, geologic "forces of unthinkable magnitude" have returned to the novel, how can we start to chart the "meaningless forces that [get] rolled in earth's diurnal course"? Although Ghosh seems to throw his hands up in defeat, claiming that climate crisis may "[resist] literary fiction" (84), I see this resistance to form as a call to arms, an impetus to keep searching for new forms, new modes of expression that might be able to articulate the continual crisis of living in the Anthropocene. It is a way to use fiction heuristically. This is what Zink is searching for, a way to imagine a new relationship between text/reader that might be able to capture the expansive scales of climate crisis in all their variance.[28]

To use fiction as a way to model Anthropocene thinking is to restructure the relationship between text and world. Crucially, this involves rethinking the relationship between author/world, text/world, and, even, reader/author. On the last page of *The Wallcreeper*, we read:

> After a while, I decided [Gernot the priest] might be on to something. I had been treating myself as resources to be mined. Now I know I am the soil where I grow. In between wallpapering, I wrote *The Wallcreeper*. Then I started on the floors. Then I took up playing the piano, I went back to school in Jena and graduated in hydrogeology [. . .] The movie version ends with a montage of Stephen in bed with different club kids (almost all girls) in Berne. Soundtrack: "Oh Very Young." (192–193)

Girded by an extractive logic ("to be mined"), Zink gives us a final reveal. The passage starts with a narrative logic that is non-agentive. The sentence "In between wallpapering, I wrote *The Wallcreeper*" suggests a hallowed intentionality; the novel's name was only incidental to the internal forces of the pun. It is almost as if the text is listening to itself, creating its own grammar. Moreover, Zink, although not identical with Tiff, implicates herself within the text. Zink-as-author is redistributed into the interior of the text, dissolving atmospherically into her novel. The text complicates the spatial relation between text and world in a way that dissipates the foreground/background distinction.[29] Tiff/Zink are inside the text, forcing us to

---

28. Taylor also describes this heuristic capacity of fiction. This is the ability, he writes, "for the novel to make visible otherwise invisible truths about the world, not in spite of its fictive status but because of it" (*The Sky*, 28–29).
29. This is something that Morton has picked up on in his descriptions of *noir* fiction. He writes, "The *noir* narrator begins investigating a supposedly external situation, from a supposedly neutral point of view, only to discover that she or he is implicated in it" (*Ecological*, 16).

reread and rethink the novel – questioning the usual types of divides we like to maintain between fact/fiction. The narrator of the novel has morphed into a weird version of Zink, as even the author is subsumed within the looping scales of crisis in the Anthropocene.

It is both author and reader, then, that exist on the inside of the text. While acknowledging that the book is "an environmental novel, if a totally surprising one," Romm describes how it strikes a similar chord to *Freedom*. "Yet even readers (like me)," she writes, "who love Zink's agenda, her irreverence, how she flips the bird at convention every chance she gets are likely to feel that her fiction loses steam when she declaims about eco-activism." Like Franzen's critics, Romm suggests that the ecological in Zink is adjacent to the text, a supplemental didacticism grafted onto the actual novel. But Romm finishes with a concession that perhaps this mode of critique is precisely the point: "Her novel defiantly resists classification as modern commodity, something easily consumed and disposed of. Wake up, this book says [. . .] You snooze and we all lose." There is a slippage here as Romm moves into the first-person plural, suggesting a textual horizon of immanence and co-implication that includes both the reader and the author. Like Zink falling into her own novel, Romm drags us all into her review. This is what it means when Tiff says, "Space, as any Kantian can tell you, is not forever" (130). Zink's transscalar critique rests in her ability to also force us to engage with the stratosphere and biosphere of her novel.

Chapter 3

Transscalar Blackness: Race and the Long Anthropocene

History doesn't unfold with one era bound to and determining the next in an unbroken chain of causality [. . .] So the point isn't the impossibility of escaping the stranglehold of the past, or that history is a succession of uninterrupted defeats, or that the virulence and tenacity of racism is inexorable. But rather that the perilous conditions of the present establish the link between our age and a previous one in which freedom too was yet to be realized.

Saidiya Hartman, *Lose Your Mother*

How terrifying it has been to realize *no one thinks my people have a future*. And how gratifying to finally accept myself and begin spinning the futures I want to see.

N.K. Jemisin, *How Long 'til Black Future Month?*

Let's start with the end of the world, why don't we? Get it over with and move on to more interesting things.

N. K. Jemisin, *The Fifth Season*

Held under a certain light, N. K. Jemisin's 2020 science fiction novel, *The City We Became,* picks up where Nell Zink leaves off. The book starts with, as one of the protagonists describes it, a picture of "*Weird New York*" in the days immediately leading up to and during a siege of the city by a Lovecraftian entity who is attempting to destroy it (32; emphasis in original). The plot of *The City We Became* is strange and complex, turning around a central conceit that cities are born into existence through individual surrogates who are made to represent each city. We start as New York is struggling to be born and the city's surrogate has only narrowly escaped defeat in a fight against a nebulous enemy, the Woman in White and her minions, a set of man-bun-donning provocateurs – the type who love craft beer, but would also be the first to line up for a slot on a Tucker Carlson broadcast. The New York surrogate (whose name is simply New York) is now hiding in a forgotten subway tunnel, only barely breathing. But New York, unlike the other city surrogates in the novel, is unique in that the city has a surrogate for the city as a whole and each borough has an individual stand-in. For the remainder of the book we follow each of the boroughs – Manhattan (Manny), Brooklyn (Brooklyn "MC Free" Thomason), the Bronx (Bronca Siwanoy), Queens (Padmini Prakash), and Staten Island (Aislyn Houlihan) – as they continue to battle the Woman in White, who wants to stop New York from being born into existence by "destroying everything that makes New York what it is, replacing it with generic *bullshit*" (357; emphasis in original). Alongside this plotline, we also witness a sibling rivalry between the other surrogates, with the perennially conservative (and racist) Aislyn allying herself with the Woman in White.

While the book itself is a far cry from the crisis realism I have traced throughout *Transscalar Critique*, its building blocks are not as different as they initially appear. *The City We Became* is very much a book about crisis and begins firmly on similar terrain to many of the works covered in the first half of the book. In the opening passages, Manny even goes so far as to describe the attacks from the Woman in White as "just like 9/11" (24). In fact, huge portions of the novel work allegorically to point back to 9/11: the initial attack is treated as a terrorist strike on the city that spawns both vehement and half-hearted calls for patriotic unity in the face of terror. This leads to a focus in the novel on a hunt for teleological closure, what Manny advocates for as "a return to normalcy" (43). In this sense, Jemisin explores how the marker of crisis has become a shorthand for contemporary authors to mark the contemporary-as-contemporary.[1] She is querying the saturation of "posts" that pockmark the contemporary from "post-9/11" to "post-George Floyd." *The City We Became*, therefore, becomes a post-9/11 novel akin to the ones I covered in the Introduction, even if it now includes alien entities and shapeshifting protagonists.

1. This is a move that Alexander Manshel, among others, has described as a hyperperiodization of the present, wherein "the crises of recent history before they become fully historical," therefore represent "both an acceleration of the novel's historical imagination and a decelerating double take at the modern news cycle" (n.p.).

But just as easily as she points to this contemporary economy of crisis, Jemisin also presents a much different picture of crisis than the ones we've seen so far. As the book unfolds, it moves centrifugally out from 9/11, morphing into a much stranger meditation on the nature of crisis in the contemporary more generally. At the center of Jemisin's weird 9/11 is an argument analogous to one at the heart of *Transscalar Critique*: a moment of crisis brings to the fore the layered and striated interconnections between time, space, and being to highlight how crisis should always be viewed from a transscalar perspective. *The City We Became* avoids crisis fetishization by reframing and rehistoricizing crisis through a larger historical framework. This, in short, is what allows us to see an alternative relationship between literary form, crisis, and scale emerge. Said somewhat differently, just as much as it is a novel about 9/11, it is also a novel about Hurricane Katrina, white flight and gentrification, climate crisis, income inequity, the long shadow of settler colonialism, and anti-Black violence, to name but a few. To understand the crisis of the contemporary, Jemisin argues that we need to think about all of these crises at one and the same time.[2] In fact, central to the novel is Jemisin's claim that to think about crisis is to think about how the infrastructure and environment of crisis are historically contingent. That is, at every moment in the book, Jemisin draws our attention to how New York itself is built upon "the bones of Black people. And Native American and Chinese and Latinos and whole waves of European immigrants and . . . everybody" (191). *The City We Became*, in short, argues for a longer conception of the contemporary that reimagines crisis not as a momentary rupture but as a constitutive state of being, looking at how crisis stretches forwards and backwards in time and space, animated through a history of specifically racialized violence. Jemisin's novel provides an opening to think about all three terms of this book's subtitle – climate, Blackness, crisis – concurrently, offering a provisional glimmer to reimagine crisis outside of the hierarchical and linear teleology of crisis realism.

This reorientation of crisis is, as I will argue in the remainder of this book, an interface of thinking about questions of Blackness

---

2. Mark Tabone makes a similar point in his reading of Jemisin: "Jemisin's fantastic worlds bear the impress of contemporary transformative politics, especially the intersectional Black feminism that infuses the Black Lives Matter movement. They also stand in critical dialectical tension with the political exigencies of the second decade of the twenty-first century and the history that led to this point" (366).

alongside questions of ecology. The second half of *Transscalar Critique* is invested in a reorganization of the crisis narratives that we have thus far followed by turning to Black Studies and Black literature as a way to disrupt the white stranglehold on crisis that has sustained and perpetuated the ongoing generic reach of crisis realism. In the first two chapters of *Transscalar Critique*, I looked at how contemporary fiction and criticism try to scale crisis through the metric of the human. Salient within these rescalings is a privilege afforded to a specific subset of humans marked as white and, more often than not, an even smaller subset of cis-gendered and middle-class white men. Although at moments I have provided fairly generous readings of these authors, the works I have read – from Michael Lewis to Nell Zink – remain inflected and infected with a determinant, if often invisible, scale of whiteness. In this sense, all these texts have remained monoscalar, hinged to a critical and literary mode that cleaves to recognizable forms without interrogating their underlying conditions.

Central to understanding the ongoing crisis of living in the Anthropocene is a full recalibration of our critical modes. Thought in the Anthropocene, Isabelle Stengers argues, requires "a struggle against probability" (17). What I argue in this chapter, and through the remainder of *Transscalar Critique*, is that to think "against probability" is not just a requisite of theorizing the Anthropocene, but also a necessity when thinking through the other seemingly intractable crisis that defines our contemporary: anti-Black and racialized violence.[3] As the passage from Jemisin limns, to think about any crisis of the present requires an acknowledgment of "the bones of Black people." Just as the Anthropocene names a crisis that preexists our naming it as such, so does the ongoing crisis of antiblackness. In her memoir, *Lose Your Mother*, Saidiya Hartman traces the long history of antiblackness from the present back to the barracoons and slave routes in Ghana. In a telling moment, she has a conversation with another American who left the country to reconnect with his ancestry outside of the architecture of US racism. In a heated late-night conversation, the expat tells her simply, "Black people have always been in crisis" (74). This observation grounds the remainder of *Transscalar Critique*.

---

3. Working at a microscale, this is a point that Katherine McKittrick also makes: "Antiblackness informs neurobiological and physiological drives, desires, emotions – and negative feelings – because it underwrites a collective and normalized, racially coded, biocentric belief system wherein narratives of natural selection, and the dysselection of Blackness, are cast as, and *reflexively* experienced as, common sense" (156; emphasis in original).

In the second half of this book, I argue that we cannot conceive of crisis in the contemporary without also thinking through the color line. Thought in the Anthropocene, simply put, must always be mediated through the lens of race. To make this argument, I argue that the critical mode I have laid out thus far as transscalar critique has an alternative lineage that emerges from and alongside Black Studies and Black literature. That is, if transscalar critique is a mode of encountering texts that thinks simultaneously about the big and the small, the epistemological and the ontological, the literary and the political in light of the perennial crisis of life in the Anthropocene, I argue that Black Studies and Black literature have always been transscalar in light of the ongoing crisis of anti-Black racism.

To make this argument, this chapter traces a genealogy of scale and the Anthropocene through contemporary Black Studies. Central to this genealogy is the work of Sylvia Wynter. Wynter's lifelong project turns around the question of the interrelationship between divergent analytic scales – from the economic to the environmental, the textual to the biological. Wynter develops a critical paradigm that has become increasingly influential and instrumental in a growing node of contemporary Black Studies that reexamines the intersection between race and the nonhuman world, particularly as this interstice is filtered through literary studies. Though scale is only a salient analytic for Wynter (and many of her theoretical successors and interlocutors, for that matter), rereading Wynter as a transscalar critic is a way to put her work in conversation with the critical landscape that I have traced throughout this book, particularly as it is situated in the field of the environmental humanities. If *Transscalar Critique* has traced a history of scale that continually bumps into the limited purchase of the human and its concomitant claims to whiteness, this chapter and the ones that follow provide a needed counternarrative, looking at how Black writing has always been transscalar. After mapping out the outlines of this critical heritage, I return briefly to Jemisin, looking at how she uses literary form to put pressure on questions of Blackness, ecology, and crisis. Not bound by the auspices of realism, Jemisin builds speculative worlds that channel the rich archives of Afrofuturism and Black speculation to circumvent the ongoing violence of a contemporary defined by anti-Black violence and anthropogenic climate change.

The Long Anthropocene

Writing about Black speculative fiction, Diana Leong presciently argues, "Blackness is the specter that haunts the Anthropocene and its possible futures" (15). This haunting, and the "possible futures" that it conjures, are not just a question of what it means to think about a spectral Anthropocene future, but also what it means to think about Blackness backwards in time. Leong's flagging of temporality is instructive for the way it signals how the time of crisis ascribed to much Anthropocene discourse remains plagued by this racial blind spot. That is, just as the Anthropocene rewrites human history at large by inserting itself onto the stratospheric record, the previous 500 years have also been imprinted with the stratigraphic marker of Blackness and colonial violence. Elizabeth DeLoughrey picks up on this claim, arguing that contemporary Anthropocene criticism has attached itself to a "discourse of rupture" that belies the ongoing legacies of systemic, colonial, and racial violence upon which it is reliant (3). This has, in effect, produced a whitewashing of the Anthropocene wherein its "rupture" is imagined as an origin point, a theoretical ground zero. "Certainly the rise of the [Anthropocene's] concurrence with the second millennium and its associated post-9/11 narratives of apocalypse and extinction are not coincidental," she writes. "Some Anthropocene discourse seems to be an elegy for a loss of the fantasy of 'western civilization' and the (overrepresented) figure of 'man'" (19–20). It is not incidental that in her historicization of the Anthropocene, DeLoughrey returns to 9/11. The types of crisis frameworks that have risen in response to the Anthropocene share an origin with the post-9/11 epistemologies we have been tracing across the pages of *Transscalar Critique*. Under this reading, the Anthropocene becomes an analogous rupture, a fungible event that occurs at, an albeit much larger, scale. Underpinning this logic is a scalar invariance where the impact of crisis is merely stretched to subsume the entirety of the *Anthropos*.[4]

DeLoughrey challenges this crisis narrative, looking at how the Anthropocene does not name a new crisis as such, but is reflective of a larger racialized history of settler colonialism and anti-Black violence.

---

4. This is a point made by Elizabeth Povinelli. Povinelli focuses in on the crisis-defined contemporary, writing "[The] Anthropocene and its companion concept of climate change should not be seen merely as meteorological and geological events but as a set of political and conceptual disturbances that emerged in the 1960s – the radical environmental movement, Indigenous opposition to mining, the concept of Gaia and the whole earth – and these disturbances are now accelerating the problem of how late liberalism will govern difference and markets globally" (*Geontologies*, 13). What I take from Povinelli's claim is the fact that the critical apparatus of the Anthropocene emerges from a contemporary that has cleaved to a circulation of crisis currency.

She argues the Anthropocene is part and parcel of a longer "historical *continuity* of dispossession and disaster caused by empire" (2; emphasis in original). This shift to a specifically racialized lens brings together the distortive and violent scalar logic of both the Anthropocene and racialized violence. DeLoughrey continues:

> Some may rightly question whether the claim of Anthropocene discourse that we have an entirely new ecological crisis is, in fact, belated. [. . .] [We] can see that catastrophic ruptures to social and ecological systems have already been experienced through the violent processes of empire. In other words, the apocalypse has already happened; it continues because empire is a process. (7)

I want to tread carefully here. When DeLoughrey claims that an apocalypse has already arrived for certain people, it is important not to fetishize Black, Brown, and Indigenous death. I will return to this point later on, but for the moment I want to pause and think about DeLoughrey's claim as it relates to the act of criticism. If the world has already ended, then what is the role of criticism? Is there even a critical scale at which we can begin to think? While the knee-jerk reaction may be to put our hands up at this juncture, flailing at what Jennifer Wenzel cites as the Anthropocene's "impasse and inertia" (*Disposition*, 1), there is also a more generative claim smuggled into the fringes of DeLoughrey's argument. If we start from the premise that the end of the world has already happened, perhaps it becomes our role as critics to begin listening to voices that are working within, through, and beyond this space of the post-apocalyptic.

To supplant the largely white canon of environmental critique that has emerged from the Anthropocene's arrival, my argument is that there is already transscalar critique discourse that has been attempting to configure and reconfigure the world differently. This is another way of saying that, beyond critical "impasse and inertia," the rest of *Transscalar Critique* takes DeLoughrey's claim affirmatively to look at thinkers who have already begun thinking about what happens after apocalypse. If the conditions named by the Anthropocene, a dissolution of epistemological and ontological scales scaffolding our sense of the present, have long been felt by Black thinkers, we can turn to their writing to build out a transscalar conception of the Anthropocene contemporary, one that reorients our understanding of a contemporary marked by crisis outside the long shadow of crisis realism.

This is a point made by Kathryn Yusoff. In *A Billion Black Anthropocenes or None*, Yusoff argues that to think the Anthropocene we need to fight back against the anti-Black and settler colonial logic that has constructed the Anthropocene as a new crisis. Yusoff, like DeLoughrey, wants to move beyond and outside of the Anthropocene's ostensible critical impasse to create what she describes as "an insurgent geology for the end of the world" (111). For Yusoff, this is an endeavor that narrates a plurality of "Black Anthropocenes." What marks Yusoff's understanding of Black Anthropocenes as transscalar is the multiplicity with which she approaches the Anthropocene outside of terminal crisis renderings. On the one hand, to identify these Black Anthropocenes requires an acknowledgment of how the Anthropocene – in the singular – signals

> an inhuman proximity organized by historical geographies of extraction, grammars of geology, imperial global geographies, and contemporary environmental racism. It is predicated on the presumed absorbent qualities of black and brown bodies to take up the body burdens of exposure to toxicities and to buffer the violence of the earth. (11)

This necessitates an identification of and attention to the salience and construction in and of the Anthropocene through anti-Black and settler colonial "toxicities" that activate extractive logics that both naturalize and denaturalize Black and Indigenous peoples. But, on the other hand, Yusoff seeks a counterpulse of possibility by creating contrapuntal Black Anthropocenes – in the plural – constituted in and through the "centrality of race" (67). To reach this horizon, Yusoff reaches for a conception of critique wherein "the Anthropocene requires a reconfiguration of the subject at the center of white liberal ethical accounts and an acknowledgment of the role of race in the production of global spaces that constitute the Anthropocene" (67). Like DeLoughrey, then, she is invested in thinking about how we can begin to manifest new worlds alongside and after apocalypse.

Literary form is key to Yusoff's plural Black Anthropocenes. Although she is trained as a geologist, her attention is plied to the way narrative has often been complicit in creating "Golden Spikes" that "endeavor to geologically map the material relations of space and time according to stratigraphic principles and scientific precedents [...] these spikes are not real places as such; they are trace effects in material worlds that infer the event/advent of this most political geology" (33). Unlike dominant geological narratives, Yusoff's charts a multiplicity of these Golden Spikes that do not claim to be exhaustive or definitive – 1610, 1452, 1800, the 1950s. These Golden Spikes are at once reflective of geological, meteorological, and climatological data emanating from ecology and geology, but they are also key postcolonial dates. The year 1610, for example, marks the first colonial contact, and 1452 is a date that she specifically derives from Wynter.[5] Yusoff's argument is not so much to stake a claim to any one of these Golden Spikes, but to make a much larger point that any origin story of the Anthropocene must be

> defined through the color line. The disembodied monuments and matter of the Golden Spike point but do not name. This is why the Anthropocene is configured in a future tense rather than in recognition of the extinctions already undergone by black and indigenous peoples. (59)

This renarration of the Anthropocene in a "future tense" creates both the heuristic and the material possibility to imagine what happens after the end of the world. "Origins also nurture," Yusoff writes. "[They] grow an armature for narratives, they root a set of emplacements or belongings into place" (71).

What is at stake for both Yusoff and DeLoughrey is a transition from an Anthropocene contemporary to a long Anthropocene. A long Anthropocene is a critical claim as much as it is a geological one. The Anthropocene is, *ipso facto*, a historically antecedent concept that predates our awareness of it. But a long Anthropocene, as I understand it here, is critically long to help undo the saturation of novelty that adheres to Anthropocene discourse by arguing for alternative histories of the Anthropocenes, histories rooted in and constituted through a foundational relationship to Blackness. This is where we can begin to pick up the breadcrumbs left across contemporary Black Studies, thinking about Blackness and the Anthropocene at a transscalar level. This is, in and of itself, not necessarily a new claim. As Katherine McKittrick argues:

> [Black] people have always used interdisciplinary methodologies to explain, explore, and story the world, because thinking and writing and imagining across a range of texts, disciplines, histories, and genres unsettles suffocating and dismal and insular racial logics. By employing interdisciplinary methodologies and living interdisciplinary worlds, black people bring together various sources and texts and narratives to challenge racism. (4)

---

5. Wynter cites 1452 as the birth of "the New World, as African slaves are put to work on the first plantations" ("Unparalleled," 44); 1800 is Yusoff's shorthand for the start of the industrial era while 1950 is tied to the period known as the Great Acceleration following our entrance into the nuclear age.

This is why it is vital to take a transscalar approach to both the Anthropocene and the ongoing crisis of anti-Black racism. We need to work across textual, material, temporal, and ontological scales as a way to think through not just racism, but also how that racism sutures and is animated through ecological violence.

Scales of Race

Conceiving of a critically long Anthropocene allows a subtending history to emerge alongside and with this conceptual framework: a counterhistory of scale, if you will. In his recent history and theorization of what he describes as "scale mania," Zach Horton looks at the ways scale has been adopted and developed across disciplinary divides over the course of the past 500 years (*Cosmic*, xx). It is an excellent, compelling, and necessary history of scale, one rooted as much in the life and material sciences as it is in the humanities and media theory. But, governing his book, we can also discern a certain claim to novelty. Horton writes, "Scales that we, as humans, had taken for granted are suddenly front and center, blocking the path both forward and backward. And when we look around, everything seems different, as if the borders between things have slipped out of focus" (*Cosmic*, 5). This is not to say that things have not changed in the contemporary – they have. Whether you are navigating rolling blackouts in Puerto Rico, watching the infrastructure literally melt in Vancouver, or experiencing flooding in Saxony, a passing glance at any newspaper will underline that the forever deferred futurity of climate crisis has arrived. But I also want to put pressure on this claim, to think about how there is an erasure that occurs with the supposition of "suddenly" that Horton offers us. This is not to say that Horton is purposely whitewashing scale. Indeed, his book is a careful ecology of scale, tracing an analogous usage of scale to the one I am tracing in *Transscalar Critique*.[6] But, his focus on the

---

6. He goes so far as to map out "trans-scalar encounters" that offer a robust picture of "scale in its full light, as ontological, construct of knowledge, and speculative ecology – all at once" (*Cosmic*, 23). And later on, he mobilizes a critique of the monoscalar imaginary I have been critiquing. "Any system predicated upon the continual appropriation and stabilization of new scales in the service of a single master scale (as a dominant and homogenizing logic)," he writes, "is bound to run up against its absolute limits relatively quickly, whether those limits take the form of a financial crash, a global pandemic, a massive loss of biodiversity" (*Cosmic*, 8).

specific media mechanics of scale as envisaged through the history of what he describes as the "cosmic zoom" and the emergence of the Anthropocene, remains somewhat myopic in attending to a history yoked to whiteness.[7] If there is a fault here, it is one in seeking out ruptures and claims to novelty where they do not necessarily exist, or do not necessarily exist for everyone. This is something that M. Jacqui Alexander describes: "The persistence of continuities ought to give us a great deal of pause about announcing the premature end to things, as in the end of history," she writes. "[For] history proceeds in a way that makes ruptures neither clean nor final" (93).

The problematic of scale, and its inability to be taken "for granted," have, in other words, an alternative genealogy that works its way through Black Studies. Indeed, as Jayna Brown so presciently puts it, Black thought has always been invested in critiquing "vast inhuman scales" (6). Consider Christina Sharpe's now canonical *In the Wake: On Blackness and Being*. Sharpe examines how anti-Black violence operates across myriad scales that remain in excess of the human. Throughout her book, Sharpe cycles through various scales to attend to the pervasiveness of antiblackness. One of her key tropes is the "weather," which she harnesses as a structural metaphor to describe the ongoing, rippling afterlife of chattel slavery:

> In my text, the weather is the totality of our environments; the weather is the total climate; and the climate is antiblack. And while the air of freedom might linger around the ship, it does not reach into the hold, or attend the bodies in the hold. (104)

First and foremost, Sharpe highlights how antiblackness is climatic, moving out into the stratosphere to structure a consumptive and toxic climate of anti-Black violence that continually sanctions the killing of Black people. But, at the same time, this passage suggests that anti-Black violence operates not just at this macro-scale of

---

7. The cosmic zoom, Horton argues, is the folly of "ordering the world in relation to the human" (*Cosmic*, 11). I should also add that Horton is aware of the way in which this history of scale is one tethered to a hegemonic whiteness. He writes, "It is not coincidental that as European colonialism faltered after World War II, a hylomorphic, trans-scalar colonialism began to take its place. It is a question of resources: when they have been fully exploited on one plane, new planes – territories – must be opened up for exploitation" (*Cosmic*, 220–221). But, even here, the question of race remains somewhat adjacent to the history he is tracing.

atmospheric violence, but also at a more insidious molecular level. Sharpe's wake is also a collection of the water molecules lapping at the hold of the slave ship, infiltrating the world at a baser, material level – from the water in Flint, Michigan, to the pathogens of COVID-19 that continue to unevenly kill people in Black and Brown communities. Sharpe is describing a world that is defined by a vast cross-section of scale that operates simultaneously to perpetuate anti-Black violence. It is no surprise, then, that McKittrick describes the contemporary as constituted by its "multiscalar injustices" against Black people (28).

To put this reading of Sharpe into the same lexicon I have used throughout this book: like the crisis signaled by the Anthropocene, antiblackness is also a transscalar crisis constituted by and through a continual proliferation of both larger and smaller scales. This does not mean that the two are interchangeable or homologous, but merely that the type of scalar dysphoria inaugurated by both has points of crucial resonance (as well as dissonance). I should be clear that Sharpe's work is not invested in querying the relationship between Blackness and the environment. She is not making an environmental claim by putting Blackness into conversation with scales of nonhuman being. What Sharpe is doing is thinking through the possibilities that exist at the intersection between Black Studies and ecology, looking at how the environment provides an animating metaphorical scale at which she can describe the ongoing afterlives and violence of chattel slavery.

No less metaphorical, but certainly more material, Wynter's work sits at a similar intersection. What differentiates her writing, however, is how Wynter is interested in thinking about ecology not unilaterally, but symbiotically, asking not just what Black Studies can learn from ecology (as is implicit in Sharpe's case), but also what ecology can learn from Black Studies. Across her œuvre, Wynter maps the possibilities of trying to envisage the human at the level of the transscalar. In an interview with McKittrick she drives this point home:

> We presently live in a moment where the human is understood as a purely biological mechanism that is subordinated to a teleological economic script that governs our global well-being/ill-being – a script therefore, whose macro-origin story calcifies the *hero figure* of *homo oeconomicus* who practices, indeed normalizes, accumulation in the name of (economic) freedom. Capital is thus projected as the indispensable, empirical, and metaphysical source of all human life, thus semantically activating the neurochemistry of our brain's opiate reward/punishment system to act accordingly! ("Unparalleled," 10)

This is an interesting passage for a number of reasons. First, Wynter offers a critique of the types of monoscalar imaginaries underpinning crisis realism. An overdetermination of economics has calcified to the point where the economic is mistaken as an ontological plane – it is now impossible to even imagine the human outside of this "teleological economic script."[8] But perhaps more than a critique of the economic, what is telling in Wynter is the way in which her work moves across myriad other scales. This passage is at once economic, but also biological, theoretical, material, and discursive all at the same time. Wynter moves with a fluidity from the "neurochemistry" of our brains to a larger "macro-origin story" of *homo oeconomicus*. These divergent scales of narrating the human are not separate for Wynter, but always present, amplifying, contradicting, distorting, and confirming one another. More importantly, they are not necessarily fungible but cause friction and tension to emerge – this is scalar variance as opposed to the homogenous mass of scalar invariance.

A scalar variance is at the center of Wynter's thought. Her theoretical project is embryonically concerned with the realm of ontology wherein she wants to conceive of life at this transscalar level, given the existential precarity signaled by anthropogenic climate change. She writes, "[For] the first time in our history, we find ourselves having to confront, *as a species*, the overall negative costs now being paid on a planetary level for the continued dynamic enactment, yet stable reproduction, of the above" ("Unparalleled," 43; emphasis in original). At first pass, this may scan as a claim to novelty: the Anthropocene has confronted us with a foundational shift in scale as it ushers in a self-consciousness "as a species." But Wynter also rehistoricizes this shift, bringing it into historical continuity and contiguity with previous moments of scalar crisis. She continues:

> [All these myriad crises] interact and are interconnected and thus, together, are constitutive of our species' now seemingly inescapable, hitherto unresolvable "global problematique." The main problem with respect to solving the cognitive contradiction with which we are now confronted is therefore how we can begin not only to draw attention to but also to *mind about* those *outside* our specific and particular *referent-we* perspective and worldview. ("Unparalleled," 43; emphasis in original)

---

8. This calls to mind the types of crisis capitalist realism I examined in Chapter 1, which are hinged, as Mark Fisher would have it, to "the way that capitalism subsumes and consumes all of previous history" (*Capitalist*, 4). I will also return to this line of argument in the final chapter on Beatty.

Wynter is quick to disavow Anthropocenic tunnel vision. For her, to think about our current moment of crisis requires us to think along larger ontological (signaled by the expansion of the "referent-we") and spatio-temporal (signaled by "worldview") scales.[9] She draws our attention to the fact that any singular claim to crisis is one that is imbricated and knotted through the contradictions that are inherent in the glossing of a particular we.[10]

Wynter, in other words, is able to think about both the crisis of race and the crisis of the Anthropocene across scales – drawing our attention to the problematics that are associated with an Anthropocene contemporary while also historicizing the current conditions of the climatic through a longer history of race. It is not that we must pretend that our present moment is not one of crisis; we just need to take a more complex and nuanced understanding of what exactly we mean when we talk about a crisis of the contemporary. Elsewhere she elaborates on this: "[The] issue of race, as the issue of the Colonial Question, the Nonwhite/Native Question, the Negro Question, yet as one that has hitherto had no name, was and is fundamentally the issue of the genre of the human, Man" ("Unsettling," 288). The scalar dysphoria of the Anthropocene is one, in other words, that is rooted in a longer history of crisis for the "genre of the human," one that can trace its origin back to the "political citizen and/or subject of the state, and, from the end of the eighteenth century onward [. . .] *as if* each such definition of *Man* were at the same time definitions of the human itself" ("On How," 123; emphasis in original). Wynter is arguing that we need to think outside the scale of the human that continues to buttress the limits of any one critical imaginary. Indeed, she is searching for a transscalar conception of humanity, what she calls a "trans-genre-of-the-human-perspective" ("Re-Enchantment," 206).[11]

---

9. Brown also picks up on this spatio-temporal mapping, arguing that Black Studies requires a larger "rescaling of the human past the bounds of recognition" through a "spatiotemporality that is not discoverable along a human timeline" (173, 8).
10. There is something akin to this sentiment in Alexander's tour de force, *Pedagogies of Crossing*. There Alexander argues that, to understand our contemporary, we need to sound out a history of Blackness built around "various sites of crisis and instability" (4).
11. Alexander Weheliye is useful in summarizing what this transscalar mode looks like in Wynter as he looks at how Wynter, alongside Hortense Spillers, "[tackles] notions of the human as it interfaces with gender, coloniality, slavery, racialization, and political violence without mapping these questions onto a mutually exclusive struggle between either the free-flowing terra nullius of the universally applicable or the terra cognitus of the ethnographically detained" (24).

Sharpe and Wynter both point back to how scale is a foundational, if unremarked upon, analytic in the Black Studies tradition, particularly for thinkers who are negotiating with the ongoing legacy and violence of chattel slavery. For Wynter, this often takes an ontological shape as she explores the outer reaches of this "trans-genre" of humanity, seeking out what she calls a "planetary" humanism ("Re-Enchantment," 207). But this focus on the human of humanity (even if that human is distorted across scales) also suggests a limit to Wynter's thought. While she provides the impetus to think through the transscalar, there is a level of scalar invariance in her thinking: Wynter wants to rescale the human from the individual to the planetary, retaining the vessel of the human even if the contents have changed. This is a point that has been critiqued by recent theorists who are keen to explore the relationship between Blackness and ecology. Brown summarizes this changing of the guard, taking Wynter to task by arguing that what is actually needed is not a "call for a new genre of the human" but "new genres of *existence*, entirely different modes of material being and becoming" (9; emphasis in original).[12]

Black Ecologies

Brown's searching for "new genres of existence" is a useful shorthand for a nascent subfield bubbling across Black Studies that builds from Wynter but thinks outside the prescription of the human. This cohort of thinkers asks what it means to theorize Blackness against the very real and pressing need to stretch questions of ethics, politics, and philosophy into messy entanglements with the nonhuman world, a world that is precariously (and self-consciously) on the edge of destruction. Equally prevalent in this subfield, and scaffolded by this first point, is the fact that these thinkers are invested in how Black Studies can teach us to think, read, and narrate the ongoing crisis of the Anthropocene alongside anti-Black violence. It is not enough to highlight the impasse signaled by the ending of the world. We need to think beyond this limit of critique to grapple

---

12. McKittrick echoes Wynter's sentiments, writing, "[In] order to be newly human, one does not only rebelliously *site* and *make* black culture in a world that despises blackness, one also *engages* cultural inventions and sounds and ideas and texts, deeply and enthusiastically, in order to affirm humanity: one grooves *out* of the logics of racism and *into* black life" (164; emphasis in original).

with whatever comes after, however provisional and tenuous it may be. Importantly, and as suggested by Wynter, this inchoate branch of environmental thinking does not occlude questions of Blackness but is animated in and through it.[13] This is an argument that Zakiyyah Iman Jackson makes pointedly: "[Racial] discourse is not simply a by-product of the discourse of species, but rather race and species discourses are homologous and symbiotic" (153). What is at stake here, then, is a sustained engagement with the racial blind spots of the Anthropocene. Said another way, to think at the level of the species is necessarily to be confronted with the question of Blackness and, in doing so, there is a dissolution of what it is that makes up the *Anthropos* of the Anthropocene.

Ian Baucom's recent work has shifted from the oceanic to the climatic as he rethinks this question of the *Anthropos* via an interrogation of climate and the postcolony:

> [How might] our understanding of the postcolony and the Black Atlantic [look] from [an Anthropocene] perspective, how they are cast into relief from this coast, from the angle of inspection, with the waters rising to the horizon line, pushing their waves, and surf, and bullions of beach sand through crumbling walls and doors in what only looks like an act of natural destruction but is, in fact, a historically natured (or alter-natured) process of violence? (73–74)

By zooming out and taking the macro-scale of a planetary perspective as his starting point, Baucom returns to the realm of Dipesh Chakrabarty, taking the bird's-eye view on what it means to think through the differentials of the Anthropocene through postcolonial methodologies. But Baucom does not opt for a universalizing lens but rather focuses in on "this coast," identifying a grounded positionality that does not succumb to a full ontological rupture and subsumes humanity *en masse* as a geologic force. He is, that is, sounding out a transscalar methodology: what does it mean to do the work of Black Studies when we have become "as humanly unified *by* the ontological (and ontology-shattering) shock of collectively *having become* the force we have become" (91; emphasis in original)? For Baucom, the

---

13. As Ian Baucom puts it, "[Any] politics of the present must be routed through the force of black reason" (24). He continues, "We see that *we* come to the planetary *through* the subaltern; that we come to the 'we' of the Anthropocene from the postcolony's shore" (88; emphasis in original).

trick in undoing the viscosity of the generic human lies in the adverb "humanly." Humanly becomes a modifier that holds at bay the temptation to collapse the world into a singular humanity; humanly is a linguistic trick that refracts the impulse to scale up to the level of species, causing us to realize that, far from being the unified humanity we perhaps thought we were becoming, our very ontological status is far more contingent. It is this shifting between scales, imagining both lived experience and what it means to become a stratigraphic force, that Baucom argues will allow for us to work through the implications of the "globally common *and* globally uneven" Anthropocene epoch (80; emphasis in original).

The shift between the "common" and the "uneven" names a mode of scalar variance by pointing to both dissonance and resonance. Baucom argues that it is a theoretical and material movement between and across scales (what he calls "part of the 'blend'" (105)) that provides a signposting for how to think through a world where sea levels are rising and, alongside and with those rising sea levels, an erasure of the Black legacy of the Atlantic is taking place. Baucom describes this as the "multi-scaled complexity of our situation" (105). He approaches this transscalar "complexity" in an additive mode, not seeking to sound out some sort of master scale, but rather looking at points of continuity and departure between scales, layering and blending them together. It is not that thinking the Anthropocene supplants or usurps other scales of critical theory and thought (for example, Marxism or postcolonialism), his argument goes, but that they work together, creating new tensions and dynamics. As a dedicated study of methodology, Baucom is particularly interested in the scale-shifting that occurs when bringing together what he calls Materialism 1 (the materialism of yore, the "cultural, economic, sociological, and political circumstances that the historian's code makes available" (43)) and Materialism 2 (the latest vanguard of nonhuman thinking, from the object-oriented ontology of Timothy Morton to the vibrant materialism of Jane Bennett). It is the interplay of these new horizons – an interplay that is at once molecular and economic, racialized and stratigraphic – that produces "not the question of irreducibility, but of the relation of times, scales, and ontologies to one another within the co-relational human and nonhuman totality" (53).

In introducing this ontological multiplicity into his analysis, Baucom is attempting to bring questions of Blackness into concert with anthropogenic climate change. Where Baucom thinks this can occur is through the scale of aesthetics and artistic form. Baucom's own close readings – from the photography of Nyani Quarmyne to the fictional worlds of David Mitchell – suggest that aesthetics plays a privileged role in how we can reimagine the world:

> [Any] method of thought adequate to encompassing this heterogeneous, epochally mixed moment must include in its appraisals of the collapsed distinction of human, natural, and sacred histories, and in its multiple encounters with the nonhuman, an encounter with the aesthetic, and an appraisal of the 'actant' power of aesthetic history. (63)

He is precise in highlighting the ways in which literary, racial, and climatic history are co-constitutional, inextricably bound and linked to one another, while also providing a causal cut back into the world as an "actant." What he is gesturing towards is how we must recalibrate our modes of reading to account for their simultaneously operative logics and realities.

There is a similar line of thought in Tiffany Lethabo King's work as she rethinks the role of critical theory in light of both anti-Black and climatic violence. King uses Wynter as a fulcrum to think through the nexus of race and the environment, picking her way through Wynter's metaphors to establish and sound out a methodology that moves across scales. "Wynter's metaphor of the ceremony," she writes, "extends beyond a mode of critique, doubling as a praxis and space where the order of knowledge and being can be ritually disassembled" (198). King's description of "ceremony" could just as easily describe her own critical practice of "the shoal." A shoal is a geological formation found off the coast where the land and water converge, "a location offshore or in the middle of the sea" which "forces one to pause before proceeding" (208, 2). For King, this becomes the locus at which to bring together Black, Indigenous, and environmental studies into a productive tension. The shoal offers both a metaphorical animacy and a material force. At the metaphoric level, the shoal represents "a process formation, and space that exists beyond binary thinking" (28). As a material force, the shoal has a distinct value, exceeding its metaphorical framework through a materiality that morphs into a praxis by reorganizing both epistemological and ontological boundaries. The shoal, put simply, is figured as a site of critical and material presence and practice that rethinks the inherited logics, syntaxes, and grammars we operate within. King is reworking the scale and modes of reading, thinking, and being in the world, simultaneously imagining and creating the possibility for Black Studies to extend into an "open state of possibility with the capacity to transform the conditions of subjection" (122). The stakes for King are high. She is invested in attempting to "interrupt the narrative commonsense and quotidian processes of making the human" (42).

Like Wynter, King also sees her work as emerging from a moment of crisis. Her work originates from what she describes as "two of the most visible mobilizations and standoffs with U.S. state violence and state-sanctioned corporate violence, the Movement for Black Lives Matter and the Standing Rock Sioux's camp of Water Protectors" (208). But against this backdrop of crisis, King theorizes an ecology of Blackness constellating and tessellating with the ever-lingering specter of anthropogenic climate change as she maps a cartography of the disproportional fallout of climatic violence on Black peoples. Indeed, her continual return to Anthropocenic scales underlines this as she seeks to "radically [reimagine] the body's relationship to life forms that have been taxonomized as plants or nonhuman" (119). The shoal, as King tells us, is "as much a dynamic and moving set of processes and ecological relations as it is a longitudinal and latitudinal coordinate that cartographers attempt to fix in time and space. It is mobile, always changing and shifting state of flux" (3). What is striking about King's writing is that it is a cartographic rendering not only of the violent histories of anti-Black and Indigenous violence and their relationship to the nonhuman world, but also of the ways in which the scales of Black Studies help us reorder the world more generally. This is to say that even if the end of the world has already happened, there is something that can be shoaled from its remains.

This is a critical movement that is central to this alternative history of scale I am outlining. Whereas the Anthropocene often remains imagined as a critical impasse to contemporary thought, reading Blackness through the climatic and climate through Blackness produces the possibility that we might be able, as Sharpe has it, to start "reading and thinking otherwise" in a world that is sutured by both environmental destruction and antiblackness (104). This gesture towards an "otherwise" runs through this branch of Black Studies querying the nonhuman world. J. T. Roane and Justin Hosbey bring together a wide cross-section of Black Studies, the social sciences, and the environmental humanities to describe this Janus-faced fluctuation. On the one hand, they write, "African Diasporas are most susceptible to the effects of climate change, including rising sea levels, subsidence, sinking land, as well as the ongoing effects of toxic stewardship" (n.p.). Key to developing a dialogue between

Black Studies and ecology, they argue, is identifying and critiquing the asymmetries of anthropogenic climate violence across the color line. But, on the other hand, it is about more than a politics of visibility that demarcates historical violence.[14] There is a need to start thinking in more expansive terms through a "corpus of insurgent knowledge produced by these same communities, which we hold to have bearing on how we should historicize the current crisis and how we conceive of futures outside of destruction" (n.p.).[15] If someone like Sharpe provides us with analytic tools to identify the countless ripples that flow across time and space from behind the slave ship, Roane and Hosbey outline not only how to collect those ripplings, but how to build alternative figurations of the world more generally. Said somewhat differently, they are not only looking for a negative critique that reifies Black death in the Anthropocene, but rather attempting to think in capacious and promiscuous terms about the possibilities of Black life.[16]

It is in this focus on Black life that this strand of Black Studies is embryonically transscalar. The transscalar is accretive, avoiding the identification of a master scale at which to read and contain the world. Central to the transscalar is a way to think about how scalar differentials bisect, intersect, and contradict one another. There is a need to identify the violent scales that conspire to create, as Sharpe describes it, a "climate of antiblackness" (106), but there is also a way to think beyond that violence. Like the transscalar, then, this nascent subfield of Black Studies turns to literature as one such site to do this doubled work. Literature thinks about the scales of antiblackness and climate crisis as they exceed any possible human metrics, while also being able to incorporate and interrogate the granularity

---

14. Wenzel makes a similar point, arguing that contemporary ecological critique cannot always be tethered to what she calls a "problem of invisibility," wherein there is an empathetic causal chain premised on "the Enlightenment ideal of bringing things to light as a catalyst for change" (*Disposition*, 14).
15. Jayna Brown also argues in this vein: "My claim is that because black people have been excluded from the category *human*, we have a particular epistemic and ontological mobility. Unburdened by investments in belonging to a system created to exclude us in the first place, we develop marvelous modes of being in and perceiving the universe. I am claiming that there is a real power to be found in such an untethered state – the power to destabilize the very idea of human supremacy and allow for entirely new ways to relate to each other and to the postapocalyptic ecologies, both organic and inorganic, in which we are enmeshed" (6; emphasis in original).
16. We will return to this at length in readings of Paul Beatty in Chapter 5.

of human experience against this ambient apocalypse. The literary provides this movement across the big and small.

Zakiyyah Iman Jackson, for example, foregrounds literature as she tries to imagine how literary form enacts a politics that corresponds to the myriad scales that bisect one another in the Anthropocene. For Jackson, this is an intervention into the question of the "common" and "uneven" posed by Baucom, but Jackson focuses her scale of critique downwards on the "infinitely malleable lexical and biological matter" to locate and bypass the critical, ontological, and epistemological vocabularies and logics that have ossified to create a hegemonic humanism (3). To read this mattering of matter, she focuses on the question of the animal and the way animality has been marshaled by discourses of antiblackness. "'[The] human' and 'the animal' are not mutually exclusive ontological zones," she writes, "but rather positions in a highly unstable and indeterminate relational hierarchy, one that requires blackness as exception, as plasticity, in the establishment and reproduction of its code or representational grammar" (77). In this sense, Jackson stretches beyond the "trans-genre" of the planetary humanism described by Wynter. While Wynter clings to a form of humanism, however modified and redefined it may be, Jackson turns to questions of animality to implode and explode the residues of an inherited humanism:

> I am interested in how African diasporic writers not only critique animalization but also exceed critique by overturning received ontology and epistemic regimes of species that seek to define blackness through the prism of abject animality. By doing so, they present possibilities that point our attention to the potential modes of worlding that are more advantageous to life writ large. (34)

Her critique, therefore, is necessarily violent and forceful.[17] She argues that the nonhuman world has been set in opposition to Black life, co-opting the scale at which to think through Blackness and

---

17. In this sense, her work is part of a larger changing of the guard that has no interest in recuperative politics. This is a point made by Chelsea Frazier, who points to how there has been a resurgence in Black Studies to conceive of "a 'new' environmental politics that cannot come as a result of liberal reform or black inclusivity within extant mainstream political discourse" (46). I also see Jackson's language as building upon Hortense Spiller's radicalism where she looks for critical modes to "break apart, to rupture violently laws of American behavior" (79).

filtering the very matter of matter through racialized terms, fomenting "an ecology of violence – pervasive and chronic" (212).

If the very molecular material of the world has been set in opposition to Blackness, the question is begged as to at what scale we can possibly conceive of a world outside of that antiblackness? And this is where we see the multiple movements of the transscalar emerge in Jackson's thought. Even against this backdrop of "an ecology of violence," there is a generative component in her disavowal of the centrality of the human. This is to say that if Jackson identifies how antiblackness operates as an ecology of violence, she also creates an alternate mode that maps Blackness outside and untethered to the "melancholic attachment" of the "elusive 'humanist prize' – the formal, symmetrical extension of European humanism" (20, 33).[18] The excess that Jackson identifies in the Black literary tradition provides the space for her to develop a transscalar mode of re-visioning the world. On the one hand, Jackson argues, "[The] icon of 'black female body' is an essential figure in the unfurling of the object, the thing, matter, and the animal in ontological discourses of Western philosophy and science" (85). On the other, the literary allows for the "gestures of potentiality" which, although "often incomplete," still hold latent possibilities of "a desire and world-upending claim that is not currently recognized in the social order that gave rise to them" (36). In this way, Jackson takes both the matter of Blackness and the matter of the nonhuman in concert, offering glimpses of what Blackness and the nonhuman without the human look like when conceived of transscalarly.

---

18. The explicit use of the "melancholic" points to another fledgling discourse in Black Studies that works beyond the negative dialectics of Black death. In *Lose Your Mother*, Hartman poses a similar question, asking, "If ruin was my sole inheritance and the only certainty the impossibility of recovering the stories of the enslaved, did this make my history tantamount to mourning? Or worse, was it a melancholia I would never be able to overcome?" (16). Thinking past this impasse has been the cornerstone of recent works by the likes of Stephen Best, who has derided the "melancholic historicism" of Black Studies that continually reinscribes the Middle Passage as the determinant metric (15), or the "counterlife" figure in Christopher Freeburg's thinking that works to reclaim Blackness from the "slavery/freedom opposition [that] informs dominant conceptual rubrics" (2). The goal in moving beyond these terms is a retheorization of Blackness that follows Fred Moten in envisaging "a perpetual cutting, a constancy of expansive and enfolding rupture and wound, a rewind that tends to exhaust the metaphysis upon which the idea of redress is grounded" (ix). This is a point I return to in my final chapter.

Using literature to conceive of race and the nonhuman world outside of prescriptive, ontological declensions is also central to Joshua Bennett's thinking. Bennett looks across the twentieth and twenty-first centuries to think about how Black writing creates a "refutation of the human as the only form of life worthy of mourning or ethical engagement" (7). By bringing to light this longer historical archive, Bennett displaces the claim to novelty of the Anthropocene by reading Black literature that has long been marred by antiblackness and its attendant scalar dysphoria. Bennett, like Jackson, focuses his first prong of critique on the micro, moving into the vexed and vacillating relationship between animality and Blackness. Bennett does not attempt to reclaim either the human or the animal as the dominant scale but looks for alternatives that exist outside this dialectic, reading authors whose works are harnessed to "the very mechanism of disaggregating human personhood itself" (32). In this way, Bennett's work is equally transscalar, turning to literature as a site in which we can think through a "kinship and commonalty among living and nonliving things alike" (154). This transscalar account of Blackness, he continues, provides a "description of an elsewhere in which the forms of life that are repressed, subjugated, and every day subdued might have room to establish a robust sociality among themselves, a commons even outside the commons, below it" (155).

In this search for a "commons even outside the commons," Bennett articulates one strategy for literature to bring new scales into view. Part of the force of his work lies in how he uses literature to reorient the historical and ontological textures of the Anthropocene. By turning to a larger historical cross-section of Black writing, he highlights how questions of navigating the scales of the human and nonhuman world have always been a concern for Black writers. In fact, this is the very condition that chattel slavery inaugurated.[19] He maps an alternative history of nonhuman thinking through Black literature, looking at the ways in which Black fiction and poetry have managed to "[cultivate]

---

19. King follows a similar line of critique: "Because conquest ushered in such a world-altering rupture, it is almost impossible for the human imagination to fully conceive of the reach of its violence. Beyond the unfathomability of the scale of conquest's historical violence, the fact that its violence does not cease makes it even more difficult for the critical imaginaries that produce critical social theories to contain it or find the appropriate level of abstraction or texture to make it legible [. . .] [Conquest] is in continual need of new language and new conceptual tools, which often exist at the margins of reason and require methods found in artistic and creative production" (49).

a poetics of persistence and interspecies empathy" (5).[20] With this as a starting premise, both Bennett and Jackson understand that the literary and the ontological do not exist separately but, in fact, animate one another, bringing into being what Bennett calls "the possibility of becoming multiple" that will, in turn, allow us to "better understand how the enslaved survived the hold, what they transformed it into, and what such transformation means for how we imagine sociality *as such*" (173; emphasis in original).

In this necessarily partial overview of work being done at the intersection of Black Studies and ecology, my goal is not to be exhaustive, but to highlight how a sampling of these readings in Black ecology preempt and coincide with the transscalar. These readings are intended to reflect the richness of a transscalar mode of critique that is bubbling up from this tradition. For all these thinkers, this transscalar disposition is as much a critical mode as it is a literary mode. Just as we will see in readings of Jesmyn Ward and Paul Beatty in the chapters that follow, the argument here is that literary form has the capacity to move both forwards and backwards across time, space, and planes of being.[21] Transscalar critique, to drive home a key point, is not just something that critics do, but something that Black literature itself demands.

The Black Fantastic

Thinking of literary form under these terms, then, is to think about what role literary and critical form can take when tasked with thinking at the intersection of climate, Blackness, and crisis.[22] The remainder of

---

20. This is a point explicitly echoed by both Jackson and King. Jackson claims "[Art] holds the potential of keeping possibility open or serving as a form of redress" (219). King similarly sees Black aesthetics as interrupting "the course and momentum of the flow of critical theories about genocide, slavery, and humanity in the Western Hemisphere" (xv).
21. Brown makes an analogous claim through her own literary archive, asking, "What if we denatured the very category of species itself, understanding it to be the product of historically specific scientific discourse? How would broadening our conceptions of life – rescaling both spatially and temporally – bring awareness to the ways in which being human has been conceived as a category of exclusion?" (110).
22. McKittrick underlines that this shift into the literary is far from incidental, explaining that "the interdisciplinary interplay between narrative and material worlds is especially useful in black studies, because our analytic sites, and our selfhood, are often reduced to metaphor, analogy, trope, and symbol" (10). A transscalar account of crisis does not fall prey to this reductive logic but thinks alongside and with its implications.

Transscalar Critique works at this intersection, looking at how Black literature provides us with an opening into the relationship between the scales of Blackness and ecology while also sketching alternate ways of being in and understanding that world. Form itself is central to this counternarration of scale. As Judith Madera puts it so pointedly and precisely, "[Black] literature confounds the logics of scale" (3).[23] This is a point made by Wynter as early as the 1970s, where her own extended project on rethinking the genre of the human turns on a formal axis, sounding out a "new aesthetic [that] could not have been audible in terms of our present order of truth and aesthetics" ("On How," 153). Wynter's emphasis on genre becomes an interface of mediation for her that allows a shift between the twinned projects of critiquing both humanist and literary form. Across her thinking, Wynter continually returns to the novel, contouring its vexed history as a colonial vessel of technology instrumental in naturalizing these "'liberal' values of individualism" alongside the emergence of the plantation ("Novel," n.p.). This is to say that the literary and ontological forms that Wynter is critiquing are inextricably linked, constantly reinforcing one another through an "*economic* conception of the human" ("Re-Enchantment," 160; emphasis in original). But the literary is also a site that she believes holds latent possibilities for Black radicalism. For Wynter, we cannot critique literary and human forms separately from one another, but rather need to think simultaneously about how both forms conspire to create anti-Black violence but can also undo that violence.

As I will examine in the next two chapters, the transscalar in Black literature takes different shapes, but, like the rest of the literature I have covered thus far, is readily intelligible in moments of crisis. This is something Brown points to: "[Times] of crisis open up possibility. A crisis could mean a total paradigmatic break, and imagining such a break is an opportunity for speculation" (87). For Brown this is not just a historical "break," but an aesthetic one. Her emphasis on "speculation" also breaks away from the stranglehold of realism in mediating crisis. While Brown's work traces speculation through

---

23. Madera's work critiques the scales inherited from human geography and, thus, remains limited in the type of scalar critique she is providing. She writes, "Scale is itself a highly flexible term. But what seems outmoded from the start, at least for new directions in literary studies, is thinking about scale in its long-standing geographical sense – as something like sequences of vertical differentiation" (211). That said, Madera's work goes on to work very much in a transscalar manner, tracing a wide swath of Black literature invested in critiquing a scalar "implicit hierarchy" tied to spatiality (213).

the work of Sojourner Truth to Alice Coltrane to Octavia Butler, an emphasis on speculation has reached an apex in our contemporary marked by crisis. Indeed, as Gabriella Friedman puts it, "Our current scholarly moment is marked by a turn not only to nonrealist literature, but to speculation in all its multitudinous forms" (205).

Speculative literature has a long history of thinking through anthropogenic climate change, sometimes at the cost of the smaller scale of lived reality and difference.[24] Mark Rifkin highlights how science fiction allows a movement across temporal scales in Black and Indigenous writing:

> Rather than solely pointing toward the future, then, speculation broadly considered points toward questions about what counts as real in the present, highlighting how varied ways of envisioning what *might be* grow out of varied ways of living and perceiving *now*. We might conceptualize speculation as an engagement with the not-known in which the tools of knowing and making become visible. (61–62; emphasis in original)

Speculative literature, in other words, provides a suture in the monoscalar imaginary. Kara Keeling continues this line of thought, describing how Black speculative writing opens up a possibility to move "with and through what exists in order to call forth something presently absent: a new relationship between and within matter. It is radical because it goes against the root, taking aim at the very foundations of a shared reality" (92). To rethink this "relationship between and within matter" is necessarily to think in a transscalar mode. As Rifkin argues: "The speculative, then, appears [. . .] less as a genre than a mode of relation, one that opens the potential for acknowledging a plurality of legitimate yet nonidentical truth claims – none of which should be taken as singularly foundational" (70). This is precisely what it is that the transscalar does by opening a multiplicity of modes focused on convergence, divergence, and simultaneity.[25]

---

24. This is something that Jerome Winter articulates precisely, arguing that science fiction and speculative literature often tackle questions of the climate but do so without attention to "their rootedness in the historical realities of colonialism and postcolonialism" (202). "By way of contrast," he continues, "Afrofuturist artists call attention to such narratives in their own storytelling practices, demonstrating both how dreams of environmental mastery lead to environmental disaster" (202).
25. This is what Rifkin calls "a vehicle through which to pluralize the potentials of the present" (68), and what Brown describes as a kinetic movement through "material, elemental, and sometimes biological incarnations" (8)

Thinking about the contemporary through the auspices of the speculative is to return to the previous chapter on climate crisis. There, I traced how questions of climate had long been the fodder of speculative literature. No longer bound by the gravities of realism, the argument goes, speculative genres provide the space for an encounter with the scalar immensity and improbability of climate crisis. What we witnessed was the way that climate had begun to filter its way back into the realist novel through the (albeit somewhat weirded) realism of authors like Jonathan Franzen, Barbara Kingsolver, and Zink. These authors attempt to mediate the scalar complexity of anthropogenic climate change through the realist novel and, in doing so, take the elasticity of realism to its tipping point. What I am pointing to here, however, is a nearly inverted trajectory. Although the realist novel has long been the privileged site for engaging with questions of race and social uplift, more and more contemporary Black authors are turning away from realism as a way to think through the violence of antiblackness.[26] This is not to say that Black literature does not have its own tradition of speculation. Indeed, the possibility of imagining Blackness outside of the violence of white supremacy has long been considered so vexed that writers, from W. E. B. Du Bois to Colson Whitehead, have looked to genre to move beyond present realities.[27] But what I want to bring to the fore is the fact that what we understand by speculative literature more generally has changed in contemporary Black writing. As Friedman puts it, there has been an insurgence of Black literature that thinks about speculation in "broader, more capacious [terms], less concerned with technical literary and generic questions" (205). In the chapter that follows, I look at how Jesmyn Ward's work sits at this interstice. At first pass, Ward's novels are recognizably realist, but the worlds she creates are always a bit off-kilter, with flecks of voodoo and surrealism that break out of the realist fixtures.

This returns us to where we started this chapter. Jemisin's *The City We Became* provides a perfect jumping-off point to think

---

26. This is a claim, for example, that underpins Kenneth Warren's *What Was African American Literature?* and which I will turn to in the final chapter.
27. This is a tradition that Richard Iton describes as the Black fantastic, which "is meant to refer to the minor-key sensibilities generated from the experience of the underground, the vagabond, and those constituencies marked as deviant – notions of being that are inevitably aligned within, in conversation with, against, and articulated beyond the boundaries of the modern" (16).

about how a recalibrated speculative literature can provide an antidote to crisis realism. Jemisin uses crisis to alert us to both a larger interconnection of multiple scales of the world and ways of envisaging the scales of that world otherwise. The novel is not explicitly about climate or racial crisis, but its structure and narrative tropes both anticipate and coincide with many of the problematics foundational to our conception of the Anthropocene, and antiblackness more generally. Jemisin's book is, in fact, an almost literal dramatization of how scales clash with one another in a moment of crisis. The plot moves through long tunnels of temporal scales, from a crisis-defined present into the caverns of New York's "Ancestral memory" before colonial contact (299). These presents and pasts, however, work centrifugally, bringing the characters into other future worlds and distant pasts. Not confined to just the temporal axis, it is also a book that moves across spatial coordinates. While *The City We Became* is very much anchored in New York, we also encounter the surrogates of São Paolo and Hong Kong, creating coalitional alliances laterally and longitudinally. But, more than just these incidental intersections with the expanded spatial and temporal scales of the Anthropocene, the book is a concretization of scalar disjuncture. As the Woman in White explains to Aislyn after a heated battle with Brooklyn and Manny, "I had no idea your kind had advanced to the point of using energized abstract monoconstructs in combat. Who expects microbes to go nuclear?" (103).

Although the Woman in White's retort comes across as a bit of sci-fi humor, it also points to a theory of the transscalar. How do we move between these scales to understand how they contradict and animate one another? Jemisin's response is not to try to unify these scales but to radiate in the disjuncture between scales. This is underlined by Bronca, the novel's Indigenous art critic and fiery mouthpiece for the Bronx, creating, "[a] mille-feuille of worlds [. . .] each building on the other, forming coral columns that rise and split and twist apart and split again" (166). Even the characters themselves in the book are unstable, moving in and out of scales as they become "the city and the land underneath" (162). This is how Jemisin imagines an ecological immanence that does not try to delineate the boundaries of inside/outside while also avoiding the abstraction performed by the scale of the nonhuman world. The Woman in White is continually imagined in the novel as a "jangling *antithesis of presence*" (219; emphasis in original).

We see this transscalar mode come to fruition towards the end of the novel, when Bronca explains what it means for a city to be brought into existence:

> All the other worlds that human beings believe in, via group myths or spiritual visitations or even imaginations if they're vivid enough, they exist. Imagining a world *creates* it, if it isn't already there ... What we are transcends the layers between worlds. Actually, when a city is born – when *we* are reborn as cities – the birth process kind of smashes through them ... What we are, what we're made of, is many worlds coming together. Reality and legends. This world where we're just people, and that world, where we can be mileswide cities that just happen to be sitting a couple of feet across each other because the laws of space, physics, don't work the same way. (302–303; emphasis in original)

This account of the city is as literary as is it material, moving between "group myths" and "spiritual visitations" alongside the "laws of space, physics." There is no ontological priority given to any one of these scales as Bronca is just as interested in the big and the small as she is the material and the imaginative. A city "transcends the layers between worlds," but this does not mean that it collapses all these layers into some sort of homogenous mass. Rather, each person remains transscalar, both "just people" and "cities mileswide." In her shift into the pluralization of the first person, we see an emergence of a new type of being: Wynter's "we" takes shape through Bronca as "many worlds coming together."

This is not just limited to the plot of the novel but is also a formal movement between scales. Unlike much of the crisis realist literature we have covered in *Transscalar Critique*, Jemisin's book does not resolve itself into any tidy or neat resolution. Throughout *The City We Became*, we patiently wait for the Staten Island proxy, Aislyn, to realize the errors of her racist and xenophobic upbringing and join with the other boroughs in a climactic fight against the Woman in White. Instead, Jemisin defers this closure; the four other boroughs (with a ninth inning assist from Jersey City) end up defeating the Woman in White and are finally birthed as a city, despite the continual racist recalcitrance of Aislyn. The suggestion here is that any resolution of crisis is messy and ongoing, not one that returns us to a pre-crisis equilibrium. As the book finishes, we see that New York has not been transformed into some sort of postracial utopia, but rather remains uneven and asymmetrical:

They are the single titanic concussion of sound from every subwoofer and every steel drum circle that has ever annoyed elderly neighbors and woken babies while secretly giving everyone else an excuse to smile and dance. It is this sound, a violent wave of pure percussive force pouring from a thousand nightclub doors and orchestra pits, that slams upward and outward from the city . . . *They* are the methane-green sewer fire that races through the streets – unreal and yet extradimensionally hot, tracing out gridlines and curbs. (427–428; emphasis in original)

Against this backdrop of perennial crisis, Jemisin's book gives us a series of metaphors that seem to be stretched to their limit. Jemisin's metaphors work across the human and nonhuman world, vibrating as the screams of babies as well as sub-bass stabs rearrange the air from a subwoofer. And the pronouns have shifted – this is not the Anthropocene's imaginary of a single, unified "we," but a pointed and italicized "they." Lines are drawn and redrawn in the sand as Jemisin is careful not to collapse identity positions. The boroughs are almost too material, composed of "pure percussive force," while remaining still ethereal, as "unreal." It may not be a resolution, but it also is not fully dejection. That is to say that Jemisin does not give us the teleological closure of crisis realism but leaves the door open to allow us a glimpse of a subjunctive "they" that remains out of reach in a forever future tense.

What this passage also brings to ground is the potential for metaphor to operate across scales more generally. There is a sense that no single metaphor can contain the imagery. McKittrick makes a similar point about the radical potentiality of metaphor: "Metaphors function to radically map existing useable (entwined material and imagined) sites of struggle and liberation and joy. Metaphors move us. Metaphors are not just metaphoric, though" (12). This description is a way to conceive of metaphor as both material and heuristic device, bringing together the unlikely assemblages that couple and recouple themselves in our crisis-defined present. McKittrick's description of metaphor describes not only the above passage from Jemisin, but the transscalar capacity of metaphor more generally. This is where the next chapter picks up, exploring how Jesmyn Ward also incorporates metaphor to blur the boundaries of realism in her transscalar account of crisis that is as ecological and racial as it is literary.

Chapter 4

Improbable Metaphor: Jesmyn Ward and the Asymmetries of the Anthropocene

We are stuck with the problem of living despite ecological ruination. Neither tales of progress nor of ruin tell us how to think about collaborative survival. It is time to pay attention to mushroom picking. Not that this will save us – but it might open our imaginations.

Anna Tsing, *The Mushroom at the End of the World*

But race in the United States is not a tidy matter.

Jesmyn Ward, *The Fire This Time*

George Bush doesn't care about Black people.

Kanye West

In the opening pages of Jesmyn Ward's 2011 National Book Award-winning novel, *Salvage the Bones*, the protagonist, Esch Batiste, starts to hear rumors about the arrival of Hurricane Katrina in her small Mississippi Delta town, Bois Sauvage:

It's summer, and when it's summer, there's always a hurricane coming or leaving here. Each pushes its way through the flat Gulf to the twenty-six-mile manmade Mississippi beach, where they knock against the old summer mansions with their slave galleys turned guesthouses before running over the bayou, through the pines, to lose wind, drop rain, and die in the north [...] We ain't had one come straight for us in years, time enough to forget how many jugs of water we need to fill, how many cans of sardines and potted meat we should stock, how many tubs of water we need. But on the radio that Daddy keeps playing in his parked truck, I heard them talking about it earlier today. How the forecasters said the tenth tropical depression had just dissipated in the Gulf but another one seems to be forming around Puerto Rico. (4)

Esch's analysis of the coming storm works across ontological, environmental, economic, and literary scales. At the start of the passage, we see Ward limn the inextricability of human and nonhuman worlds. Esch thinks about how beach, in this rendering, is a metonym for both a transgression of the human/nonhuman dyad and how this particular beach, with its "summer mansions," is also a byproduct of class hierarchy. Focusing solely on the beach as manmade or as class symbol would either dematerialize or depoliticize the passage. Ward also picks up where the Intergovernmental Panel on Climate Change left off: drawing our attention to the ways in which climate crisis is distributed asymmetrically across geographies, both physically and socially. Once the summer holidaymakers have left the beach, it is Esch and her family that must contend with the battering of the hurricanes. This asymmetry, moreover, is explicitly racialized. Richard Crownshaw, in a special issue of the *Journal of American Studies* dedicated to Ward, makes a similar claim in his reading of the novel: "As Esch puts it, hurricanes have always revealed a history of slavery" (227). In this passage, the veneer of racial progress is peeled away to reveal how the legacy of slavery is a topographical feature of the Mississippi Delta's landscape. This reaching across scales also occurs at the level of literary form. Although the majority of the passage is written in what is clearly Esch's voice, there is a slippage in the final sentence. Esch parrots voices from the radio by moving into a pseudo-technical language that shifts the understanding of the hurricane from the lived materiality and pathos of her family hoarding "tubs of water" into the abstracted scale of "tropical depression." Through this syntactic code-switching, Ward is both modeling and critiquing the abstracted language of climate change as she parodies its official lexicon, disconnected from felt realities.

Esch's understanding of Hurricane Katrina moves across scales to capture the specificity of Black life in the Anthropocene. This early scene in *Salvage the Bones* offers a blueprint for fiction in the era of anthropogenic climate change that is just as much concerned with syntax and nonhuman agencies as it is with race and history. It is not just Hurricane Katrina that Ward is analyzing in the above passage, but the continual crisis of being a poor Black woman in the

South when the weather and atmosphere have gotten weird. This decidedly transscalar account of crisis is at the heart of Ward's work beyond just *Salvage the Bones*. From her memoir, *Men We Reaped*, to her other novels that continue to build her fictional Mississippi Delta town, Bois Sauvage, 2008's *Where the Line Bleeds* and 2017's *Sing, Unburied, Sing,* Ward's work moves across scales to interrogate questions of climate, Blackness, and crisis through literary form. Her work is almost paradigmatic in its sketching of a transscalar mode of critique, responding to the divergent couplings and assemblages that are called into being in the ongoing wakes of both anti-Black violence and climate crisis. In doing so, her work rehearses a new model of crisis literature beyond the teleological auspices of crisis realism.

In this chapter, I focus on how Ward's portrayal of Hurricane Katrina offers a history of crisis on the Mississippi Delta that is environmental, racial, and literary, a symbiotic history of the transscalar crisis of antiblackness and the Anthropocene. *Salvage the Bones* is told through the eyes of Esch Batiste, the teenage and pregnant middle sister of the Batiste family, and follows her impoverished family living in the rural Mississippi Delta in the days leading up to and immediately following Hurricane Katrina. After Katrina hits, Esch surveys the damage across Bois Sauvage, and thinks, "Katrina surprised everyone with her uncompromising strength, her forcefulness, the way she lingered; she made things happen that had never happened before" (248). In part, this understanding of Katrina seems to replay some of the crisis realist logic of the first two chapters. Crisis appears as unprecedented, rearranging the world in its slipstream. This is, after all, what it means to think about Katrina through the lens of an event "that had never happened before." But Ward's work moves past the stale coagulation of the crisis realist tradition, understanding that crisis for Black people in the Mississippi Delta is a continual condition of being.

This is a central premise to all of Ward's work as she thinks about the long shadow of Hurricane Katrina and the other storms that have wreaked havoc on the Gulf Coast alongside the surrounding infrastructure of anti-Black violence that pockmarks and constitutes that same geography. The Mississippi Delta is a place where people, as the matriarch in her debut novel, *Where the Line Bleeds*, puts it, are "perpetually waiting for something astounding to happen: a tornado, a flood an earthquake" (89). This is to say that Ward's work thinks about crisis as continual rather than a momentary rupture. In doing so, her novels foreground the fact that crisis itself is not a uniform category but remains contingent upon myriad factors. This is a far cry from the type of species-imaginary often activated in the Anthropocene as Ward traces the uneven distribution of climate crisis across geographies and, even more intimately, across the bodies of the characters in her books.[1] In this attention to the gradients and valences of both the Anthropocene and anti-Black violence, Ward is able to rethink crisis in the contemporary and the shape narrative form can take to capture a contemporary marred by these crises.

In this chapter, I argue that Ward offers a corrective to the crisis realist tradition by rethinking the ontological and literary logics that seek to contain crisis in a singular moment. Indeed, Ward's work is transscalar in its DNA, offering us a glimpse of an alternative critical and narrative mode to crisis. To make this argument, I focus on her novels.[2] My focus on her novels is to allow a longer historical framework of Katrina to emerge. *Where the Line Bleeds* is purposely set in the summer of 2005 right before Katrina came bearing down. The following two books, however, are explicitly interested in the relationship between Blackness, climate, and crisis as mediated through Katrina. Equally important for this chapter is the fact that all of her books spend time querying realist form. *Where the Line Bleeds* is her most traditional domestic realist novel. In it, we follow the twin brothers, Christophe and Joshua DeLisle, in the dog days of summer after they graduate high school and try to find work and fight temptation in a depressed rural economy. *Salvage the Bones*, in many respects, carries on this traditional realist narrative form as the book follows Esch before, during, and immediately after Hurricane Katrina. But, like the authors in Chapter 2, Ward starts to weird her realism by blurring its bounded lines and turning to something slightly stranger, at moments resembling a refracted image of a realist novel. *Sing,*

---

1. To a lesser extent, this is also true of Ward's nonfiction. Ward is clear about the ways in which she wants to identify this scale of intimacy that reaches across time and space. Her work, taken together, performs a transscalar corralling. As she puts it in the Preface to a collection of essays she edited, *The Fire This Time*, "I remember that in choosing to identify as black, to write about black characters in my fiction and to assert the humanity of black people in my nonfiction, I've remained true to my personal history, to my family history, to my political and moral choices, and to my essential self: a self that understands the world through the prism of being a black American, and stands in solidarity with the people of the African diaspora" (15).
2. In this sense, I follow Arin Keeble, who has argued that there is a strengthening "when her work is read and considered together, and that the shared settings of the texts invite such a reading" ("Siblings, Kinship," 41). I develop this critical model further in my reading of Beatty in the chapter that follows.

Unburied, Sing moves the furthest from realism proper. While not quite the fully speculative world of N. K. Jemisin, it is as much a ghost story as it is a realist novel. Part mother/son story, part road novel, part ghost story, the book is a knotty and nebulous exploration of the violence embedded in the Southern topography. These novels, taken together, provide a transscalar critical and literary mode that explores the twinned history of environmental and racial oppression in the Mississippi Delta. At every pass, Ward is aware of the ways that race and the environment are inextricable from one another and how this requires exploratory forms to imagine the world otherwise.

When the Levees Broke

In many ways, Hurricane Katrina was understood from the outset by both popular pundits and critics as a transscalar crisis. There is a central scale shifting that occurs in almost all accounts of the crisis, from the moment the levees broke right up until Katrina's ghost that is dredged up with increasing regularity each time a storm forms on the Gulf. It was a natural disaster, but it was also hard to deny the fact that it felt very much like a manmade crisis. Indeed, as Nancy Tuana describes it, Hurricane Katrina limns the "viscous porosity between humans and our environment, between social practices and natural phenomena" (193). Wai Chee Dimock, in her reading of Katrina, goes so far as to say that the storm created a mode of world history "according to Katrina." Katrina, she writes, becomes instructive, nearly pedagogic, in the sense that it calls for an "unbundling" that exerts pressures on fantasies of "the sovereign claim of the nation" and, by extension, the individuals that constitute that national fantasy ("World," 35–37). Dimock argues that Katrina offered an alternate model of reading crisis that "makes it clear that climate, geology, and human and nonhuman life are all complexly intertwined, part of the same fluid continuum" ("World," 49). Dimock is clear, however, that this does not mean we swap one monoscalar imaginary for another, scaling Katrina exclusively through an ecological metric or the level of the planetary but that we think of the crisis across a "fluid continuum" of scales.

Understanding world history according to Katrina requires narrating the crisis by paying attention to its uneven distribution. It is not just the images of flooded neighborhoods that are called to mind when "Katrina" is mentioned. Alongside people trying to escape from the flooded lower parishes of New Orleans, the lasting images of the storm are of Black people packed into the Superdome and of Black men from a flooded prison stranded atop freeway overpasses as guards stand at attention with their guns raised. These images pointed to a subtending crisis that had been trumpeted as vanquished by the Bush Administration in the wake of 9/11. For, as much as it was a natural disaster, Katrina signaled, as Henry Giroux puts it, "a return of race" (10).[3] As pointedly put by Kanye West in the epigraph to this chapter, it was not long before the conversation around Katrina shifted its focus – from the architectural failures of the levees and subsidence of specific New Orleans neighborhoods to the inequity experienced by racialized people in contemporary America. Katrina was a watershed moment for both the climatic and the racial imaginary as it moved across scales, a crisis of both meteorology and racial politics. "Unlike the 9/11 story," Anna Hartnell argues, "which presented the western world with a deceptively simplistic face, Katrina immediately confronted us with its complexity, its challenge" (5).

This is, to return to Esch's reading of the storm in *Salvage the Bones*, the critical juncture at which Katrina demanded to be mediated in its transscalar complexity. To read one of these renderings of crisis without the other is to miss the interconnected ways in which they are always entwined, animating and informing one another. I want to be clear from the outset here that the America of 2005 is a much different place than the one we live in now. As I write in the winter of 2022, the worst floods on record wreaked havoc on Germany and Australia last summer. Twenty-one different named storms swept through the Mid-Atlantic from May to November, ending another record-shattering hurricane season, and record temperatures are being recorded across Alaska and Greenland as I type this. It is impossible (and rightly so!) to discuss ostensibly natural disasters in the current cultural and actual climate without also acknowledging the impact and acceleration of these events due to anthropogenic climate change. But, in 2005, we were only just understanding the scale and textures of the Anthropocene and Katrina was one of the first events to drive home to America where and how its asymmetries

---

3. And in doing so, Giroux continues, "Hurricane Katrina broke through the visual blackout of poverty, low-income blacks, and the pernicious ideology of color-blindness to reveal the ineptness of the government's response efforts and the dire conditions of largely poor African–Americans who were bearing the hardships incurred by the full wrath of the indifference and violence at work in the racial state" (26–27).

would unfold. While 9/11 and the 2008 financial crisis were largely mediated and cloaked in the invisibility of whiteness, Katrina did the opposite: it forced a reckoning with the transscalar crises of both climate and anti-Black violence.

If Katrina signaled a sea change in our understanding of crisis, it also provided an opportunity to rethink the narrative architecture which frames and supports these narratives: What sort of literary frame might be able to mediate a transscalar Katrina? It is curious, although perhaps unsurprising, that in that moment of crisis there was a resurgence of crisis realist tendencies. To return to one of our earlier straw men, Dave Eggers, his post-Katrina narrative, *Zeitoun* (which ended up as one of the most commercially successful post-Katrina texts), preempts some of the same tricks of *A Hologram for the King*. *Zeitoun* is a loosely fictionalized biography of Abdulrahman Zeitoun in the days before and months after Katrina. Zeitoun, a Syrian immigrant who had married a local New Orleans woman, started a painting company, and raised a family in the city, is presented to us as a heroic everyman (in some ways, the hero to Alan's antihero in *A Hologram for the King*) in the aftermath of the storm. He returns to his flooded neighborhood to paddle around rescuing dogs and protecting homes from the threat of the mobs of looters that never materialized. Eventually, however, Zeitoun is arrested and held in a Guantánamo-evoking purgatory, guilty of being Brown in the days following the racially charged storm. A compelling, tragic, and horrifying story unfolds as we follow Zeitoun through his post-Katrina nightmare. Eggers's choosing of Zeitoun as his protagonist makes sense: he is opening up the scale of crisis, looking at how Katrina unfolded differently, depending on the color of your skin. But just like the narratives in Chapter 1, the book ultimately stagnates within the doldrums of crisis realism. The fulcrum of the story pivots on Zeitoun trying to restart his business and ends up as a celebration of his entrepreneurial self and his economic relations "woven so thoroughly into the fabric of [his] adopted city" (24). That is, the brief moments of environmentalism and racial critique largely go nowhere but appear adjacent to the actual plot of the text, which focuses on Zeitoun's economic and marital reconciliation.[4]

Ward's novels take a different tack. For the most part, they are realist texts focused on the domestic concerns of realist novels – these

---

4. The domestic abuse scandal that consumed Zeitoun in the years afterwards only makes this more troubling.

are books about families and the emotional, financial, and physical hardships families face. But there is an elasticity to how Ward thinks about literary form that allows the texts themselves to imagine the thick and heavy crises of anti-Black violence and anthropogenic climate change. Towards the end of *Salvage the Bones*, for example, Ward offers us a glimpse of how these crises put pressure on literary form. As the storm hits, Esch tries to sort through the detritus and debris to find a narrative frame with which to mediate Katrina. In a harrowing series of scenes where she and her family barely survive, her brother and confidant, Skeetah, loses his prized fighting pit-bull (and his confidant), China, to the rising waters.[5] Upset and inconsolable, Skeetah refuses to leave the family compound while Esch and the rest of the family seek refuge on higher ground. As Esch takes stock of the damage, she tries to figure out a mode in which she can "tell [Skeetah] the story of Katrina and what she did to the coast" (254):

> I will tie the glass and stone with string, hang the shards above my bed, so that they will flash in the dark and tell the story of Katrina, the mother that swept into the Gulf and slaughtered. Her chariot was a storm so great and black the Greeks would say it was harnessed to dragons. She was the murderous mother who cut us to the bone but left us alive, left us naked and bewildered as wrinkled newborn babies, as blind puppies, as sun-starved newly hatched baby snakes. She left us a dark Gulf and salt-burned land. She left us to learn to crawl. She left us to salvage. Katrina is the mother we will remember until the next mother with large, merciless hands, committed to blood, comes. (255)

Borrowing heavily from the Medea story that permeates the text, Esch tries to imagine how narrative can stretch itself out across time

---

5. It is worth mentioning that Ward's decision to focus in such detailed fashion on dogs and dog fighting in *Salvage the Bones* is another moment when we see her interrogating the relationship between the human and nonhuman world via race. Dog fighting is deeply personal to Ward and is a theme she returns to in her memoir, *Men We Reaped*, while remaining pointedly political. In her critical account of how Blackness is naturalized and equated with the nonhuman world, Claire Kim argues that one such strategy of naturalization has been equating Black men with dogs as a way to violently erase their personhood (4). Ward understands this vexed history. We see this in *Sing, Unburied, Sing* when Jojo's grandfather, Pop, tells him, "But it was something about a colored man running the dogs; that was wrong. There had always been bad blood between dogs and Black people: they were bred adversaries – slaves running from the slobbering hounds, and then the convict man dodging them" (138).

and space.⁶ While reaching towards classic mythology, she is quick to realize that this offers only a partial diagram and one that remains limited in the way it suggests crisis is fleeting and temporary. As she surveys the coast, Esch is quick to realize that there is not going to be a return to a pre-crisis equilibrium. In fact, Katrina loses its primacy even as it is occurring; Esch cannot help but imagine "the next mother." While the damage may be exceptional, its underlying conditions certainly are not. This means that Esch does not harbor any fantasy that crisis is something that can be resolved. With this as her starting point, she feels an inadequacy in trying to relay the chaos to her brother, particularly as the storm seems to move across temporal (from Ancient Greece to a to-come horizon of another storm), spatial (encompassing the entirety of the Gulf), and ontological scales (Esch moves quickly across registers of being – cycling through dog, snakes, and babies). Esch, in turn, looks towards nonhuman modes of writing as a way to articulate a mode of narrative interdependency that crosses the human/nonhuman threshold. Esch seeks a way to "tell the story of Katrina" in a form that cannot be circumscribed by the human metrics of crisis realism as she reaches for the refracted interplay between "glass and stone."

Landscapes of Crisis

Ward's insistence throughout *Salvage the Bones* on inserting Katrina into a larger history of crisis on the Mississippi coast ends up as a refusal to reify Katrina's status as event. Arin Keeble makes an analogous point in his reading of Ward, arguing that she avoids the impulse to "exceptionalize Katrina as a moment of rupture" ("Siblings," 45). But more than just inserting Katrina into a larger history of hurricanes on the Gulf, Ward makes a larger claim about the constitutive nature of crisis for her characters. Ward's work provides a twinned history of environmental degradation and racial oppression on the Mississippi Delta that begins in *Where the Line Bleeds*. Ward's initial characterizations of Bois Sauvage in the book are through the sometimes rose-tinted glasses of the DeLisle twins. There is a hint of pastoralism that

---

6. The use of the Medea frame narrative is convincingly detailed by Benjamin Stevens's reading of the novel. Stevens argues that the Medea story offers us a hermeneutics of "salvage." For Stevens, this involves an act not just of retelling, but "of recuperation after the fact that is at once richly creative and a reflection of impoverished necessity" (162).

runs throughout the novel as we see a tracing of the aquatic memory of Bois Sauvage via the Wolf River:

> The river was young and small. At its start it seeped from the red clay earth in the piney woods of southern Mississippi, and then wound its way, brown and slow, over a bed of tiny gray and ochre pebbles through the pines, shallow as a hand, deep as three men standing, to the sandy, green lowlands of the gulf of Mexico [. . .] Near the river's end, at one such bridge, two teenage boys, twins, stood at the apex. (1)

While this passage does not suggest any environmental violence, what it introduces is a very specific concern and focus on the nonhuman world. Ward moves across time and space and outside of human ontologies as the river becomes the subject, introducing "two teenage boys, twins" only through a subordinate clause towards the end of its dense, syntactical structure. As the book progresses, there is a focus on how this nonhuman landscape has been subject to a violent history. This much is made clear in the following chapter where Ward offers her most comprehensive history of the town:

> Joshua could understand why Ma-mee's and Papa's families had migrated here from New Orleans, had struggled to domesticate the low-lying, sandy earth that reeked of rotten eggs in a dry summer and washed away easily in a wet one. Land had been cheaper along the Mississippi gulf, and black Creoles had spread along the coastline. They'd bargained in broken English and French to buy tens of acres of land. Still, they and their poor white neighbors were dependent on the rich for their livelihood just as they had been in New Orleans: they built weekend mansions along the beach for wealthy New Orleans expatriates, cleaned them, did their yard work, and fished, shrimped, and harvested oysters [. . .] Like the oyster shell foundation upon which the country workers packed sand to pave the roads, the communities of Bois Sauvage, both black and white, embedded themselves in the red clay and remained. (7)

This passage, which so clearly and elegantly anticipates the scene full of summer mansions with which she starts *Salvage the Bones*, looks at how race is "embedded" within the landscape. Although Joshua tries to import his mode of the pastoral into the landscape,[7] Ward

---

7. This is par for the course for Joshua. He is characterized in the preceding passage as "[loving] the country; he loved the undulating land they moved through, the trees that overhung the back roads to create green tunnels that fractured sunlight" (5).

alerts us to the hierarchies and asymmetries that are coded into the topography, from the subprime agriculture yield of the land to the sinking foundations that underpin the coast itself (a fragility that will be exasperated when Katrina actually hits). This reaches its apex later in the novel as the brothers drive to New Orleans. Once outside of Bois Sauvage, they pass several gated communities and Joshua begins to daydream about the people who live in the grand houses cut off from the road:

> If it weren't for the bright paint and the neatly shelled driveways and the cut grass, he would've sworn that no one worked or lived there, that the place existed as a mirage, as an idea, as a foreboding relic to black people to remind them that outside their own communities, there existed enmity and history and dread hidden in the pines and the marsh that was based on the color of their skin. (164)

Ward doesn't pull any punches. As the brothers drive through the countryside, they read the legacy of the plantation and the Jim Crow South through its new valences. The pastel colors outside may try to dull the violence, but it is just a new shade of a blood-stained gray.

More of this environmental violence is manifest early in *Salvage the Bones* when China gives birth to a litter of puppies. As excited as Skeetah is by the birth (and the potential income they will generate when he sells them), his excitement quickly turns to horror when one of the puppies dies. Almost instantly, Skeetah realizes that the dog has caught the highly contagious and fatal parvovirus. As soon as he figures this out, Skeetah understands what is at stake for the rest of the litter and tries to decontaminate himself, his clothing, the bedding, and area where he has holed the puppies up:

> He stands for a second in the firelight, still, breathing hard. He throws his shirt into the fire.
> "What are you doing?" Marquise asks around the squirrel bone he is sucking on. He slurps and almost swallows it, chokes it back up.
> "It's all contaminated," Skeetah says. "Everything."
> He shucks his pants, throws them into the fire. (52)

This moment points to a crisis beyond the immediacy of Katrina. Parvo takes on an allegorical heft as his clothes, the very dirt on the ground, simply, "everything," has become "contaminated." It is in a moment like this that the world-at-large is revealed to be complicit in the crisis that Ward is narrating. Kelly McKisson argues that *Salvage the Bones* reveals a foundational ecological precarity for the residents of the Gulf Coast of which Katrina is only the latest manifestation. In fact, McKisson claims, "Katrina is depicted as the continuation of a longer legacy of oppression figured by land destruction" (488). This is a way of saying that, instead of being a site of discontinuity, Katrina is continuous and contiguous. Sure, Katrina may appear to be unprecedented in the speed of the destruction, but as Skeetah makes clear above, the environment itself has already been poisoned: everything is contaminated.[8]

We see this further concretized in *Salvage the Bones* by the Batiste family home, the Pit. The Pit is a dugout plot of land on which Esch's house and the house of her deceased maternal grandparents are set. Early in the book, Esch relays the story of how her maternal grandfather bought the land, only to watch it get hollowed out from underneath him:

> Papa Joseph who let the white men he worked with dig for clay that they used to lay the foundation for houses, let them excavate the side of a hill in a clearing near the back of the property where he used to plant corn for feed. Papa Joseph let them take all the dirt they wanted until their digging had created a cliff over a dry lake in the backyard. (14)

This passage sets up a very clear register to understand Esch's version of the Pit alongside Bois Sauvage and the Mississippi Delta more generally. Returning to the red clay of *Where the Line Bleeds*, Ward suggests the social and geological foundation of the Gulf Coast is built upon the exploited labor and stolen resources of Mississippi's Black people, leaving them to salvage the dry and cracked dirt. This is unstable ground, ground that has become, as Skeetah's puppies make clear, toxic. The Pit literalizes the inequities and asymmetries of the Mississippi landscape in which the entire narrative takes place, where the topsoil itself becomes a living palimpsest "where everything else is starving, fighting, struggling" (94).

For Joshua Bennet, this is indicative of how *Salvage the Bones* creates a "narrative landscape in which no categories remain stagnant and pure" (165–166). This is nowhere truer than within the family home itself. It is easy to dismiss the Pit as merely a record of

---

8. Leonie names something similar in *Sing, Unburied, Sing*, describing Bois Sauvage as "[some] kind of bad earth" (177).

an environmentally and racially charged exploitation.[9] But, at the same time, as the center of Batiste familial life it becomes something close to what Bennett describes as "a spatial description of an elsewhere in which the forms of life that are repressed, subjugated, and every day subdued might have room to establish a robust sociality among themselves, a common even outside the commons" (155).[10] Ward is careful not to collapse these two understandings of the Pit into one another. It remains knotted and contradictory, both a fugitive counter-commons and one that remains ephemeral as its center cannot hold over the extractive architectonic that turns to quicksand to drag the characters in.

To pause for a second, what I am arguing is that, unlike the accounts of crisis I covered in the first half of *Transscalar Critique*, the singularity of crisis, its imaginary status as punctum, is constellated across a much longer and much Blacker history of crisis in *Salvage the Bones*. This effects a redistribution of Hurricane Katrina across a preexisting landscape of racialized crisis. If the *longue durée* of crisis is hinted at in these types of allegorical moments in *Salvage the Bones*, the formula is inverted in both *Sing, Unburied, Sing* and *Where the Line Bleeds*, where Katrina only ever appears as spectral flicker against a present defined by the continuity of crisis. *Sing, Unburied, Sing* follows a road trip where Jojo, his sister, Kayla, his mother, Leonie, and Leonie's friend Misty are traveling from Bois Sauvage up to Parchman prison to retrieve Jojo's incarcerated father, Michael. As the drive unfolds, Ward reveals a post-Katrina landscape where the hurricane remains an undulating presence that increases and decreases in amplitude over the terrain. The storm is only ever mentioned once when Leonie follows Misty home to do some cocaine after working a nightshift: "[We] went to [Misty's] pink MEMA cottage she'd had since Hurricane Katrina,

---

9. The fact that it is also called the Pit is not coincidental. This name gestures towards the types of extractivist logics that Imre Szeman and Jennifer Wenzel describe as "a human instrumentalization of nonhuman nature: the use of nature only as a means toward human ends – or, to be slightly less universalist, a means towards the end of some subset of human" (511). Even at a more granular level, the name is evocative of the excavation of tar, coal, and oil. This resonance taps into what Elizabeth Miller describes as a long history of environmental extraction and exploitation, ending with the realization that "extraction-based life is a future-depleting system" (12).
10. Sarah Cervenak provides a similar description of a "common even outside the commons" that suggests an adjacent conception of Black spatiality, seeking out "another imagination of earthly relation that pushes against capture" (3).

and she pulled out an eight ball" (32). This shift in status is something hinted at in *Where the Line Bleeds*. Although the book is set in 2005 in the summer before Katrina, as the DeLisle brothers drive to New Orleans to see their mother, we read:

> The whole city seemed on the verge of collapsing, of coming apart and spewing into the streets to slide and submerge into the river. Joshua imagined it all gone: the levees, the sea of white aboveground tombs, the French Quarter, the flickering sparkle of the knot of shiny skyscrapers called downtown, and the huddling rows of high-windowed, wooden-sided houses warped soft by the salty, sulfurous air and the rain. (166)

Taken together, these two passages from two separate books bookmark Katrina to contour its hovering presence on the horizon.[11] As Joshua tells Christophe towards the end of *Where the Line Bleeds*, "'Got a storm out in the gulf. On the other side of Cuba. They say it's coming right for us'" (208). Ward is creating a desensationalized sense of crisis that helps transition from the type of claims that buttress crisis realism to an understanding of crisis as a state of being. Indeed, Christophe tells Joshua, to chill out, reminding him, "'It's the third one we done had this summer – ain't no reason for you to be so nervous'" (210).

Said somewhat more dramatically, Katrina is not a crisis in the way we tend to think of crisis, but something much more boring, an infrastructural presence.[12] Jessica Hurley and Jeffrey Insko describe the way that an elongated sense of slow violence is built into the rusting and dated infrastructure that surrounds our daily lives. They

---

11. There is an interesting way in which Ward represents a history of hurricanes in the Gulf in *Where the Line Bleeds*. Consider, for example, a scene where Joshua feels envious of Christophe's ability to sleep, remembering: "Once he'd fallen asleep during the eye of a hurricane that hit the year they were eight, and he hadn't woken up until after the storm had passed. While he had slept, Joshua had stayed awake, transfixed, staring out the window at the hundred-mile-per-hour winds uprooting pecan trees from the field next to the house" (30–31). What would, elsewhere, be a fairly traumatic encounter with climatic violence is used merely to give a sense of just how deeply Christophe can sleep.
12. Tellingly, Sophia Beal, Michael Rubenstein, and Bruce Robbins also point to how infrastructure only makes its presence felt in acute moments of crisis: "[Infrastructure] tends to go unnoticed when it's in fine working order. Infrastructure is supposed to go unnoticed when it works" (576).

focus on how infrastructure itself is particularly vulnerable to racialized violence and anthropogenic climate change. In a special issue of *American Literature* dedicated to the relationship between infrastructure, crisis, and climate change, they point to how the previous decade has seen literature attempt to come to grips with "not the sensational event but the routine character of infrastructural violence, not the singularity of disaster but its ongoingness under conditions of colonial racial capitalism" (346).[13] And, indeed, *Sing, Unburied, Sing* very pointedly dramatizes a crisis of infrastructure. Just as much as the book is about Hurricane Katrina, it is also about the Deepwater Horizon explosion. Michael had previously been an oil worker on the Deepwater Horizon oil rig, owned and operated by British Petroleum, when it exploded and killed eleven people and spilled hundreds of millions of gallons of oil into the Gulf. But even with this key node in the plot, the explosion itself appears only in fits and starts. If you do not know what you are looking for, it is possible you might misread the underlying conditions that lead to Michael "[coming] home with severance money and nightmares" (92).[14] But these allusions are explicitly detailed by Jojo later on, when he remembers a fishing trip with his father:

> *I actually cried*, Michael told the water. He seemed ashamed to say that, but he went on anyway. How the dolphins were dying off, how whole pods of them washed up on the beaches in Florida, in Louisiana, in Alabama and Mississippi: oil-burnt, sick with lesions, hollowed out from the insides. And then Michael said something I'll

13. This work follows a larger turn towards infrastructure in sociology and anthropology. Infrastructure's critical ascendancy is part and parcel of reaching for scales beyond the human concomitant with the Anthropocene. As Hannah Appel, Nikhil Anand, and Akhil Gupta write, infrastructure in the Anthropocene allows us to "decenter humans [. . .] to think about other time spans, the lifetimes of other things that shape life on the planet" (20). But, Appel, Anand, and Gupta are careful not to treat infrastructure across a temporal scale only, arguing that infrastructures are complex "sites of conceptual and scalar trouble" (28).
14. Interestingly, when Leonie first brings up the Deepwater explosion, she does so from within an almost hyperbolic mode of crisis realism: "I'd spent the days after the accident with Jojo in the house watching CNN, watching the oil gush into the ocean, and feeling guilty because I didn't give a shit about those fucking pelicans, guilty because I wanted to see Michael's face [. . .] He'd called me not long after the story broke on the news, told me he was safe, but his voice was tiny, corroded by static, unreal. *I knew those men – all eleven of them*" (92; emphasis in original). She wants to rescale the crisis into a more manageable scale – the environmental catastrophe becoming a blip in her own domestic drama.

never forget: *Some scientists for BP said this didn't have nothing to do with the oil, that sometimes this is what happens to animals: they die for unexpected reasons. Sometimes a lot of them. Sometimes all at once.* And then Michael looked at me and said: *And when that scientist said that, I thought about humans. Because humans is animals.* And the way he looked at me that night told me he wasn't just thinking about any humans; he was thinking about me. (226; emphasis in original)

Although the above is ostensibly about the Deepwater disaster, it also points to how there is a more insidious cause of death. These "unexpected reasons" that "some scientists" cite to deflect British Petroleum's willful negligence and culpability are symptomatic of a longer history of environmental (and racial) destruction. Although Michael is one of the few white characters in the novel, Ward is creating an account of an environment of crisis on the Mississippi coast that stretches beyond and above any of the types of the causal crisis markers signaled by "Katrina" or "Deepwater." Indeed, this is a landscape constituted in and through environmental destruction that sees the humans surrounding it as replaceable and part of that nonhuman world.

Wakes of Crisis

A topography of crisis that stretches across the Delta is not contained to a spatial axis but moves along a temporal one as well. Indeed, as the openings of *Where the Line Bleeds* and *Salvage the Bones* both suggest, crisis is part of a long history of racialized violence and environmental exploitation that is imprinted on the stratigraphic record of Bois Sauvage. When Esch thinks about the slave galleys on the coast, she is tapping into the wake described by Christine Sharpe where Black people exist in the "continuous and changing present of slavery's as yet unresolved unfolding" (13). To exist in this wake is to be forced to confront wide swaths of time to come to grips with antiblackness. Indeed, as Sharpe has it, anti-Black violence becomes "the atmospheric condition of time and place" (106). Sharpe is pointing to a scalar vastness of antiblackness akin to the way we think about anthropogenic climate crisis. It is not enough to think of a crisis defined now; we must think of a much longer sense of crisis, one often marked by its belated arrival. We see crisis as constituting "time and place" across *Sing, Unburied, Sing*. As the family and Misty near Parchman, Jojo thinks, "I see the men bent at the waist, row after row of them, picking at the ground, looking like a great murder of crows landed and chattering and picking for bugs in the ground" (125). The landscape here becomes a chronotope of crisis where past and present blur to give Jojo a glimpse of a racialized landscape and history.

The fact that Jojo is given some clairvoyant-adjacent powers is one way Ward explores the elongated temporality of anti-Black violence. Keeble has described her novels as containing a "surface realism" ("Siblings," 42), but this realist laminate is peeled back as ghosts and ghost stories begin to fray the novel with their hauntings. Leonie is visited by the ghost of her dead brother, Given, whenever she does drugs and, as the road trip unfolds, Jojo is visited by the ghost of Richie, a twelve-year-old boy who was sent to Parchman in the 1950s for petty larceny alongside Jojo's grandfather, Pop. Although nearly two generations separate Richie and Given, they both introduce the long wake of anti-Black violence. Given, a star high-school athlete, is killed by a jealous white classmate on a hunting trip. The classmate, whose family is connected to the Bois Sauvage police, gets off scot free after claiming that he did not see Given in the woods. While Given presents us with a modern-day lynching, Richie is the intended victim of an actual lynch mob. Much of Jojo and Pop's conversations revolves around Pop retelling Richie's story and, as the book progresses, Richie is given sections of the text to narrate himself. Eventually, we learn that Pop shot and killed Richie after he escaped from Parchman and a lynch mob is set to hunt him down after he is (falsely) accused of harassing one of the white prostitutes who visit the prison on the weekends for conjugal visits.

Richie's sections of the novel provide a long view into the history of antiblackness in the postbellum Gulf. His experience of Parchman becomes a stand-in for the larger failures of Reconstruction and the violence of the Jim Crow South as anti-Black violence consumes the "past, present, and future all at once" (186).[15] Richie himself is unbound from any temporal constraints, seemingly able to move across time in an instant. Immediately following his death at the hands of Pop, we read:

> [When] I slept and woke, I was in the Delta before the prison, and Native men were ranging over that rich earth, hunting and taking

---

15. A similar Black temporality is voiced by Jojo's grandmother, Mam, who tells Leonie: "Because we don't walk no straight lines. It's all happening at once. All of it. We all here at once" (236).

breaks to play stickball and smoke. Bewildered, I burrowed and slept and woke to the new Parchman again, to men who wore their hair long and braided to their scalps, who sat for hours in small windowless rooms, staring at big black boxes that streamed dreams. (186–187)

This is not just about Richie but a larger critique of the wake of racialized violence. Richie's movement across history provides latitude for Ward to time-travel, opening her narrative into a temporality not available via crisis realism. The sad reality that Richie sees, however, underlines that while the signifiers may have changed, the underlying violence remains the same. In this moment we see how it is not just Black life that is erased, but also Indigenous life as Richie looks across the entirety of human history on the Delta.

Alongside this movement across temporal and spatial scales, Ward also works across ontological ones. Throughout *Sing, Unburied, Sing*, and hinted at by Michael thinking of "humans as animals," Ward explores an extended and protracted contact with the nonhuman world as characters interact with animals. From the opening scene of Jojo and Pop killing a goat to barbecue for his birthday, we are brought into sometimes too close a contact with the animal world:

> The goat is inside out. Slime and smell everywhere, something musty and sharp, like a man who ain't took a bath in some days. The skin peels off like a banana [. . .] He's slicing and the smell overwhelms like a faceful of pig shit. It smells like foragers, dead and rotting out in the thick woods, when the only sign of them is the stink and the buzzards rising and settling and circling. It stinks like possums or armadillos smashed half flat on the road, rotting in asphalt and heat. But worse. (5–6)

Ward stretches simile to its tipping point as she cycles through images to contain this moment of deathly proximity. Jojo moves fluidly through human and nonhuman imagery, trying to find a way to describe his grandfather killing the goat, but is unable to articulate the stench as he compares it to this wide cross-section of tropes borrowed from the animal kingdom.[16] Read a certain way, the violence of this passage continues to link the long history of Black people and the animal world to a dual erasure. This is a history elegantly

---

16. Goats also feature in *Where the Line Bleeds* when the DeLisle brothers, like Jojo, barbecue a goat for the Fourth of July and watch a man kill it "the old way" (142).

critiqued by Zakiyyah Iman Jackson, who describes how, since the arrival of chattel slaves in the New World, there has been a rhetorical and ontological linkage between Black people and animals: "The black body's fleshiness was aligned with that of animals and set in opposition to the European spirit and mind" (6). This vexed history works its way across the canon of both Black and environmental literatures and bubbles up across *Sing, Unburied, Sing*.[17] Leonie concretizes this historical narrative:

> Once, my grandmama told me a story about her great-grandmama. She'd come across the ocean, been kidnapped and sold. Said her great-grandmama told her that in her village, they ate fear [. . .] She learned that bad things happened on that ship, all the way until it docked. That her skin grew around the chains. That her mouth shaped to the muzzle. That she was made into an animal under hot, bright sky, the same sky the rest of her family was under, somewhere far away, in another world. I knew what that was, to be made an animal. (69)

Here we map out a very clear yoking of antiblackness and the nonhuman. It is a literal animalization that is being described by Leonie's great-great-great-grandmother where the chains of chattel slowly transmogrify into animal skin. And while this is certainly prevalent throughout the book, there is a critique of the linkage between animals and Blackness that is also a bit more complex.

Said differently, there is another way to read the type of ontological rescaling that Ward is performing in her books through this intimacy with animals. This is true not just of *Sing, Unburied, Sing*, but of her earlier novels as well. At the end of *Where the Line Bleeds*, Joshua and Christophe go out fishing with their cousin Dunny. As they catch mullet and return them back to the bayou, Joshua's mind drifts off into the ether and he starts to think of himself as a fish:

> He could imagine them sliding along other slimy, striped fish and laying eggs that looked like black marbles as the sun set again and again over the bayou and hurricanes passed through, churning them to dance. He could imagine them running their large tongues over the insides of their mouths and feeling the scars where the hooks had bit them, remembering their sojourn in the water-thin air, and mouthing

---

17. This, it should be noted, is the history that is at the center of Paul Outka's seminal study, *Race and Nature*.

> to their children, the smell of the metal in the water, the danger of it [. . .] Out and through the spread of the bay until their carcasses, still dense with the memory of the closed, rich bayou in the marrow of their bones, settled to the bottom of the Gulf of Mexico and turned to black silt on the ancient floor of the sea. (239)

There is a type of closeness with the nonhuman world that transgresses ontological, temporal, and spatial scales. In this extended echo of William Faulkner's Vardaman Bundren, Ward allows Joshua to slide in and out of both the fish's mind and body, moving through the water and across time to sediment on the ocean floor.[18] It is a powerful scene and one that works through a conditional tense. The modal possibilities of the "could" in this passage are not definitive or closed, but rather open a whole new realm of the possible through Joshua and this nonhuman kinship.

This type of ontological recalibration also permeates *Salvage the Bones*. We see this brought into relief most distinctly in the relationship between Skeetah and China. Skeetah carries on Joshua's fishy ontology to create a new type of relationality, a human/nonhuman kinship with his pit-bull. This is the way Joshua Bennett reads their relationship, arguing that China and Skeetah seek to "complicate, and ultimately subvert, the bourgeois sensibilities that give shape and form to any strict, hierarchical relationship between pet and human master-subject" (142). The book, after all, starts with a scene of China giving birth where Esch cannot help but imagine China as a proxy for her own mother ("What China is doing is nothing like what mama did when she had my youngest brother" (1)). At the end of the novel, we see very clearly how China and her relationship with the family have undercut the human/nonhuman dyad:

> Skeetah rubs his head from his neck to the crown like his skin is a T-shirt he could pull off and over his skull. Like he could pull who he is off and become something else. Like he could shed his human shape, in the dark, be hatched a great gleaming pit, black to China's white, and run off into what is left of the woods, follow the creek, and find China. (257–258)

---

18. It is worth noting that since the earliest days of Ward criticism, there have been linkages to Faulkner. Bois Sauvage, as Vincent Cunningham puts it, is a "duskier Yoknapatawpha." Or, even more forcefully, as Greg Chase has argued, the town "becomes a means not just of supplementing Faulkner's legacy but also of correcting its racial blind spots, offering a kind of redress to the rural Southern communities about which they both have written" (201).

Skeetah is trying to "shed his human shape," wanting to move out of his self and into something else with China. The repetition of "like" in the passage is also telling. With each appearance, the word seems to present Skeetah momentarily stumbling and pausing as his body is opened outwards. His humanness is slowly refracted as merely a vessel seeking to contain a self that is easily hollowed out and turned into "something else." This compounds the temporal slippage in the passage where Ward imagines Skeetah running into a future that does not exist.

If this "something else" remains somewhat elusive and unnamed in *Salvage the Bones*, Ward circles back to it with Jojo in *Sing, Unburied, Sing*. There is a lineage in Ward's work that starts with Joshua, moves through Skeetah, and ends with Jojo, who can speak directly to animals. Kayla and his uncle, Stag (and, to a lesser extent, his grandmother and Leonie), also share this ability to communicate with the nonhuman world, but it is Jojo who most frequently tunes into animal frequencies: "But it was impossible not to hear the animals, because I looked at them, understood, instantly, and it was like looking at a sentence and understanding the words, all of it coming at once" (14–15). For Jojo, this means that there is a co-constitutional relationship with the animal world that allows him to understand his sense of being differently. Part of this has to do with the added elasticity in the realism of the book where the supernatural brushes into the corners of the novel as this zoolingualism provides space to imagine a world outside cycles of endless violence and crisis. We see this emerge as Jojo approaches Parchman Prison: "I hear the tail end of their chatter, of all those voices calling at once, and I wish I could feel their excitement, feel the joy of the rising, the swinging into the blue, the great flight, the return home, but all I feel is a solid ball of something in my gut, heavy as the head of a hammer" (123). The birds figure alternate coordinates for Jojo, promising a fleeting glimpse of a line of flight above and beyond a land marred by violence. Importantly, the passage returns to the "solid ball of something in my gut" at the end, highlighting that this is only ever provisional and still subject to the passage's final gravity.

By infusing this element of the telepathic, Ward interrogates the joint legacy of racialized violence and environmental exploitation. There is an identification of this joint legacy of abjection, but there is also something else at play here, a generative understanding that emerges from the savaged landscape of the Delta as Jojo turns his eyes to the sky. It is, as Leonie describes it to Jojo, "like the plants following the sun across the sky" (151).[19] In an article on *Salvage the Bones*, Crownshaw begins to bring this alternate horizon into focus: "Here, then, subjectivity is to be found forever breaking its bounds, oscillating between the world of subjects and objects, the human and the nonhuman, environmentally dispersed, or, more accurately put, ecologically constituted" (228). This is even truer in *Sing, Unburied, Sing*. As Ward moves across spatial, temporal, and ontological scales simultaneously, she begins to think in alternate ways about the continual crisis of being.

Improbable Metaphor

To confront crisis as a continual state of being, Ward has been very explicit about how her work thinks capaciously about literary form. In interviews, Ward has described an almost associative logic to her writing that helps usher her towards the transscalar. As she relays to Anna Hartnell in an extensive interview following the publication of *Salvage the Bones*:

> When I was writing Esch in *Salvage the Bones*, I would think about the ways what she's seen, in the place where she's from, would influence the way she's seeing the world in those twelve days. On the level of language, I would think about what are the metaphors for what she would see, and what are the similes that she'd see, what will stand out for her, what is informing what she's seeing, giving her context for what she's seeing. (212)

---

19. We even get passing glimpses of Jojo as an aspiring environmentalist: "I like the heat. I like the way the highway cuts through the forests, curves over hills heading north, sure and rolling. I like the trees reaching out on both sides, the pines thicker and taller up here, spared the stormy beating the ones on the coast get that keeps them spindly and delicate. But that doesn't stop people from cutting them down to protect their houses during storms or to pad their wallets. So much could be happening in those trees" (63). Jojo, in this scene and throughout the book, is expanding upon the arboreal imaginary that Ward creates in *Where the Line Bleeds*. There, we read, "Christophe watched the tree line, smiling faintly when he realized he could tell where he was going in Bois Sauvage by the tops of the trees, that he recognized the big oak at the corner of Cuevas and Pelage" (50). And later, as the boys enter New Orleans, "Everyone [they] watched in the streets seemed cut from the trunks of the ancient, bowing oaks" (166).

Ward is describing an interdependent form of metaphor where metaphor becomes a site that moves across scales while also remaining very much grounded in a specific positionality. Metaphor becomes distributed across an environmental continuum to describe crisis, but it is one that arises from Esch's specific "context." That is, metaphor moves between the big and the small at the same time. At the level of metaphor and simile, Ward's rhetorical tropes are grounded in their very specific sense of place and environmental immanence. To get a sense of this, consider a description of Skeetah:

> For once he doesn't smell like dog. He smells like the constant wind that pushes the tide in over the Gulf of Mexico, but not the tide at the beach. The tide at the Bay of Angels, which smells of oysters fresh dug from the mud. Daddy used to take us swimming there when we were younger, in a little cove. (84–85)

Human and nonhuman memory are tangled together, layering and pushing up against one another in a way that is not contestatory but co-constitutional and contrapuntal. The text is scaling outwards, only to scale back down. Esch moves transscalarly from Skeetah's body to the "Bay of Angels" before she returns to the scale of the personal with the image of her father swimming. This is a scale-shifting that moves across layers of being. There is no hierarchy in the structure of these metaphors, just continual displacement and substitution across scales.

This centrifugal movement occurs throughout the text. After the Batiste father has an accident and loses part of his hand while trying to fix his tow truck, there is a collapse between the layers of space that separate the human/nonhuman world:

> He shuffled along next to Randall, his hand wrapped up to the wrist in gauze and tape so that it looked like a webworm moth nest wound tight in a pecan tree, a yarn of larvae eating at the ripe green leaves beneath to burst forth in black-winged flurry in the throat-closing heat of fall. Only Daddy's hand would not emerge whole and quivering. Daddy's hand would be not the moths but the bare branches, like bones, left under the husk. (132–133)

What we see is a contemporaneous revision to metaphor where the initial image of the tree is not quite able to describe or capture the violence that has taken Esch's father's hand. Unable to find the generative possibility of rebirth like the larvae, Esch's father remains "bare branches." This image is both invasive and a literal marker of the transgressed boundary between human/nonhuman that ultimately uses ecological violence to animate a human condition. There is a residual image of invasion and environmental destruction in the warped bodies of the novel's characters.[20] This is a way of imagining climate at the intimate level of the individual body through a simultaneous proliferation of imagery. More importantly, this is not the harmony of a pastoral narrative, but a violent image of nature.[21]

Yet the direction of these metaphors is not unilateral. Ward does not simply take the environmental as a reservoir from which to give depth to the people in her texts. In *Salvage the Bones* she also uses metaphor as a dialogic site wherein the human can animate the nonhuman. Sound becomes one such a location where we see this interdependence as an animating back-and-forth.[22] As Esch waits in a park for her brothers, she thinks:

> I listen for the boys and the dogs somewhere out in these woods, but all I can hear is the pine trees shushing each other, the oak bristling, the magnolia leaves hard and wide so that they sound like paper plates clattering when the wind hits them, this wind snapping before Katrina somewhere out there in the Gulf, coming like the quiet voice of someone talking before they walk through the doorway of a room. (159)

20. This is also picked up in the temporal multipolarity that Sinead Moynihan reads through the organizing trope of recycling. She describes this as constituting an entangled sense of being: "The fluidity that exists between Ward's characters suggests that this is a family unit in which identities overlap, in which cooperation and empathy rather than atomization and selfishness are the distinguishing features" (557).
21. It is important to avoid romanticizing or naturalizing Esch's relationship to the environment. Kim describes how this type of "intimate relationships with animals and nature" that has saturated racial rhetoric ends up creating a racialized "fraught zone of ambiguity, menace, and transgression" (24).
22. In this way, Ward is both building upon the type of acoustic aesthetics we saw in Nell Zink, while also pointing to the centrality of listening and the aural in Black literature more generally. This is a point Nicole Furlonge makes: "Black literature *sounds*. The critical power, possibility, and promise of the acoustic permeate African American and black feminist literary criticism, traditions that actively work to understand, think through, and know difference heavily through describing the sonic lives of difference" (7; emphasis in original). Jayna Brown goes further into the ecological possibilities promised by listening, arguing that the aural provides "the pulse of other levels of consciousness" (10).

Although this may initially read like a retreat into the quietude of nature, there is a foundational violence to these images as Katrina enters the novel. Ward doubles down on this when Esch listens to the sound of the storm from the attic of their quickly flooding house:

> The dog barks loudly, fast as a drum, and something about the way the bark rises at the end reminds me of Mama's moans, of those bowing pines, of a body that can no longer hold itself together, of something on the verge of breaking. The high notes are little rips. It circles the house, its bark near and far. (223)

This is to say that metaphor in *Salvage the Bones* is not about reestablishing the centrality of a specific image or giving depth to any fixed object or character. Metaphor does not operate on one scale. Rather, metaphor is about showing how language is part of a larger ecology, dispersed across a world in excess of any determinant human metrics. As Esch says during the middle of the hurricane, "But the wind grabs my voice and snatches it out and over the pines, and drops it there to die" (205).

Ward makes this point clear in an interview that accompanies the paperback edition of *Salvage the Bones*. In a reflection on what it was like for her mother to live through another category five storm, Hurricane Camille, Ward describes how language is frayed beyond recognition when confronted with the scalar vastness of a hurricane: "*The wind sounded like a train*, my mother said every time she told me the story, and even though the metaphor made sense, I couldn't hear it" (261; emphasis in original). This is, however, until Katrina, when Ward's own experience with the storm allows her to understand her mother's metaphor. "I understood then how hurricanes, like Camille," she explains, "had unmade the world, tree by water by house by person [. . .] Even in language, it had reduced us to improbable metaphor" (262).[23] This captures perfectly what it means to write and think crisis outside the logic of crisis realism. Both the Anthropocene and anti-Black violence inaugurate a world of "improbable metaphor" where the couplings of disparate entities are brought into being. Ward does not think across the divergent

---

23. This is also integrated diegetically into the text: "Daddy has faced a category 5, but we're too young to remember the last category 5 hurricane that hit the coast: Camille, almost forty years ago. But Mama told us stories about that one" (213).

scales of crisis, then, just at the level of plot and content, but at the very level of language.

Christopher Clark makes a similar point when he describes the novel's form: "The dreamlike environment of Ward's South becomes a haze through which one body can be confused with another" (350). This is a way of describing how the metaphors of the novel slip into their environment, formalizing what it means to think through the perennial crises of Black life in the Anthropocene. When Esch looks at China, she thinks that even China's appearance is imbricated within a larger ecological and historical fabric:

> [China] looks up and her whole body shimmies like a woman down at the Oaks, a blues club set on six acres of woods and baseball diamond in the middle of Bois. They hold baseball games for black town teams every Sunday during the summer. (92)

This comparison continues for another three paragraphs. The simile diffuses out across time, space, and memory in a new constellation that has placed China into a larger historical, environmental, and ontological continuum. The image starts with a memory of China before Esch starts to think about her own childhood and the other women in her community, linking China into a matriarchal kinship across species lines. This carries on through the history of the Delta as Esch thinks about the segregated baseball teams and the speakeasy bars.[24] This is not a metaphor that is contained to a single scale – it moves across lifeforms and history, stretching itself to make sense out of the world with words to theorize literary form at the transscalar level.

The transscalar structure of the metaphors that Ward diagrams in *Salvage the Bones* are expanded in *Sing, Unburied, Sing*. From the outset, there is a deluge of metaphors that cut across human and nonhuman planes of being. Our introduction to Kayla is arboreal, "tangled as the sticker vines that hang from pine trees" (19). When Richie describes Pop for the first time, he mines the epipelagic zone, thinking of Pop as "the scent of leaves disintegrating to mud at the bottom of a river, the aroma of the bowl of the bayou, heavy with water and sediment and the skeletons of small dead creatures, crab,

---

24. The Oaks is a key site in all of the novels. In *Where the Line Bleeds*, the mother of the DeLisle brothers has a confrontation with their drug-addicted father in front of the bar, and in *Sing, Unburied, Sing*, Leonie works at The Oaks alongside Misty.

fish, snakes, and shrimp" (132). This is later contrasted to Leonie's memory of Pop where he has taken "the hardship of the world into him and let it calcify him inch by inch till he's like one of them petrified trees" (207). This is everywhere in the book, from descriptions of music, to stories, to smoking a cigarette. The ambient background music that Leonie hears while working a shift in the bar takes on an atmospheric lilt ("The music, all violins and cellos, swells in the room, then recedes, like the water out in the Gulf before a big storm" (112)), while Pop's story about himself and River becomes tangled with insects ("a moth-eaten shirt, nibbled to threads" (137)), and Leonie even imagines an aquatic self as she steals a smoke ("the nicotine laps at my insides like a placid lake" (101)). The book is dizzying with these tapestries of richly improbable metaphors that move across scales of time, being, and space. My point in listing a few of them here is to give a sampling of the crosscurrents that work across *Sing, Unburied, Sing*. Every character, nearly every sentence, is inflected by a cohabitation with nonhuman scales.

Key to the effectiveness of these improbable metaphors is the fact that they draw our attention to the long, Black history of crisis on the Mississippi Delta. For Leonie, there is a lingering violence that hovers at the periphery of her metaphorical scalings of the world. Early in the book, when she does coke with Misty, she catches a glimpse of Misty's bra and begins to spiral outwards, as the blue of the bra becomes

> the color of the deep water off in the Gulf of Mexico. The kind of blue in the pictures that Michael took when he worked on the oil rig offshore, and the water was a living wet plain around him, making a great blue bowl with the sky. (64)

This is a dense and winding image that pans further and further out, blurring the ocean with the stratosphere as Leonie's mind moves from the ocean to the sky to describe this "living wet plain." But, as powerful an image as it is, it is one that is coded and colored by the Deepwater disaster. In fact, Leonie cannot think of the water outside of the past tense, a previous era when the "water was a living wet plain." In her crisis-defined present, the water has blackened and become tarry as the oil continues to spill and pollute the world around her.[25]

25. The darkened water is a constant for Ward. We first see it in *Where the Line Bleeds*, when Joshua contemplates the Wolf River: "Joshua knew that there were some place in Alabama where the water was blue, where it was clear enough to see the sandy bottom, but here in Mississippi, it was so gray" (90).

This metaphor allows Ward to make visible the Deepwater crisis in a way that brings to the fore the invisibility of our dependency on oil. This is a point that Jennifer Wenzel has made precisely: "*Oil is everywhere and nowhere* [. . .] Oil is everywhere, ubiquitous in our daily life, and yet we so rarely *see* oil, either literally or metaphorically" ("How To," n.p.; emphasis in original). At the same time, oil is, at its core, a transscalar entity, one that is both, as Wenzel puts "geopolitical and [. . .] personal" ("How To," n.p.). Oil, like its actual existence in our own lives, is everywhere in Ward's work as it laps at the shores of her metaphors. In an offhand remark early in *Where the Line Bleeds*, for example, the DeLisle twins speak to a classmate and ask what he is doing after graduation. He responds, "'I'm going offshore. My uncle already got my application in'" (20). Oil does not even need to be named in this scene - "offshore" becomes a metonym for the extractive enterprise that defines the Gulf's economy.[26]

The salience of oil also helps gloss the way that oil itself is a transscalar entity, constantly slippery and nebulous. This is a point Stephanie LeMenager argues forcefully in her personal, literary, and energetic history, *Living Oil*. LeMenager theorizes oil as concept and as energy force, pointing to how it disrupts our attempts at ontological stratification:

> Oil challenges liveness from another ontological perspective, as a substance that was, once, live matter and that acts with a force suggestive of a form of life [. . .] the microbial life in oil, in addition to oil's deep geologic history as life-through-time, forces questions of how biology, geology, and culture come together to define what counts as living matter. (6–7)

This is a critique that works across both ontological and temporal planes as oil demands an understanding that moves across "deep geologic history" while it also challenges what is considered living.[27] Mark Simpson approaches the relationship between oil and scale

---

26. We can also trace this in the way that driving appears in Ward's work. The car that Joshua and Christophe inherit from their mother acts as their entrance into adulthood, as they think, "Why show up when you give us a car? Guess she's really done, now" (26). The cars, unlike the fear of the road in *Sing, Unburied, Sing*, become a place of agency and autonomy for the boys as they move up and down "the coastline" tracing "[solitary] sparse stands of pine trees [that] dotted the sandy median as they rode along" (49).
27. It is not incidental that LeMenager also looks at the "U.S. Gulf Coast in the wake of the BP blowout and Hurricane Katrina" in her work (*Living Oil*, 16).

from the other end of the spectrum, arguing that oil's "lubricity" has enabled the development of a scalar invariance wherein oil facilitates a fantasy of "smoothness as cultural common sense," hiding its inherent shift between scales in order to perform a magic trick that obfuscates "the violent asymmetries of movement and circulation globally" (289). Ward counters this type of narrative lubricity, using these twinned moments of crisis to bring our attention to these "violent asymmetries" that are concomitant with crises of oil.[28]

We see in *Sing, Unburied, Sing* how an extractive petro-imaginary becomes, like the oil that gushed into the Gulf, pervasive and viscous, attaching itself to the way that Leonie reads both herself and the world at large. As she drives homes from Misty's trailer after their coke bender, the figurative animacy of the oil becomes even more topsy-turvy as she opens her car window to "gas fumes thick with the smell of wet earth [. . .] The rain presses my eyes closed, kneads them. I think I hear a whisper of a whoosh of a word, but then it's gone as the tank pings and the nozzle goes slack" (65). Like the dialogic relationship between the human and nonhuman world in *Salvage the Bones*, the oil cuts both ways. The oil becomes imbricated with not just the sea water, but also the moisture in the air, enveloping Leonie in its fossilized toxicity. For Leonie, the natural world does not have the type of liberatory potential that Jojo is able to read in it.

Although Leonie's mother had tried to teach her to attune herself to the nonhuman assemblages that surround her, Mam is ultimately unsuccessful in providing her with "a map of the world as she knew it, a world plotted orderly by divine order, spirit in everything" (105). Mam, that is, tries to introduce Leonie to an alternative epistemology as a counterforce to this oily toxicity. Once Mam realizes Leonie is pregnant, she begins summoning "Our Lady of Regala. On the Star of the Sea. That she was invoking Yamayá, the goddess of the ocean and salt water, with her shushing and her words, and that she was holding me like the goddess, her arms all the life-giving waters

---

28. In this way, Ward is also taking part in a larger critical conversation around narratives of oil. In their Introduction to the seminal *Petrocultures: Oil, Politics, Culture*, Sheena Wilson, Adam Carlson, and Imre Szeman write, "'Oil transformed everyday life in the twentieth century. In the twenty-first century, we are finally beginning to realize the degree to which oil has made us moderns who and what we are, shaping our existence close at hand while narrating us into networks of power and commerce far, far away" (3). Ward is participating in this more nuanced attention to oil itself as constituting entity.

of the world" (159).²⁹ But, for Leonie, these "life-giving waters of the world" have only become oily and murky, tarred by the pollution that sticks itself not just to the animals and sea life, but also into every corner of her own atmosphere. As we read later, "[There] is none of that [knowledge] inside me. Just some water oak limbs, dry and mossy, burned to ash, smoldering" (194).

Black Anthropocenes

If Leonie remains ensnared within a determinant reading of the world that cannot think past the gelatinous muck of the oil, defined and constituted through the crises that pulsate through the text, Ward still wants to think about what Black life looks like outside of terminal crisis. This is true in both *Salvage the Bones* and *Sing, Unburied, Sing*. Said another way, Ward is just as interested in critiquing the legacy of Black death while also imagining the possibilities of Black life. To highlight this dual movement, consider a scene from *Salvage the Bones*. There is a sense of climatic violence that clings to the family that we see when Esch battles through morning sickness: "It all disappears and I wonder what I am feeding. I imagine the food turning to mush, sliding down my throat, through my body like water through a storm drain to poll in my stomach" (41). Her sense of self is diffused through images of waste and extraction akin to Leonie's: it is not just a baby that is being theorized, but also a self that becomes liquid passing through – "a storm drain." Esch imagines herself as part of a larger nonhuman continuum, unthinkable outside an environmental immanence that is figured as refuse.

But there is also something that escapes this ubiquitous waste and extraction. Sharpe writes that to think outside of determinant humanist categories is a way to reorient ontology, a way to begin to "attend to, care for, comfort, and defend" new positions and relationalities despite the ongoing crisis of antiblackness (38). This is what Ward is sounding out, a way to imagine what it means to be, as Esch thinks, "human debris in the middle of all the rest of it," where

---

29. The matriarch in *Where the Line Bleeds*, Ma-mee also holds this knowledge but seems to understand that it may die with her, thinking, "It bothered her that she often dreamt in a language that no one around her spoke any longer, that she woke still thinking in Creole French, to a wide, lonely bed, an emptying house" (64). Christophe describes Ma-mee in similar terms: "Ma-mee always say we got that blood in us, the kind that know things, that Bois Sauvage blood" (130).

that "debris" crafts new relationalities (237). In the final scene of *Salvage the Bones*, we see how Ward imagines this care and comfort as Esch imagines China returning from the floodwaters unscathed:

> We will sit with him here, in the strange, insect-silent dark. We will sit until we are sleepy, and then we will remain until our legs hurt [. . .] She will return, standing tall and straight, the milk burned out of her [. . .] She will know that I am a mother. (258)

Motherhood again moves across species, forming a human/nonhuman kinship between both Esch and China. Motherhood acts as a surrogate site at which Esch can figure herself beyond the human. But Ward is careful not to romanticize this relationality either. It is only in a futural tense that Esch can begin to create new animative possibilities and fantasies. Let me be clear: China does not actually return, but the book still leaves this door open as a to-come possibility for what sorts of human/nonhuman kinship ties can emerge from the debris of the human. Esch is thinking outside of the teleology of crisis by using her pregnant body to imagine a future world that scales between the micro and the bodily, the macro and the planetary. I want to return here to a claim from the Introduction of *Transscalar Critique* that transscalar critique is not just something that we do to texts, but something that texts themselves do. This is at the heart of Ward's fiction. The texts themselves make it impossible to think these scales of crises independently: to be a young Black woman in the Mississippi Delta is to live at the intersection of myriad crises. If literary form is to have any political or social efficacy, it must also be able to mediate and move between these scales.

This is also what we see in the relationship between Pops, Richie, and Jojo at the end of *Sing, Unburied, Sing*. As Pops finally finishes telling Jojo the story of Richie's death and his role in it, Ward moves into a similar mode to think across scales. As Richie leaves his body and assumes a spirit form, freed from the purgatory in which he has been forced to circulate, we read:

> Across the face of the water, there is land. It is green and hilly, dense with trees, riven by rivers. The air is gold: the gold of sunrise and sunset, perpetually peach [. . .] There are people: tiny and distinct. They fly and walk and float and run. They are alone. They are together [. . .] They are never silent. Ever present is their singing: they don't move their mouths and yet it comes from them. Crooning in the yellow light. It comes from the black earth and the trees and the ever-lit sky. It comes from the water. It is the most beautiful song I have ever heard, but I can't understand a word. (241)

This passage is striking for the type of perspectival shift it signals, moving out into the atmospheric firmament as Richie reorients his sense of human scaling, imagining the people as "tiny." But this does not necessitate a collapse into an undifferentiated mass; instead, the people also remain "distinct." And from this, there emanates a type of relationality that is brought together across "black earth and the trees" but also "from the water." The fact that the earth is imagined as specifically Black is a reclamation; the Black earth does not return to the oily death of Deepwater but rather becomes the generative locus of the "most beautiful song" that glistens across a water no longer toxic from acidification.

What is also key to this passage, and the final scene in *Salvage the Bones*, is that Ward has left the realms of realism. Gone are the gravities, logics, and whirlpools of realism as Ward explores the perspective of Black Anthropocenes that are mediated through what Jojo calls "language flipped inside out" (241). In this revision to literary form, a new Black ecological kinship model emerges in the texts; even the trees in *Sing, Unburied, Sing* are given a second life as "a great dark green tangle: oaks reaching low and wide, vines tangled around trunks and dropping from branches, poison sumac and swamp tupelo and cypress and magnolia growing up around us in a circular wall" (251). This is a protective enclosure and one which brings the characters into the fold rather than pushing them out – we finally see in these moments a way to reinhabit the world despite and because of the ongoing crises of anti-Black violence and environmental destruction. As the story ends and Richie's ghost leaves the text, there is a moment of peace: "There is soft air and yellow sunlight and drifting pollen where he was, and me and Pop embracing in the grass. The animals are quieting in grunts and snorts and yips. *Thank you*, they say. *Thank you thank you thank*, they sing" (257; emphasis in original).

Like *Salvage the Bones*, Richie's ecological reconciliation is not final, but provisional and tempered. In diametric opposition to the types of familial reconciliation of crisis realist fiction, in the scenes immediately afterwards, Mam dies and Leonie and Jojo end up in a yelling match that ends with Leonie viciously beating him.[30] The book finishes with this tension, not allowing the family to come back

---

30. Throughout the book, Leonie struggles with motherhood as she is never able to fully love Jojo. The violence she feels towards him, tellingly, is toxic in much the same way that she thinks about water in the text: "[When] I hit his face, pain cracks through my palms, pings through my fingers [. . .] And Jojo's straight, straight as Pop, all the little boy gone from his eyes: the tide gone out, the sun scorching the residue of water away, leaving hot sand baking to concrete" (272).

together to heal. Leonie and Michael relapse into drug abuse and Jojo and Kayla are abandoned to Pops and have to fend for themselves as they remain haunted by their own respective ghosts. Even Richie's ghost cannot leave the family alone. He remains haunted by a landscape that has been defined by a climate of antiblackness. In one of his final exchanges with Jojo, "'There's so many of us,' Richie says. His voice is molasses slow. 'So many of us,' he says. 'Hitting the wrong keys. Wandering against. The song'" (282). And this is Ward's point: this "song," this promise of a different type of relationality is one that can never be fully realized. It is ephemeral, always at risk of being swept up in the undertow of violence.

Ward's attention to these asymmetries in the Anthropocene is a rebuttal to the now common argument that the Anthropocene's scalar vastness runs the risk of depoliticization. The planetary mode of Anthropocenic thinking has been productive for the ways in which it has expanded the horizon of literary theory and nonhuman agencies. But much ecocritical thinking has been rightly critiqued for the interpellation of humanity into a monolithic entity without the valences of lived difference. This is where Ward intervenes. She is able to attend to all of these scales simultaneously, thinking through the scales of Blackness and climate, while also theorizing how literary form is able to attend to crisis. What Ward does is develop a transscalar form of literature that is able to think through this interconnection, just as attentive to the racial as it is the linguistic, providing us with a way to begin building out new narratives of Black Anthropocenes.

Chapter 5

Unmitigated Blackness: Paul Beatty's Transscalar Satire

> Maybe the reason so few people are funny these days is that nothing is identified as being absurd anymore [. . .] The word is rarely even used, because for the dutiful American to acknowledge the absurdity of life implies responsibility.
>
> Paul Beatty, *Hokum: An Anthology of African–American Humor*

> What is it – here, now, in a world of modern blackness – that Black America indicates?
>
> Fred Moten, *Black and Blur*

Towards the end of Paul Beatty's Man–Booker prize-winning novel *The Sellout*, the narrator takes stock of contemporary Black art. The protagonist, known only by his last name, Me, is at a comedy club when a comedian abruptly stops his performance as a white couple start laughing hysterically at his jokes. The comedian yells: "'Do I look like I'm fucking joking with you? This shit ain't for you. Understand? Now get the fuck out! This is our thing!'" (287). Me is both awed and confused by the performance:

> I respected that he didn't give a fuck. But I wish I hadn't been so scared, that I had the nerve to stand in protest. Not to castigate him for what he did or to stick up for the aggrieved white people. After all, they could've stuck up for themselves, called in the authorities or their God, and smote everyone in the place, but I wish I'd stood up to this man and asked him a question: "So what exactly is *our* thing?" (287–288; emphasis in original)

Me picks up on the comedian's phrase "our thing" to ask what qualifies as contemporary Black art and aesthetic expression. How can the comedian, Me wonders, draw a line between our thing and an idea of their thing? Extrapolating from Me, I finish *Transscalar Critique* by looking at how this is not just a question about comedy, but also a question of literary form. Through Me, Beatty's novel joins a conversation encapsulated by Kenneth Warren in his controversial but essential *What Was African American Literature?* There, Warren claims that African American literature as an aesthetic category and enterprise existed only in relation to Jim Crow laws in the period following the failure of Reconstruction until the passage of the Civil Rights Act of 1964 and the Voting Rights Act of 1965. This is not to say that "racism has disappeared from the nation's sociopolitical landscape," but rather that African American literature was constituted as a dialectical "function of Jim Crow and the fight against it" (5, 110). With the end of *de jure* segregation and the ascendancy of *de facto* racism, there is the loss of a distinctly African American aesthetic vernacular. Contemporary Black art in America, Warren goes on to argues, lacks a grounding referent.

Warren is making more than a claim about the periodization of African American literature, but also a political claim about the role of African American literature. African American literature, Warren contends, provided the space "in which the black literary voice could count for so much because, in political terms, the voice of black people generally counted for so little" (156). Warren is arguing that African American art is grounded in a reciprocal relation between the aesthetic and the political made possible by the obvious structural oppression of Jim Crow. This is where Warren and Beatty diverge. While Warren laments the loss of a distinctly African American literature, in this chapter I argue that Beatty, throughout *The Sellout* and his three other novels, critiques this idea of a stable African American literature having ever existed, crafting instead a transscalar form of Black writing.

The plot of *The Sellout* turns on Me's relationship to Hominy Jenkins, the former understudy of the *Our Gang* minstrel, Buckwheat, and the sole surviving "*Little Rascal* stunt coon" (71). Hominy sets off a series of events that eventually lead to the narrator being charged by the Supreme Court with "willfully ignoring the Fourteenth Amendment" and resegregating the fictional Los Angeles ghetto of Dickens (23). As well as segregating Dickens, the narrator is charged with possessing Hominy as a slave. In some senses, this regressive plotline seems to revolve around what Warren describes as a tired trope within contemporary literature wherein "'the discovery' [is] made again and again by recent scholarship, that despite news to the contrary, 'racism' still exists" (85). But *The Sellout* does not merely uncover the racist bias of some minor character. By staging the segregation of Dickens and the reinstitution of slavery, Beatty goes much further than the "discovery" that "'racism' still exists." *The Sellout* stages a radical erasure of the gains of not only the Civil Rights movement but postbellum Black political culture more generally, imagining a return to chattel slavery as offering the only way out of our current moment of, to highlight this book's central term, racial crisis.

In this sweeping revision, *The Sellout* satirizes the politics of intelligibility that underpin Warren's idea of African American literature which remain circumscribed within a specific version of American liberalism constituted by a nostalgic pining for "the coherence of African American literature" (2).[1] Beatty's polemical intervention into contemporary racial politics is brought into crystalline relief as the novel concludes with a scene where Me drives around in the days after Obama's inauguration. Me runs into his occasional sparring partner, Foy Cheshire, the text's Black intelligentsia straw man, who he finds waving a flag from his car in celebration of the election:

> "Why are you waving the flag?" I asked him. "Why now? I've never seen you wave it before." He said that he felt like the country, the United States of America, had finally paid off its debts. "And what about the Native Americans? What about the Chinese, the Japanese, the Mexicans, the poor, the forests, the water, the air, the fucking Californian condor? When do they collect?" I asked him. (289)

In the afterglow of Obama's election, Foy is celebrating the ostensible end of American racism. Me, however, reminds Foy that systemic violence is not undone by the elevation of one individual, thus short-circuiting the postracial end-of-history narrative trumpeted in the wake of Obama's election.[2] Moreover, this passage pushes against

---

1. This type of logic is symptomatic of what Stephen Best, in a survey of contemporary Black Studies, describes as a tendency to read "history arrayed as teleology [. . .] fundamentally recuperative in its orientation" (12).
2. There are numerous discussions and critiques of the postracial proclamations that followed Obama's election. Frank Wilderson, for example, argues that the "election of Obama enables a plethora of shaming discourses in response to revolutionary politics" and thus ghettoizes discourses of race into "the rebar of . . . intellectual (political discourse), that is, as unspoken grammars" (4–5). This "unspoken grammar" is taken up in *The Sellout* when Me recalls going to a zoo after the election: "At the zoo, I stood in front of the primate cage listening to a woman marvel at how 'presidential' the four-hundred-pound gorilla looked [. . .] When her boyfriend, his finger tapping the informational placard, pointed out the 'presidential' silverback's name was Baraka, the woman laughed aloud, until she saw me" (5). This joke not only highlights a syntax of racism but also reveals a circular temporality of race relations, as "Baraka" slides between Obama and Amiri Baraka (see note 8).

Warren's singular focus on African American as a singular aesthetic and political category. Me, in effect, is asking Foy to imagine Blackness in much the same way that Ward did in the previous chapter, outside the liberal imaginary and yoked to myriad other scales of being, in this case, from the Mexicans to the air.

By focusing on race as a broader category, Me understands contemporary Blackness more expansively than Warren. Blackness is a tangled category that intersects not only with other racialized beings but also with class, the environment, and even animals. This type of entanglement is counter to Warren's political imaginary. In language that feels as if it could be leveled directly at Me, Warren argues that "the turn to diasporic, transatlantic, global, and other frames indicates a dim awareness that the boundary creating [African American literature's] distinctiveness has eroded" (8). Whereas Warren sees this erosion as politically corrosive, Me's inclusion of "other frames," whether they be condors or the Chinese, is precisely the point. These other frames form the basis of a contemporary politics of Blackness for Me. The addition of frames does not represent a loss of cohesion but a way for Me to theorize race as part of what Sylvia Wynter calls *the global problematique*.[3] As I covered extensively in Chapter 3, at the heart of Wynter's political project is an argument for how Blackness bisects and intersects with other categories as a nexus "together constitutive of our species" ("Unparalleled," 44). For Wynter and Me, that is, Blackness does not exist in a vacuum but is dispersed across an environment, creating, as I argued earlier, the foundations for a Black ecology. *The Sellout* approaches this head on by not seeking to shore up a fixed definition of contemporary Black aesthetics that would understand the world only through the analytic frame proposed by Warren. By returning to the tropes and political structure of Jim Crow America, *The Sellout* argues that there never was any such thing as singular African American literature in the first place.

The Sellout, then, is a novel about the contemporary crisis of Blackness aesthetically, politically, and ontologically. In this chapter, I think through this crisis as an opening towards literary and critical forms that, as Saidiya Hartman puts it, "do not simply traffic in the obviousness of [racial] common sense" (*Scenes*, 119). In what follows, I argue that Beatty's fiction models another mode of transscalar critique that thinks past the saturated commonsense epistemes of race towards a

---

3. Wynter is borrowing this term from Gerald Barney, but I find it useful to index the ways in which her thinking works across divergent frames.

broader ontological investigation of contemporary Blackness. In an interview with Frédéric Sylvanise, Beatty makes it clear that to think race in the contemporary requires a new vocabulary: "It's like when you watch something on the news, like the Trayvon Martin thing. You can hear things like 'Did they get justice?' But what does fucking justice mean in this sense? I think we gotta talk a little differently somehow" (7). Beatty's version of "justice" follows Me's invocation of the "forests, the water, the air, the fucking Californian condor," to bring questions of race into conversation with the Anthropocene. In making this argument, I read Beatty as providing literary form focused on the scalar co-constitutionality of the racial and the environmental. For Wynter, the fact that "global warming and climate instability now confronts us" means that we have to "replace the ends of the *referent-we*" of both racial *and* ontological common sense ("Unparalleled," 24). This requires moving between divergent scales simultaneously. Like the other iterations of the transscalar in Black literature that I have followed in the second half of this book, Beatty's work imagines how it is possible to use literary form to attend to the macro-scale of the planet at the same time that we think about the lived reality of Blackness. Talking about Blackness, as I have contended throughout *Transscalar Critique*'s second half, requires a model that is able to think about these scales simultaneously.

A key aspect of the transscalar in Beatty is the way he avoids making equivalencies or hierarchies between marginalized positions. The transscalar is an integration of the planetary, the biological, and the geological within our political vocabularies in an ongoing moment of environmental and racial crisis while also avoiding the claim that any one type of crisis or analysis should take precedence.[4] Transscalar critique does not imagine oppressive power dynamics as equivalent by adding the "environmental" to the holy trinity of race, class, and gender, but instead imagines both human and planetary metrics as simultaneously operative and contrapuntal in intersecting ways. This claim – that race cannot be thought of in the singular – is not new in itself; indeed, in many respects it evokes long-running claims made by and through intersectionality. However, intersectionality as a term and concept has been defanged at both the critical and institutional levels. Jennifer Nash, for examples, describes a critical reappraisal of

---

4. To read Beatty in these terms is to follow the work of Sarah Pfaff, who has also argued that Beatty's fiction models a "relational, networked belonging as a solution to the cultural politics of crisis" (110).

intersectionality as a necessity resulting from how the term has been detached from its situated history within Black feminism and mobilized "to migrate across entrenched disciplinary divides" as it, "neatly and coherently," is employed to "describe complexity" ("Intersectionality," 11). This is to say that the complex interplay of power relations that was originally mapped by intersectionality has now given way to a reductive shorthand for complex layerings of oppression deployed without attention to the specificity of each of those positions.

Furthermore, intersectionality remains limited in what I see as its critical scale. As Nash writes,

> Intersectionality's reliance on black women as the basis for its claims to complex subjectivity renders black women prototypical intersectional subjects whose experiences of marginality are imagined to provide a *theoretical value-added*. That is, black women enable scholars to "ask the other question," to expose the specters of racism and sexism, which leave their traces even in progressive analyses. ("Re-Thinking," 8; emphasis in original)

This is to say that even within intersectional analyses, the Black female body, the generative locus of intersectionality itself, is often erased or imagined as "a unitary and monolithic entity" ("Re-Thinking," 8). Imagining the Black female body in these limited terms comes at the price of lived reality. This limit is what Calvin Warren identifies as an analytic that "seeks to understand blackness through forms of *equivalence* with human identity" (409; emphasis in original). This problem of equivalence "with human identity" suggests a limit in the reification of humanity that cannot think outside the strictures of a humanism that is historically contingent upon whiteness. This limit is symptomatic of Foy's reading of Obama's election. For Foy, Obama's election is allowed to stand in for the continually asymmetric and incommensurable ways that Blackness is entangled with other forms of being in the contemporary US through a cosmetic multiculturalism.

The institutionalization of intersectionality, in short, has limited its critical scale, relying upon the human even as it tries to situate and resituate the historical conditions of the Black female body.[5] To get

---

5. In this sense, the transscalar is able to sidestep these terms of critique while simultaneously following Wynter's ontological critique of the "genre of the human that reifies Western bourgeois tenets," and, by extension, underpins hegemonic modes of thought, including, in our contemporary moment, intersectionality ("Unparalleled," 9).

outside of this critical limit, a key part of the transscalar's project is what Alexander Weheliye calls a "global approach to racialization" that prioritizes the category of Blackness over the category of African American (29).[6] But, to reiterate a central claim of this book, the transscalar is not merely a zooming out or a zooming in, substituting one category for another. Whereas identity becomes calcified in the equivalencies and hierarchies intersectionality can produce between subject positions, the transscalar gestures toward a fluid understanding of being: identity is wrapped within and through large and small scales without prioritizing any singular mode. We need to attend, transscalar critique argues, to the macro-scale of the planet at the same time that we think about the lived reality of Blackness and the histories of inequity upon which that planet is structured. As I have made clear throughout this book, the transscalar takes intersectionality's critical ecology and fuses it with Anthropocenic thought and literary studies in order to interrogate and continually remap and rescale our units of critique.[7]

As I have argued throughout, by using the term scale as my central analytic, I make the case that the transscalar reaches critical horizons

---

6. This is where Wynter and Weheliye depart from Warren. As opposed to using the signifier "African American," both Wynter and Weheliye take a multivalent approach to Black Studies to highlight how *Black* denotes a break from "an identarian marker of cultural and/or ethnic specificity" at the same time that it does not reify "transnational frames of reference" (30). But I also want to be careful in respect to this type of reading of Beatty. While Beatty's work is *transscalar* in its breadth, this does not neatly map into an expanded, globalized model of Blackness versus African American identity. In fact, his work still emphasizes and builds upon a more local satirical, and distinctly *African American*, tradition where, as Daryl Dickson-Carr describes, Beatty "addresses questions that have haunted African American politics since the assassination of Martin Luther King, Jr." (202). Indeed, Beatty is carrying on a long tradition of African American satire running from George Schuyler to Ishmael Reed that is consistent only in its inconsistency. Dickson-Carr continues: "[The] African American satirical novel is not entirely consistent ideologically within the twentieth century, outside of a few essential characteristics: unremitting iconoclasm, criticism of the current status of African American political and cultural trends, and indictment of specifically American forms of racism" (16). My point is that Beatty's focus on Black Americans and "American racism" does not preclude the incorporation of other frames. Whereas Warren argues you can only have one or the other, Beatty's work moves between these scales fluidly and fluently.
7. Although transscalar critique certainly does seek what Weheliye cites as "the liberation of humans from all 'isms' versus only one specific form of subjection," the transscalar is not wholly concerned with this type of liberatory work, but wants to think more capaciously about Blackness and ecology more broadly (23).

unavailable to other modes. Our modes of critique have to simultaneously scale outwards to account for the planetary, while also remaining focused on the micro that makes up the asymmetrical distribution of the *Anthropos* of the Anthropocene. In this way, then, this chapter is a continuation of the two that precede it while also signaling a return to where I started. This is a chapter that is as concerned with the environmental and racial implications of Beatty's work as it is with the literary, returning to the question that Don DeLillo posed at the beginning of this book: what literary forms can map a contemporary that is defined by its sense of crisis? Turning to satire, Beatty disavows any stable ground beneath his object of critique, looking at the way that the scales of crisis continually shapeshift and redraw one another. Beatty continually refashions both the aesthetic and the political boundaries of his texts to respond to the expansive scales of an Anthropocene present while remaining focused on the way in which the Anthropocene is also partially an interface of a history of anti-Black violence.

For Beatty, this is a literary function of satire. The shifting scales of Beatty's satire are a way of formalizing a new critical and literary genre of and for the Anthropocene. The efficacy of satire is that it does not operate at any single scale, but rather foregrounds the processual act of moving between scales, in what I see as a transscalar genre *par excellence*.[8] Julian Murphet takes up a similar argument in his theorization of satire in the Anthropocene:

> Satire knows that the space of being is not *full* but riven by irreconcilable interests that cannot be arbitrated other than by being "fought out" in the open. There is no metadiscourse with which to portray this cloven space, only immanent language games that can be hijacked to expose their limits and, with them, the social tectonics that subtend them. (666; emphasis in original)

What we read in this passage is a moment of transscalar critique. Murphet starts out with an ontological claim about "the space of being" and moves into the linguistic and formal qualities via "immanent

---

8. Dickson-Carr makes a similar claim about Black satire more specifically: "[Racism] is just but one ideological system interrogated within the African–American satiric novel" (32). There is a similar transscalar logic in the way that Ishmael Reed describes another satirical predecessor of both himself and Beatty, Amiri Baraka: "But part of Baraka's genius was that he could take scraps of culture and ideologies and quilt them together" ("LeRoi Jones," 21). I find that the term "quilt" lends itself nicely as a trope for the transscalar.

language games," before finishing with the "social tectonics" of the political. In these three sentences, Murphet is modeling the type of transscalar critique I will go on to describe in Beatty. Satire is attendant to the ontological, the syntactical, and the political simultaneously. Beatty's satire models, in short, an aesthetic that conjures a transscalar critique of the molecular and the molar. Beatty does not prioritize striated layers (environment or race, biology or geology, politics or genre) but strives for a transscalar *and*.

Moreover, satire in this iteration is both critical and creative. That is, this continual movement between the ontological, linguistic, and political limns the ways in which satire is a muddying of the line between fiction and critique, a point that I have returned to throughout this book. This is something that Aaron Matz highlights in his twinned history of realism and satire in the nineteenth-century novel:

> Satire and realism are two ways of understanding literature's relationship with the world it represents. The first has to do with a moral attitude toward the world: satire isolates conditions or truths in order to chastise the mankind responsible for them. Realism has generally been understood as an expository or demonstrative stance – or posture, or method, or (like satire) attitude – that is interested in those same truths, in those same conditions, without necessarily operating on the assumption that it has set forth to mock them. (2)

Although Matz's book goes on to complicate this binary, I find it useful for demonstrating the ontological stakes that are at play within satire. Satire, that is, is invested in making a cut "toward the world" rather than the "demonstrative stance" of verisimilitude that dominates the aesthetic logics of literary realism. In this sense, I see satire as another transscalar mode of both literature and criticism that responds to the demands of literary criticism against the ambient backdrop of both the Anthropocene and anti-Black violence. This is why "the Chinese, the Japanese, the Mexicans, the poor, the forests, the water, the air, the fucking Californian condor" remain present at every turn in Beatty's writing: Beatty is constantly seeking out a way to "chastise the mankind responsible" for not just racial injustices but environmental ones as well. To return to a quote that I started this book with, living in the Anthropocene is to be aware of a world composed of these myriad scales. As Wai Chee Dimock puts it, "This is a moment in the history of the planet, and the history of the institution of literature when a plurality of scale might turn out to be a matter of necessity rather than a matter of indifference" ("World History," 614). In other words, the Anthropocene's "plurality of scales" requires us to think across scales simultaneously, and this is precisely what satire allows Beatty to do.

Like my reading of Ward in the previous chapter, I read each of Beatty's novel alongside one another to try to capture Beatty's diffuse and expansive scalar imaginary, weaving the prose, plots, and ideas of *The White Boy Shuffle* (1996), *Tuff* (2000), *Slumberland* (2008), and *The Sellout* (2015) through one another. Bookended by Rodney King and Eric Brown, each of Beatty's books is a book about the crisis of Blackness in America in the late twentieth and early twenty-first centuries, a time when the police killing of unarmed Black men continues unchecked.[9] At the same time that Beatty explicates these very material and real crises, each of his books is simultaneously invested in satirizing the ways in which the category of Blackness remains a tenable political category in a contemporary moment of racial crisis. This is not to say that Beatty is somehow proffering a postracial horizon. This is exactly what Beatty is not doing. Rather, Beatty's work explicitly makes the case that discourses – critical, political, or literary – that prioritize either the economic, the national, the biological, or the geologic all attempt to rescale Blackness through their own limited hermeneutic apparatus. This is what Beatty's work combats by using the transscalar as "a matter of necessity." Moreover, by working across the entirety of Beatty's œuvre, I model in miniature a transscalar mode of reading: to capture the complexity of his satire, it is necessary to think through Beatty's work as an ecology, rather than as singular texts.

Class Consciousness and the Crisis of Blackness

As the tension between Me and Foy limns, discussions of Blackness in the contemporary often oscillate between two contradictory poles. The *New Yorker* critic Hua Hsu's reading of *The Sellout* alongside

---

9. The Rodney King riots feature graphically in *The White Boy Shuffle*, and the plot of *The Sellout* is inaugurated by the narrator's father being shot in the back and killed by the police. In *Tuff*, the narrator's former ex-Black Panther father "drummed into his head" the names of people killed by police (61). This culminates with the protagonist Winston's political platform being: "Anti-cop, Anti-cop, Anti-cop" (172). Even in *Slumberland*, a novel purposely set away, both temporally and geographically, from our contemporary in Soviet-era Berlin, there is this pervasive sense of police violence. The narrator, for example, watches his girlfriend's sister kill herself, which leads to a riot after the "callous treatment of the deceased [by the police] set the black Germans off" (190).

the rapper Kendrick Lamar's opus *To Pimp a Butterfly* is particularly instructive in highlighting this impasse of racial dynamics as they play out in the realm of contemporary Black art:

> [Beatty and Lamar capture] a time when diversity has gone completely mainstream. [Their work] is animated by a desire to understand the paradoxes of that time – of a multitudinous America that contains both Barack Obama's election and Trayvon Martin's murder. A time when the conversation on race seems both terminal and never-ending, when the promise of ever more conversation is offered as an end itself. (n.p.)

There is a crisis of Blackness, Hsu argues, but it is one that is both ongoing and already foreclosed upon. Although the election of Obama was touted by many (both Fox News and MSNBC pundits) as the zenith of a postracial horizon, churning underneath this veneer is a "terminal and never-ending" crisis of Blackness. Beatty captures this impasse midway through *The Sellout*:

> [The] difference between most oppressed people of the world and American blacks. They vow never to forget, and we want everything expunged from the record. We want someone [. . .] to present our case to the world with a set of instructions that the jury will disregard centuries of ridicule and stereotype and pretend the woebegone n****s in front of you are starting from scratch. (98)

There is, on the one hand, the impulse to expunge. However, this is impossible when held against "centuries of ridicule and stereotype." These are the two scales between which the crisis of being Black in America continually shuttles. Me puts it simply: Black Americans represent "an entire race that was raceless on the surface, but quietly understood by those in the know to be very, very black" (10).

One strategy some contemporary theorists have deployed to wiggle their way out of this gridlock has been a reprioritization of economic critique. While we explored this in Chapter 1, it is important to highlight how the abeyance of race under neoliberalism has been taken as a measure of the futility of cleaving to identity categories as generative political sites. Race trumps class, so the argument goes, as the neoliberalization of multiculturalism usurps structural critique. Walter Benn Michaels, alongside critics like Warren, has been one of the foremost promulgators of this critical genre.[10] "We like the idea of cultural equality better than

---

10. Michaels is also continually critical of what he derides as "the literature of identity" ("Model", 107).

we like the idea of economic equality," Michaels writes, "and we like the idea of culture wars *much* better than we like the idea of class wars" (*Trouble*, 17; emphasis in original). This fixation on the cultural apotheosizes into a horizon wherein the "economic gap between rich and poor remains, but the economic gap between black and white is gone" (*Trouble*, 129). There has been an acceptance of a diluted version of a neoliberal multiculturalism, Michaels argues, fixated with "pictures of the US as a country composed of many different minorities rather than of a large majority falling further and further behind the one minority that matters most – the rich" ("Model," 1024). Although clearly polemical (not to mention intentionally trading in rhetorical caricature), Michaels's point is that a preoccupation with identity politics has rendered race ineffective in addressing material political change.

This type of critique is redolent and present in Beatty's debut novel, *The White Boy Shuffle*. The protagonist, Gunnar Kauffman, attends elementary school at "Mestizo Mullatto Mongrel Elementary, Santa Monica's all-white multicultural school," where "everything was multicultural, but nothing was multicultural" (28–29). The school satirizes the empty politics proffered via platitudes like, "'Eracism – The sun doesn't care what color you are'" (29). This is a parody of an incorporative, neoliberal multiculturalism that rescales politics to the level of the individual.[11] This individualization, however, is a problem for thinking politically. As Hominy tells Me in *The Sellout*, "'Well you have to stop seeing us as individuals, 'cause right now, massa, you ain't seeing the plantation for the n*****s'" (80). A hermetic individualism, Hominy argues, misses the forest for the trees. Another way of saying this is that this scale of the political misses, as Adolph Reed puts it, that the "race line *is* the class line" (288; emphasis in original):

> The problem is that the discourse of racism or racial disparity [. . .] does not help either to identify the precise mechanisms through which even many decidedly racialized inequalities are produced or to guide development of strategies for challenging them. Analytically, its taxonomic impulse abstracts away from the discrete characteristics of relations and phenomena to extract whichever of their features can be construed as generically racial. To that extent, it privileges category over content, labeling over description. (290)

---

11. Beatty is satirizing the bland corporatization of multiculturalism that David Theo Goldberg derides as "convenient public relations and advertising modalities for corporate interests" (17).

This "taxonomic impulse" is the project of a representational politics mired in the morass of "category over content." The loss of class solidarity to representational politics, according to this argument, is the victory of neoliberal abstraction over alternative formations of a political imaginary.

At one level, this is the critique that Beatty is offering. However, claiming that politics can be constituted only by the economic is to miss the transscalar ways in which Beatty thinks Blackness. Beatty's second novel, *Tuff*, dives into this debate from the other end of the spectrum. Instead of critiquing the way in which identity politics obfuscates class, Beatty critiques the ways in which economic analysis obfuscates and erases Blackness. The novel follows Winston "Tuff" Foshay, a Harlem neighborhood staple and occasional low-budget criminal, as he decides to run for city council, representing New York's 8th District of East Harlem. During the campaign, Winston's patron, Rabbi Spencer Throckmorton, writes an article titled "The Hip-Hop Populist" to galvanize Winston's quest for office (206). After the article comes out, Winston is courted by a number of fringe political parties over increasingly lavish dinners:

> The feasts followed more or less the same agenda. His hosts, often a white charter member and two or three colored officers, opened up with a statement that Party X was a multiracial organization. But if during the ensuing conversation Winton mentioned race, the dithyrambic chorus was quick to tell him that race was a dead-end issue. That if history has taught us anything, it's that using ethnic oppression as the basis for social and political upheaval is doomed to fail. No matter what you do, racism will still be, if not prevalent, at least present. Social and economic class must be the rallying points of the future struggle for democratic dignity. (211)

The claim that Winston continually hears at these lunches is that politics can include Blackness only at the cosmetic level. Racism, after all, will always remain "at least present." Any attempts for "political upheaval" and change must work through the economic as "rallying points." Politics, what Winston cites as "the struggle for the future for democratic dignity," is only possible as an interface of class. As Winston reflects on these political luncheons, he notes the ways in which reading the political as the economic ends up reproducing a "political rectitude [he] found condescending" (211). Eventually, this circumscription within the economic is what frustrates his semi-revisionist politics. Winston becomes fatigued with "the tautology of third-party politics" and "leftist liturgy" that forces his Blackness to play second fiddle to class consciousness (211). As Winston suggests, this desire to rescale the economic as the *sine qua non* of the political also falls into the double-bind that misses that neoliberalism is always racialized.[12] This type of class-versus-race hierarchization loses any nuance as it attempts to categorize subject positions in the homogenization of an imaginary polity.

This is where Beatty's work departs from the economic scales of Warren and Michaels. Beatty is sounding out a transscalar conception of the political that works beyond this type of economic overdetermination. In this sense, Beatty is again more aligned with the thinking of Wynter. For Wynter, an understanding that "successive modes of economic production" are the sole causal inputs of politics misses the way we actually exist within the world ("Unparalleled", 39).[13] Indeed, Beatty is satirizing an ideology that believes that once class solidarity is achieved, "everything else [will] follow" as politics is "subordinated to a teleological script that governs our global well-being/ill-being – a script therefore whose macro-origin story calcifies the *hero figure* of *homo oeconomicus*" ("Unparalleled", 41, 10; emphasis in original). Beatty wants to think outside and beyond this deterministic modality. It is not that politics cannot include economic critique. It is, rather, that politics is not a zero-sum game.

A *Tuff* Liberalism

If Michaels and company represent an attempt to use the economic to rescale race through class, we see a similar company line in arguments

---

12. On the other side of the coin, that is, we need to be cognizant of what Jodi Melamed describes simply as "the reality that neoliberalism remains a form of racial capitalism" (42).
13. In an earlier piece, Wynter describes how her genre of critique works as a supplement to "Marx's class struggles in the terms of a 'politics of being'" ("Unsettling", 319). This is her way of describing a sort of ontological addendum to Marxism. Tiffany Lethabo King has similarly taken up this position, examining how this type of Marxist critique is limited in its purchase over contemporary Black experience. "While labor is important, when it is used as the exclusive governing analytic in the scholarship on U.S. Slavery and U.S. Settler colonialism, it hides more than it reveals," she writes. "Specifically, labor as a governing frame obscures other processes, relations, locations, and symbolic economies that Black bodies and representations of Black embodiment produce and sustain within New World spatial expansion and geography's attendant project of human-making" (118). This, in many ways, resonates with the work of Cedric Robinson and his monumental

that prioritize the scale of the national. This is particularly clear in the work of political scientist and cultural talking head Mark Lilla, and his post-Trump diagnostic book that raced up the Amazon and *New York Times* bestseller lists, *The Once and Future Liberal*. Scrambling to understand why the left lost the 2016 presidential election, the proliferation of op-eds and *Medium* think pieces alike on how to regain America via the mythical white working class were a dime a dozen.[14] Citing a liberal "crisis of imagination and ambition," Lilla traces the history of what he calls the "great liberal abdication" that started with the presidency of Ronald Reagan and climaxed in the early 1990s with "a pseudo-politics of self-regard" (5, 8, 10). Identity politics have been effective only in catalyzing a loss of "what we share as citizens and what binds us as a nation" (114). Lilla advocates for the dissolution of "political agreement" within the public sphere while maintaining that the political must be soldered to a normative nationalist logic of citizenship and consensus (114). What we need to recreate, Lilla argues, is a syntax of nationhood via citizenship in order to resuscitate "a political language for speaking about a solidarity that transcends identity attachments" (123). Although Lilla pays passing attention to how citizenship may be "extendable and its meaning expandable," his prescriptive political grammar does not account for racialized people (122). Put differently, although Lilla is quick to set his sights on critiquing identity politics, he is less invested in the other half of this critique: interrogating the way in which liberalism-as-common sense has failed to redress the ongoing crisis of Blackness. As Richard Iton writes, "The remakings of the racial architecture that occurred post-1965 also suggest that the traditional frameworks for discussing and distinguishing black politics and discourses might need to be abandoned or, at the very least, troubled" (22). Lilla's dream of consensus in a deracinated national sphere is the determinant scale that "might need to be abandoned."[15]

Returning to *Tuff*, we see the novel take the nation and its metrics of citizenship as a structural problem. Winston's run for political office

---

Black Marxism, where he argues "The Black radical tradition cast doubt on the extent to which capitalism penetrated and re-formed social life and on its ability to create entirely new categories of human experience stripped bare of the historical consciousness embedded in culture" (170).
14. I take Lilla as the paragon of this mode as Lilla's book, with his Columbia pedigree and ascendant public intellectual status, received both mainstream and academic attention and accolades.
15. Elizabeth Povinelli is more forceful here, arguing that, in fact, we need to rupture these "core frameworks of liberal justice" (*Economies*, 26).

is steeped in a sense of incommensurability: "Just contemplating the absurdity of a n****r like him running for political office was making Winston's head hurt. He knew that there was no point in talking about the future" (122). Winston's necro-logic renders him outside of citizenship as he realizes there is "no point in talking about the future" because, simply, the future does not exist for him. The national scale of the political, Tuff suggests, is not capable of responding to the long caesura after the Civil Rights movements that produced "a n****r like him."[16] To combat this incongruity, Winston attempts to restructure the terms of American politics through his anti-partisan manifesto for his anti-partisan political party, A Party. His mentor, the jaded 1960s revolutionary Inez Nomura, thinks of how his party platform seems to subvert nationalist political paradigms: "A Party. Inez mulled the phrase over. A Party. She liked the way the name shifted between egalitarianism and hierarchy: A Party, one political party out of many; A Party, as opposed to B Party and C Party" (141). On the one hand, Winston is working in a revisionary mode. He is attempting, à la Lilla, to remake the tenets of citizenship in a way that can accommodate his own iteration of a liberal imaginary. He is trying to reconstitute how the conditions of intelligibility are distributed from the inside. On the other hand, Winston bypasses fantasies of consensus. Winston's politics are not tethered to Habermasian communicative rationality. "'I'd sit in the [council] meeting,'" he says from his jailhouse soapbox, "'take my shoes off, and put my funky feet on the table, and say, 'I don't know what you stupid motherfuckers is making laws about, but don't forget the poor smelly motherfuckers like me'" (181). Winston reworks the content of liberal justice by nullifying the content of the law by using his feet as a material reminder of Blackness. This is Beatty's two-pronged attack: he expands the umbrella of citizenship while also remaining doubtful that Blackness can be collected under that umbrella.[17]

16. Nikhil Singh also argues that the nation, echoing Hartman, is an exhausted mode of "common sense" (11). Thinking through the scale of the nation and the citizen, Singh argues, is to remain within normative forms of politics "at the expense of a full rendering of black political subjectivity" (43).
17. In this way, I also see Beatty as offering a critique of the resurgence of an interest in liberalism across the political spectrum. Amanda Anderson, for example, has recently formulated a "bleak liberalism." Like Lilla, Anderson is advocating for a capacious understanding of liberalism that is not monolithic but rather "involves a broad spectrum of values associated with complexity, difficulty, variousness, ambiguity, undecidability, hermeneutic open-endedness, and threshold experiences – experiences that prompt or tease one into an apprehension of

This generative possibility of opening up the category of citizenship becomes even more complicated as Winston's political campaign begins to feel stifled by the "tedium of democracy" (233). His revisionary aspirations diminish when he concludes that politics are still inflected with the maxim that "people like me can't run people like you" because "'that vote shit ain't for n*****s like me'" (212, 230; emphasis removed). As he prepares for the first and last debate of his campaign, Winston finds himself wrestling with this tired national formalism. Debating the incumbent German Jordan, Winston is adamant about an irreducibility of race:

> 'I wasn't listening too hard, but I heard him say something about we need to imagine ourselves beyond race. Look at me,' Winston said, raising his arms to crucifixion height. 'What you see is what you get, a big black motherfucker from a low-budget environment. If I'd been to outer space, written books, had dollars, drove a Mercedes-Benz, I'd imagine myself beyond race, too ... "Imagine yourself beyond race." Shit, imagine owning a brand-new Mercedes-Benz. If you goin' to fantasize, go all the way.' (236–237)

Two interrelated but separate things are made clear in this passage. The first is that Winston argues that the post in postracial is an aspirational designation that requires the maintenance of its antecedent term.[18] The second is that Winston's critique here is transscalar. It is impossible for Winston to think "beyond race" because "big black" and "low-budget environment" are indelibly linked. What are also brought into relief are the ways in which Beatty's transscalar imaginary refuses to think Blackness outside of the environmental. Moreover, it is not just

> the new, the unrealized, or the buried" (7). While certainly a laudable number of characteristics, I find her history limited in accounting for those marginalized subjects that are unable to perform "local response or individual agency" which, in turn, "form a complex whole and together constitute the very kind of liberalism this project aims to reconstruct" (50–51). This again strikes me as a reactive capitulation to the limited terms of contemporary politics attached to nationalisms in various hues.

18. This is akin to what Ramón Saldívar sees as the vexed "post" of the postcolonial. Saldívar argues that the postracial does not designate a "triumphant posteriority," but is "more like the *post* of postcolonialism, that is, a term that designates not a chronological but a conceptual frame, one that refers to the logic of something having been 'shaped as a consequence of' imperialism and racism" ("Historical", 575; emphasis in original). Or, as Gunnar says in a letter to his basketball coach in *The White Boy Shuffle*, "Guess I'll never be one of those black role models who 'transcends race,' will I?" (150).

a linking of the environmental and the racial; there is also the return of the economic. Winston's critique of postracial fantasy is transscalar in its shifting between the national, the economic, and the environmental, all in a few sentences. The scale of the national, time and time again, Winston argues, has proved unable to incorporate race. Beatty's liberal critique in *Tuff* amounts to what Fred Moten describes as "the refusal to fall for the ruses of incorporation and exclusion that say all we can and should desire is citizenship and subjectivity" (167). Beatty wants something more than that, something beyond the "all we can and should" of liberalism's recognition and consensus.[19]

Transscalar Politics

But, as I have made clear throughout *Transscalar Critique*, what constitutes a beyond means more than just finding a scale that substitutes one level of thinking for another. Beatty does not want the scale of the nation, for example, but he also does not want the economic.[20] Alongside the limit of these scales, however, Beatty remains cautious about how quickly we scale up or down to sidestep their limited political efficacy. There are equal problems in scales that sidestep the national or economic by way of the biological or the geological. Critiquing the biopolitical turn, stretching from Foucault to Agamben, Weheliye describes how biopolitical theory excludes "subjectivity in theoretical discourse" and "leads to the neglect of race as a critical category" (48). This is, Weheliye contends, what is at stake when political imaginaries find refuge in the biological, as "bare life and biopolitics discourse aspire to transcendent racialization via recourse to absolute biological matter" (4).

---

19. As an alternative, Stefano Harney and Moten imagine a transscalar mode of the political called "the undercommons": "[In] the hold, in the undercommons of a new feel, another kind of feeling became common. This form of feeling was not collective, not given to decision, not adhering or reattaching to settlement, nation, state, territory or historical story" (97–98). Moving through sedimented scales of political form ("settlement, nation, state, territory, or historical story"), Moten and Harney are thinking outside a logic "given to decision" to rethink a "common" that is not yoked to racialized common sense.
20. George Ciccariello-Maher makes this point forcefully: "The idea that class is 'real' whereas race is simply a backward idea, or that nations are 'imagined communities' and nothing more, is bound up with the idea of reason in history that is so central to the same conservative dialects we hope to bury" (18–19).

This "transcendent racialization" is also a risk for the biological and material scale of thinking congealing under the banner of "new materialisms." Min Hyoung Song makes this point forcefully: "What in short might be most troubling about a move toward the new materialism is the potential that it might lead us to ignore how our very social order is propped up, maybe even driven, by a dizzying intersection of inequalities" (58).[21] Indeed, this material turn runs the risk of not only leaving Blackness and race uninterrogated, but, at worst, reproducing some of the most pernicious modes of racist thinking.

Throughout *The Sellout*, Beatty's notion of "the Stank" satirizes the apparently generative horizon proffered by new materialism and biopolitics. The Stank first appears in the novel after Me draws a border around Dickens to demarcate the fictional ghetto's boundaries:

> Dickens, despite its newly painted barrier, has the Stank, an eye-burning, colorless miasma of sulfur and shit birthed in the Wilmington oil refineries and the Long Beach sewage treatment plants. Carried inland by the prevailing winds, the Stank gathers up a steamy pungency as the fumes combine with the stench of the lounge lizards returning home from partying in Newport Beach, drenched in sweat, tequila shooter runoff, and gallons of overapplied Drakkar Noir cologne. (113)

On the one hand, this scene captures the promised "vibrant matter" of new materialism in the Stank's emergence as a heterogeneous entity composed of human and nonhuman actants (Bennett, *Vibrant Matter*, 3). On the other, Beatty is suspicious of the political impact of this material entanglement as the Stank remains distinctly Black. The Stank hovers only over Dickens, compounding the literal color line that Me has drawn, imposing itself as "celestial flatulence" (187). Moreover, the Stank indexes the asymmetries of material relations. The Stank arises from industrial and human waste, acting as a cesspool of runoff for Los Angeles that collects in its Black ghettos.

---

21. Derek Woods makes an analogous point, highlighting how it is a particular scalar reinscription that new materialism tends towards: "Written as a substance rather than simply a provisional genre that includes diverse particles and forces, matter becomes the underlying identity from which specific entities differentiate. When this is the case, new materialism risks reiterating the same reductionism that it constantly works to avoid, privileging matter as the foundational scale or substance" ("Scale Variance," 200).

I highlight this passage as it points to how Beatty's work moves across scales, equally suspicious of the big and small at the same time. On the flip side of this coin, Beatty is anxious about scaling up through the geologic immensity of the Anthropocene. Beatty's work is, in many ways, an explicit rebuke to the type of scalar invariance that, as Françoise Vergès, among others, argues, performs a "de-historicizing" impulse to chart a "charismatic mega-category" of the Anthropocene that falls beyond the pale of lived difference (168–169). The vastness of thinking the Anthropocene, put simply, runs the risk of imagining the scale of the Political without doing any politics. To counter this depoliticization, Elizabeth Povinelli imagines how the Anthropocene can actually facilitate a mode of transscalar critique:

> Indeed, the shift of scale entailed in the study of Anthropogenic climate change is what allows biologists to link the smallest unit of life and death to planetary life and death (the planetary carbon cycle). And this shift in scale allows the thought of extinction to scale up from the logic of species (species extinction) to a planetary logic (planetary extinction). (*Geontologies*, 42–43)

Povinelli is offering us a glimpse of a scalar shifting where there are links between "the smallest [units] of life" and the planet as a whole. Conversely, Povinelli is also resolute in arguing that we must scale down. That is, we do not lose the "smallest unit of life" to the planetary, but rather think through these units co-constitutionally and relationally. Povinelli takes this further to make explicit how this involves integrating Blackness into discussions of the Anthropocene. The "disorganizing principle of a postclimate politics" entails a shift "from the demand 'listen to me' to the statement, 'I can't breathe'" (*Geontologies*, 42, 124). This shift outside the logos of the citizen who has the capacity to "demand" to an evocation of the ghost of Eric Garner suggests that we attend to both scales simultaneously. I want to be clear that my argument throughout this book is not that new materialist, biopolitical, or Anthropocenic thinking and theory is necessarily racist and/or vacuum-sealed from politics. What I am arguing is that there is a certain risk in overly valorizing the biological and the geologic without attending to other contemporaneous scales. This is where the transscalar offers a more inclusive analytic range. The transscalar is concerned with all these scales all the time, the biological and the planetary, just as much as it is concerned with, as the extended meditations in *Tuff* make clear, the economic and the national. Beatty is not choosing between these scales but is comfortable moving between and through them.

Beatty's querying of the relationship between Blackness and the environmental is most pronounced in *The Sellout*. Similar to the petro-imaginary of Jesmyn Ward, the extractive imaginary of the Anthropocene is mapped onto Black bodies at the end of the novel when Me unearths Hominy's film archive, including a "low-budget one-reeler called 'Oil Ty-coons!'," featuring Hominy and Buckwheat, but also a "heretofore unknown member of the Little Rascals, a moppet credited as Li'l Foy Cheshire, alias Black Folk" (281). Bringing back the text's straw man, Foy, Me describes a film where the three Little Rascals galivant through the streets of Greenville, SC, betting at the horse races and eventually spending money to construct movie sets around the town. Finally, Foy and Hominy demand that Buckwheat tells them where the money that is funding this shopping spree is coming from. Buckwheat turns to them and says: "'We'z in oil!'" (281). This, however, still does not quite appease his colleagues:

> Still harboring doubts and unable to find an oil derrick, the gang follows Hominy to a hidden warehouse, where they discover the nefarious darkies have all the kids in N****rtown hooked up to IVs and, for a nickel a pint, filling oil cans with crude drop by black drop. (281)

In this scene, Beatty links explicitly climatic and anti-Black violence. The twinned exploitation of the environment and Black people is brought forcefully into the foreground. Like the Stank, this scene links the micro-scale of Black blood and bodies to the macro-scale of oil to argue that the environment and racialized bodies have been used as resources upon which Western liberalism and neoliberalism have propped themselves up. At the same time, there is an inoperative analogy at play. Black blood would not actually be able to power Greenville. At one level, the movie appears to offer a veneer of oppressive equivalency wherein Blackness and the environment are fungible, both reservoirs of energy powering societal mechanisms. But something more complex is at play as well. Beatty is actually pointing to the incommensurability between the environment and Blackness, making us aware of how it is misguided to try to collapse one into the other.[22]

---

22. For Me, this symbiotic relationship between the environmental and Blackness is a constant in the text. Me is a farmer and his agricultural knowledge is the driving force of his retrograde racial politics: "I'm a farmer, and farmers are natural segregationist. We separate the wheat from the chaff. I'm not Rudolf Hess, P.W. Botha, Capital Records, or present-day U.S. of A. Those motherfuckers segregate because they want to hold on to power. I'm a farmer: we segregate in an effort to give every tree, every plant, every poor Mexican, every poor N****r, a chance for equal access to sunlight and water; we make sure every organism has room to breathe" (214).

Blood and oil, although linked in certain ways, still remain separate entities, operating, we might say, at different scales.

While they are most prominent in *The Sellout*, throughout his work Beatty invests in identifying these types of moment where the racial and ecological act as co-constitutional inflection points without collapsing into one another. At the start of *Slumberland*, for example, the protagonist, the expat DJ, Ferguson W. Sowell, awaits his weekly respite from Berlin's gray skies at the Electric Beach Tanning Salon, where he queries the logic of speciation:

> You would think [Germans would] be used to me by now. I mean, don't they know that after fourteen hundred years the charade of blackness is over? That we blacks, the once eternally hip, the people who were as right as Greenwich Mean Time, are, as of today, as yesterday as stone tools, the velocipede, and the paper straw all rolled into one? The Negro is now officially human [. . .] It doesn't matter whether anyone truly believes it; we are as mediocre as the rest of the species. (3)

The novel starts with an announcement that race is no longer a metric: Black people have finally achieved status as "officially human." As opposed to an *a priori* ontological condition, Beatty uses Ferguson to argue that speciation is an achievement of varying granularity. It is posterior to Blackness, only possible once "the charade of blackness is over." Beatty is denaturalizing the question of species and turning it inside out by arguing that there is a rivenness between Blackness and being. The ontological intelligibility of both these positions, he contends, is slippery, never fixed but relational.[23] Later on, this idea of Blackness being "passé" returns in a conversation between Ferguson and the reclusive jazz musician he moves to Berlin to hunt down, Charles "the Schwa" Stone. Ferguson turns to the Schwa and asks him what he was thinking about when he soloed over Ferguson's hip-hop beat. The Schwa responds, "'I was thinking about the phrase on the banner, 'Black Passé.' How being passé is freedom. You can do what you want. No demands. No expectations. The only person I have to please is myself'" (230). Being passé is the privilege of those who can circulate and signify as human. It is a type of "freedom,"

---

23. As Cristin Ellis would phrase it, Beatty is interrogating how the human "is an ideology masquerading as a species" (144).

a latitude to inhabit an unmarked and undifferentiated category of species. But this position is forever impossible as Ferguson tells the Schwa, "'You'll never be passé'" (230). Ferguson reminds us that being a member of a species is like being a citizen. It requires, as Wynter would argue, a recalibrated humanism that cannot account for all bodies.

We see a similar back-and-forth in Beatty as early as *The White Boy Shuffle*. In the prologue to the novel, Gunnar finds himself filling "the perennial void in African–American leadership" as a begrudging "Negro Demagogue:"

> In the quest for equality, black folks have tried everything. We've begged, revolted, entertained, intermarried, and are still treated like shit. Nothing works, so why suffer the slow deaths of toxic addiction and the American work ethic when the immediate gratification of suicide awaits? [. . .] Every day they wishfully look heavenward, peering into the California smog for a metallic gray atomic dot that will gradually expand until it explodes some one thousand feet over our natural and processed heads. It will be the Emancipation Disintegration. Lunch counters, bus seats, and executive washrooms be damned; our mass suicide will be the ultimate sit-in. (2)

For Gunnar, liberalism's politics of intelligibility have atrophied against the *longue durée* of "slow deaths."[24] Beatty's critique of *de facto* racism is imagined through the environment, where "bus seats," "toxic addiction," and the "California smog" all exist simultaneously. That is, Gunnar describes "toxic addiction" and the nuclear logics of the "California smog" as part and parcel of his Black being. In fact, the image "natural and processed heads" puns on the way in which Black bodies are both naturalized and denaturalized, even at this micro-site of hair. Like the petro-imaginary in *The Sellout*, the modality of climate in *The White Boy Shuffle* is one of toxic waste that is distributed unevenly on racialized people. At the same time, it isn't that one of these sites offers the definitive hermeneutic key to reading the racism of the present. Rather, Beatty's work moves between the climatic and

---

24. Suicide, in effect, would make visible the type of violence and death indicative of the racialized violence of environmental segregation: a violence that Rob Nixon argues "occurs gradually and out of sight, a violence of delayed destruction that is dispersed across time and space, an attritional violence that is typically not viewed as violence at all" (2).

Blackness without prioritizing either or collapsing the two, looking at the ways in which they are entangled with one another.[25]

Part of the issue here is that, like thinking the Anthropocene, thinking Blackness always already requires thinking a scalar relation that is too large for human comprehension. Returning to Christina Sharpe's "wake work," we can see why she evokes this inhuman scale as she looks to the environmental as a way to capture the scalar distortion of racism. Describing the ways in which racism becomes "pervasive *as* climate," Sharpe theorizes what it means to be Black by thinking through the lexicon of ecological crisis "when the only certainty is the weather that produces a pervasive climate of antiblackness" (106; emphasis in original).[26] In effect, Sharpe's description of the ongoing crisis of Blackness works symbiotically with environmental crisis: "It is not the specifics of any one event, any one set of events [. . .] but the totality of the environments in which we struggle; the machines in which we live; what I am calling the weather" (111). Although, as I argued in Chapter 3, Sharpe is not considering the Anthropocene as such in her writing, she is pointing to a scale that operates as "the totality of the [environment]," irreducible to the punctuation of singular events. This is a scale that Sharpe identifies as "living the history and present of terror" which "grounds [. . .] our everyday Black existence; living the historically and geographically dis/continuous but always present and endlessly reinvigorated brutality" (15). As Sharpe makes clear in her reading of the ongoing wake of slavery, the quotidian crisis of Blackness in the contemporary requires scales in excess of the present.

This problem of thinking through multiple scales simultaneously is taken up again in *Slumberland* as the text interrogates the ongoing temporality of slavery. One of Ferguson's favorite pastimes is submitting words to *The Kensington-Merriweather Dictionary of Standard American English* in order "to improve linguistic repression from afar" (14). As he thinks about his latest submissions, he finds himself pondering the restrictive temporality of English:

---

25. This type of immanence is mirrored by Ferguson in *Slumberland* when he listens to the Schwa's wall of sound for the first time: "Barely able to keep my head above water, I gave myself up to the current. Surrendered to the sound, waiting, praying, for the next eddy of cacophony to pick me up, smash my head against the rocks, and put an end to my misery" (222).
26. Sharpe is also inverting the type of climatic racism that has overdetermined Black people since chattel slavery.

Most languages have a word for the day before yesterday. *Anteayer* in Spanish. *Vorgestern* in German. There is no word for it in English. It's a language that tries to keep the past simple and perfect, free of the subjunctive blurring of memory and mood. (13)

Although Ferguson is not explicitly dredging up the history of slavery, the language echoes how Ferguson's temporal experience is one that is defined by the violent reverberations of a past that is not quite past. The "simple and perfect" is a privilege for those that can live outside "the subjunctive." Ferguson, however, is trying to think outside this inherited mode, looking for a way to move between "memory and mood."

We also see this at the midpoint of *The Sellout*. As Me prepares to celebrate Hominy's birthday, he realizes that, through the regressive, racist logic of Hominy, the best present that he can give him is a segregated bus. To help facilitate this present, Me asks his on-again, off-again bus-driver girlfriend, Marpessa, if he can put up a plaque that reads "For Whites Only" on one of her buses as Hominy's present. After the expected back-and-forth, Marpessa agrees and, as Me and Hominy sit on the bus waiting for a white passenger to enter so that Hominy can give up his seat with bravado, Me thinks:

> That's the problem with history, we like to think it's a book – that we can turn the page and move the fuck on. But history isn't the paper it's printed on. It's memory, and memory is time, emotions, and song. History is the things that stay with you. (115)

What we see in this scene are multiple scales competing with one another. Me is thinking through four different scales of history simultaneously: he is querying "memory," "time," "emotions," and "song." History, in this iteration, is transscalar. It is, as Me says, "the things that stay with you." In effect, history is all of these things all the time, a tangled and messy temporality that cannot be solely mediated through "the paper it's printed on." We cannot just "turn the page," but have to contend with its continual cohabitation across scales.

In this passage, Beatty sounds out a new way to think through the historical entanglements that constitute contemporary Blackness at the same time that his transscalar critique offers a way of drawing together past and present without prioritizing or valorizing either. To think through the contradictions of the historical is not so much to disavow history as to reckon with how history is inflected with the modal possibilities of the subjunctive, the possibilities of the otherwise worlds outlined by Ward and Sharpe. Stephen Best approaches the question of the legacy of anti-Black violence from a similar vantage to Beatty, disrupting an overdetermined "melancholy historicism" that has been the mode of Black Studies and, by extension, Black identity in the post-Civil Rights era. Best offers a successor to Warren's African American literature, sounding out a new "'style' of freedom: freedom from constraining conceptions of blackness as authenticity, tradition, and legitimacy" (23). Beatty is also looking for a way to think outside this melancholic mode, using satire to allow for both authenticity and inauthenticity, tradition and perversion of that tradition, at the same time. While Best believes that to identify a new style of Blackness requires a severing of "the omnipresence of history in our politics" (3), Beatty works in a mode both revisionary and radical. He tries to think through contemporary Blackness as inflected with the historical while also still imagining an otherwise to a teleological historical narrative. In terms of the two competing modes of Black aesthetic form I have traced thus far, Beatty squares the circle between Warren and Best. For Beatty, that is, the transscalar embraces not only the large and the small but also the past and the present. At every moment, we are pressed to remain aware of "the Chinese, the Japanese, the Mexicans, the poor, the forests, the water, the air, the fucking Californian condor" as we also reckon with, as Me says, "the things that stay with you."

The ultimate effect of this entanglement is a confrontation with a historical and aesthetic excess that is impossible to confront through the types of monoscalar imaginary that saturated the first half of this book. Beatty inculcates us with an immensity of scale in the first pages of *The Sellout* as Me awaits the Supreme Court Justices:

> It's a trip being the latest in the long line of landmark race-related cases. I suppose the constitutional scholars and cultural paleontologists will argue over my place on the historical timeline. Carbon-date my pipe and determine whether I'm a direct descendent of Dred-Scott [. . .] They'll scour the plantation, the projects, and the Tudor subdivision affirmative-action palaces, digging up backyards looking for remnants of ghosts of discrimination in the fossilized dice and domino bones, brush the dust off the petrified rights and writs buried in legal volumes. (8)

This passage makes clear that it is not just a matter of appending the environmental to the racial. Me moves through scales of carbon-dating and paleontology just as easily as he reimagines "dice and domino bones." The "plantations" and the "projects" are alliteratively linked as they offer a transtemporal reading of contemporary Blackness. Reversing the triumphant narrative of the Civil Rights Movement, *Me* is holding a funhouse mirror up to Black literary and political form. This idea that "segregation would be the key to bringing Dickens back" is a perversion of Warren's argument, unveiling the tenuousness of his claims (167). Simultaneously, this is an inversion of Warren's longing for the coherence of African American literary and political identity. Beatty's satire is a critical rereading of post-Dred Scott America that highlights how anything as solid as the nominal African American that Warren stakes out remains enshrined in arguments that run the risk of being reduced to biological determinism.

Laughing B(l)ack

Returning to Warren also helps illuminate how Beatty is invested in thinking about the literary status and form of his work. Midway through *The Sellout*, Me name-drops Beatty's most obvious satirical predecessor, Ishmael Reed, thinking, "Thanks to years of my father's vernacular pop quizzes and an Ishmael Reed book he kept on top of the toilet for years, I knew that 'reckless eyeballing' was the act of black male deigning to look at a southern white female" (175–176). Crucially, Reed is linked here to "reckless eyeballing." Just as "reckless eye-balling" described the plight of Black people in the Jim Crow South, so too does Reed's version of satire describe an earlier version of literary form that was suited for the political agenda of Warren's African American literary project. This signals Beatty's critique of a historical mode of satire that is not quite up to the task of thinking through the present.[27] Darryl Dickson-Carr, in

---

27. This self-conscious sense of where he falls within the canon is pervasive throughout Beatty's work. As Ferguson rereads the Black literary tradition in *Slumberland* while speaking to a pseudo-academic "slash asshole" in a Berlin bar, "Like everything else he read, it invariably bore a series of blurbs comparing the author's biting satire to Ralph Ellison and Richard Wright, a comparison that I never understood because Richard Wright isn't funny [. . .] I loved reading these books. The black tweed-jacketed eruditeness mixed with street-corner irreverence, the honesty about racial turpitude coupled with the dishonesty about its manifestations" (103). Funny enough, Beatty makes sure his protagonists are decidedly unfunny. Me is described as having "absolutely no sense of humor" (243). Winston's best friend, Fariq, describes him as having only "two emotions: serious and serious as fuck, straight up'" (125). Although Gunnar plays the part of the "funny, cool black guy" in Santa Monica, this is just a momentary guise that is lost when he moves to Hillside (27).

his genealogy of African American satire, identifies the change from writers like Reed to Beatty as generated from a collapsed "distance between the sacred and the profane" that maps onto the *de jure* racism of the present (163). Moreover, Dickson-Carr suggests that it is the inclusion of "previously denigrated considerations of gender, sexuality, and class" that sets apart the work of contemporary satirists (167).[28] It is, for Dickson-Carr, an interrogation into the granularities of Black identities that changes in contemporary satire. While I agree with the general contours of Dickson-Carr's argument and the way it opens up an intersectional scaling, this does not account for the entirety of Beatty's transscalar approach.

Writing about another contemporary satirist, Mat Jonson's, novel, *Pym*, Kate Marshall argues that in *Pym* we see a "a virulent and obligingly satirizable racism, an affection for the narrative pull of an ancient, alien past, and a fascination with the indifferent neutrality of the nonhuman" ("Old," 632).[29] Marshall's description of Jonson makes clear that it is not just the intersectional trifecta that is at stake for contemporary Black satire, but a larger constellation of literary form, history, and ontology. Just as Chapter 3 surveyed how contemporary Black Studies is attempting to rethink the genre of the human through a sustained engagement with ecology, Beatty is rethinking literary genre by melding together a critique of literary form with contemporary ecological and racial politics.[30] Beatty is involved in the speculative project of imagining a transscalar world that moves as comfortably between questions of geology as it does

---

28. Reed, above and beyond the misogyny attributed to him, has also been criticized for the ways in which his work sometimes "[reproduces] core capitalist institutions" while "incorporating multiculturalism" (Donofrio 101, 112). Beatty continues to remain suspicious of multiculturalism as much as a dogmatic Marxism.
29. We could add Colson Whitehead's *Zone One* or *The Underground Railroad*, Esi Edugyan's *Washington Black*, or Jason Mott's *Hell of a Book* to this list of contemporary satires interrogating Blackness, literary form, and the nonhuman.
30. This is precisely what Reed misses in his review of *Tuff*, where he suggests that "this book will be hailed not for its artistic form, but for its issues" (n.p.). While it is certainly a book about issues, it is also a compelling and aesthetically interesting book. Part of the issue may be that Reed remains too attached to the liberal aspirations of the Black novel in the model of Warren. This is what Michael Collins diagnoses in Reed as portrayals and defenses of "the delicate fulcrum of American democracy: the consent of the governed" (422). This is another place where Reed remains circumscribed within a monoscalar imaginary.

intersectionality.[31] What I will spend the rest of this chapter arguing is that Beatty's use of satire captures this transscalar mode of critique. The satire of Beatty's work creates a perpetual turning, moving between layers and scales of critique. This is again to underline the way that satire itself is both literary and critical, not just representing the world, but actively invested in its remaking.

Murphet builds upon this conception of satire's transscalar capacity, arguing that it is the ideal genre for thinking the Anthropocene's scalar reverberations. Conspicuously absent from contemporary Anthropocene criticism, Murphet claims that satire "is the time-honored genre" for thinking outside "the ideological current of humanism and the inhumanity of the industrializing marketplace" (659).[32] Murphet sees satire formalizing a genre for and of an Anthropocene defined by its divergent and contradictory layers. Although satire, following those like Northrop Frye, is often read as a conservative genre serving as a social corrective, Murphet limns an alternative lineage. This thread weaves through Matz's claim that satire loses its generic identity "when the task of representing the human in its natural habitat could no longer be distinguished from the act of scorning the entire category of human, and that entire habitat known as the world" (157). Although Matz is critiquing this near-nihilistic undercurrent in contemporary satire, this description is precisely what I see as productive in Beatty. It is the "entire category of human" and the "entire habitat known as the world" that need to be reevaluated and lampooned in the Anthropocene. Marshall, Matz, and Murphet, then, are making cases (albeit with markedly different levels of enthusiasm and amplitude) for the efficacy of satire for mediating the transscalar. It is, like Ward's work that frays realism, a literary form trying to think outside inherited categories.

The complete reevaluation of the world in Beatty's satire is amplified at moments when his texts seem to critique just about everyone and everything. We can glimpse this in *The White Boy Shuffle* when

---

31. Howard Rambsy describes this as Beatty "[defying] reality" by using "speculative narrative" to "[envision] the unforeseen" (652–653).
32. Although not explicitly referencing satire, Mark McGurl sees humor more generally as a genre of Anthropocene thinking "that names those literary forms willing to risk artistic ludicrousness in their representation of the inhumanly large and long" ("Posthuman," 539). The intersection of humor and environmentalism has been taken more seriously in recent years, highlighted by Nicole Seymour's recent *Bad Environmentalism: Irony and Irreverence in the Ecological Age*.

Gunnar's friend, Psycho Loco, accidentally kills his fellow gang member, Pumpkin, in a botched liquor store robbery. Feeling remorseful and vengeful, Gunnar and his pals drive around the posh Cheviot Heights neighborhood vandalizing property and shooting guns. When Gunnar returns home, his mom asks where he's been:

> 'Shooting the neighborhood. Ma, I'm becoming so black it's a shame.' I wanted to explain to her that living out there was like being in a never-ending log-rolling contest. You never asked why the log was rolling or who was rolling the log. You just spread your arms and kept your feet moving, doing your best not to fall off [. . .] I wanted to chew my runny eggs and talk with my mouth full. Tell her how much I missed the calm equipoise of my old life but how I had grown accustomed to running in place, knowing nothing mattered as long as I kept moving. I wanted to say these things to her, but my breath smelled like wet dog shit with a hint of sulfur. (102)

In this scene, Blackness emerges as an agentless agency, static and yoked to the formal inheritance of "becoming so black it's a shame." Gunnar inhabits the perpetual crisis of never being able to "ask why the log is rolling" while making sure you are "doing your best not to fall off." The pathos of this scene, however, is offset by its humor, undercut first by the "runny eggs" and then by the "dog shit with a hint of sulfur." The humor removes the grounding of the transcendent and transhistorical thinking that Gunnar parodies. This satire, anticipating the imagery of waste so prevalent in *The Sellout*, acts as a conduit for performing an ungrounding through form.[33]

The tension produced between political critique and humor is particularly pronounced and productive when Beatty critiques contemporary Black politics. As Me gets ready to resegregate the Dickens School District, the novel pauses:

> But if you asked me, Chaff Middle School had already been segregated and re-segregated many times over, maybe not by color, but certainly by reading level and behavior problems [. . .] Made me realize that for many people integration is a finite concept [. . .] The problem is we don't know whether integration is a natural or unnatural state. Is integration, forced or otherwise, social entropy or social order? No one's ever defined the concept. (167–168)

---

33. By reading Beatty's satire as performing an "ungrounding," my argument dovetails with Saldívar's recent work on race and the Anthropocene's bisection in contemporary fiction. Saldívar describes a "permanent parabasis" wherein "the turn from illusion to reality and back again is not stifled but revolves perpetually" ("Historical," 17).

Beatty interrupts the flow of narrative to pose a version of a crucial question about contemporary Black politics. How can inherited markers (here, integration) of Civil Rights activism be used now? How can a politics of visibility combat a racism that has become invisible? Should questions of equity, Beatty asks, still oscillate between segregation and integration? For Beatty, the terms of the debate are limited as a "finite concept." By instead running through biological and evolutionary metaphors, Me grasps at the limits of what the political is and how it can be reconstituted outside the dialectic of integration/segregation. Yet at the very moment this reading appears to offer a hermeneutic key to the text, it is destabilized: "So that summer I didn't worry about fecal matter and microbes. I agonized over my satsumas and segregation. How do you grow the world's most water-sensitive citrus under monsoon conditions? How do you racially segregate an already segregated school?" (169).[34] Beatty reverts to the fecal in this scene. His scatology moves between political allegory and parody, forcing us to wonder if we can tell the difference between the two (or if it even matters). The slippage between satsumas and segregation means that Me even begins to think of his satsumas in racialized terms: "I never n****r-whispered to my plants. I don't believe that plants are sentient beings, but after Hominy went home I talked to [the satsumas] for an hour. Read them poetry and sang them the blues" (173). Satsumas and segregation are linked syntactically and phonetically in this passage, creating an ecological mode of thinking about Blackness that has to jump between monsoons and the Los Angeles Unified School District in an instant. In effect, Beatty's satire forces a thinking outside of terminal, decisional logic by prioritizing entanglement over discreteness.[35]

---

34. This passage, with "satsumas and segregation," is one of many places where Beatty uses agrarian metaphors to animate racism in *The Sellout*. We see this earlier when Me tries to come up with a way to start actually segregating Dickens: "I know why I couldn't get the potatoes to grow, because the climate's too warm. But when it came to ideas for separating the races by race, all of a sudden I had a racism block" (210).
35. Beatty is complicating the type of argument that thinkers like Lisa Guerrera, another theorist of contemporary Black satire, have made: "Black satire in the post-racial age gives voice and legitimacy to black rage – not the black rage that post-racial has imagined to justify racial violence and injustice against black people, but the black rage that gives form to the black subject in a time and place that have rendered all aspects of black life to be invisible, unimaginable, or wholly impossible" (276). That Beatty pushes back on this is demonstrated by the fact that it is not just a matter of working between the dyad of visibility/invisibility; rather, it is thinking outside the circumscription of this logic.

Unmitigated Blackness

Beatty's satire is always turning in on itself, undercutting any singular or monoscalar position of critique. Stability and discreteness in Beatty are offset by a continual logic of the satiric riff. This is what Madhu Dubey calls the "slippery limits" of Beatty's work (372). Beatty does not choose between layers but allows the satire to destabilize any type of grounding from which we might try to offer a conclusive reading. For Beatty, there is just the continual addition of more and more scales. We see Ferguson provide a surrogate description of this literary mode with his "phonographic memory": "I remember everything I've ever heard. Every dropped nickel, raindrop drip-drop, sneaker squeak, and sheep bleat [. . .] I remember every sound I've ever heard. It's like my entire life is a song that I can't get out of my head" (14–15). Ferguson is creating a new mode of memory through "the confluence of melody and groove" that "transcends mood and time" (29). This is a way to inhabit a transscalar turning, a continual accretion of "every sound I've ever heard."[36] We see this most explicitly articulated in descriptions of the Schwa's music. After discussing Wynton Marsalis with the music critic and his friend Lars, Ferguson critiques the inherited modes of both critical and aesthetic form: "And I don't know whether or not Marsalis's music is an allegory, for race, American democracy, or black fascism, but I do know the Schwa's music is anarchy. It's Somalia. It's the Department of Motor Vehicles. It's Albert Einstein's hair" (97). Beatty's listing performs an extemporaneous revision as he tries to locate something more than what is being described. Having run through a list of potential metaphors to capture the complexity of Marsalis's music, Ferguson routes anarchy into Somalia into the DMV into Albert Einstein. There is no ground here, just the continual dissolve of satire, each term laughing back at the one that preceded it. To try to trace a single line through these three images is impossible. Or, rather, to try to allegorize Blackness, Beatty suggests, is impossible; the three terms deflect any extractive hermeneutic, making us question which way the joke is cutting. This is what is at the heart of *Transscalar Critique*: there isn't one single critical vantage

---

36. This is an update of a concept Gunnar's friend Nicholas Scoby explains to him in *The White Boy Shuffle*: "Because a musician has they own sense of time and experience of time [. . .] That's why your poems can never be no more than descriptions of life. The page is finite. Once you put the words down on paper, you've fossilized your thoughts. Bugs in amber, n****r. But music is life itself. Music is time [. . .] Backward, looped, whatever" (204). Equally interesting is the Anthropocenic time-slice Scoby identifies with music via "bugs in amber."

that transcends the others, but it is this tension and movement between the disjuncture of scales that produce the space where transscalar critique itself is made possible.

This lack of grounding is further theorized when Ferguson is at the annual Bundestreffen music festival in the German countryside ("the annual Afro-German get-together" (177)). Finding himself on stage, Ferguson tries to tell a group of enthusiastic dancers about the Schwa. Ferguson describes his music as feeling like "Wile E. Coyote walking on air for those precious few moments before the bittersweet realization he's walking on air" (180). To be suspended in the air in "sensate harmony" is to be outside the logic of gravity (180). As Christian Schmidt writes, *Slumberland* "[refuses] to cling to material boundaries" and, therefore, "calls for a change of epistemologies. It moves away from a predominately visual model that focuses on bodies, borders, and blackness and invokes an aural regime that highlights the fluidity of demarcations" (157). Schmidt's point is that the "aural truth" of the text makes it resistant to taxonomic fixity as it locates an alternative epistemology (157). This is what Ferguson calls the synesthetic possibility of "the touch of sound" (157). It is to realize, as Lars says to Ferguson, "'You've turned this motherfucker out. Permanently fucked shit up. Shit is no longer okay, but that's a good thing'" (231).

If Beatty uses *Slumberland*'s musical mediations as a proxy for his transscalar critique, he returns to this idea of being "permanently fucked" in *The Sellout*. At the end of *The Sellout*, Me shares a blunt with the white courthouse sketch artist Fred Manne. In between tokes, Fred turns to Me and says, "'I know it's been a trying day. I know that in this culture 'race' is especially hard to talk about, in that we feel the need to defer'" (273). In his misquoting of Langston Hughes, Me thinks about this idea that widely circulates about race as a conversational faux pas. Unwilling to cede the debate, Me tries to think through this holding pattern:

> I'm high as hell, but not high enough not to know that race is hard to 'talk about' because it's hard to talk about. The prevalence of child abuse in this country is hard to talk about, too, but you never hear people complaining about it [. . .] I actually think the country does a decent job of addressing race, and when folks say, 'Why can't we talk about race more honestly?' What they really mean is 'Why can't you n*****s be reasonable?' or 'Fuck you, white boy.' (273)

Me pinpoints the limits of signifying in inherited syntaxes. For Me, working through these types of logic means that race is always simultaneously foreclosed upon and circuited through what he identifies as "'mitigating circumstances'" (273). Me is diagnosing the way in which the crisis of Blackness is politically neutered, clothed in perennial euphemism (preempting Donald Trump's "both sides" comments in Charlottesville that will come a few short years later). This is what Warren describes in the contemporary Black novel as "personal victories" and "petit bourgeois aspirations" rather than the larger structural critiques of a previous generation (131). We hear this from Fred. He does not want to talk about collective politics; he thinks that the entire situation can be written off by the fact that Me has had a "trying day." But Beatty departs from both Fred and Warren by actually thinking about the difficulty of Blackness that resists mitigation or conflation with "bourgeois aspirations" in a contemporary novel. Beatty uses Me to put his finger on the pulse of a different type of critique, a new form of Blackness, a transscalar Blackness.

This alternative political mode is articulated in the final pages of *The Sellout* as "Unmitigated Blackness."

> I'm not sure what Unmitigated Blackness is, [Me thinks,] but whatever it is, it doesn't sell. On the surface, Unmitigated Blackness is a seeming unwillingness to succeed [. . .] Unmitigated Blackness is simply not giving a fuck [. . .] It's the realization that there are no absolutes, except where there are. It's the acceptance of contradiction not being a sin and a crime but a human frailty like split ends and libertarianism. (277)

Unmitigated Blackness names the possibility of inhabiting multiple, contradictory scales simultaneously: "there are no absolutes, except where there are." This is counter to Warren's belief that "the idea that sustains the possibility of an African American literature is a belief that the welfare of the race depends on the success of a black writer and those who are depicted in their texts" (139). Me forecloses on this success, pushing back against an overly commercialized version of Blackness turning in the permanent gyres of a transscalar critique that doesn't "[give] a fuck". This is a way out of commonsense: a way, as Sharpe writes, "toward seeing and reading otherwise; toward reading and seeing something in excess of what is caught in the frame" (116). This is the transscalar horizon of critique: a thinking outside the cuts that demarcate inherited forms.

Whereas Warren bemoans the atrophied politics of contemporary Black writing, Beatty rejects this mode of taxonomizing fixity and fangless critique, creating a new type of contemporary Black literature. Beatty is thinking outside of "absolutes," thinking through "contradiction" beyond inherited identity categories. Set in the Supreme Court, moreover, Beatty makes it clear that this mode of Unmitigated Blackness is the naming of a form that is beyond the pale of the liberal imaginary, an iteration of the "otherwise" that requires a larger recalibration of politics and ontology. In his varying definitions of what actually constitutes Unmitigated Blackness, Me models the way in which any type of consensus is impossible. It is not one thing, but rather a provisional "whatever it is."[37] This is where Unmitigated Blackness becomes a transscalar critique of the contemporary crisis of race. Beatty imagines "blackness in the present" as the continual eddies and flows of definitions that push up against one another and contradict one another. Unmitigated Blackness, in short, is an appropriate place to finish *Transscalar Critique*. It is a final iteration of a horizon of transscalar critique, one that remains always in flux beyond the reach of absolutes.

---

37. I find an analogue to Beatty's thinking in Michelle Wright's work. Wright, arguing specifically against critics like Walter Benn Michaels (whom she name-checks), claims "[Locating] Blackness as a determinable 'thing,' a 'what' or a 'who,' gives us a conceptualization that exhibits the unnerving qualities of a mirage: from a distance, it appears clearly cogent, but up close, Blackness evanesces" (2).

Works Cited

Alaimo, Stacy. *Exposed: Environmental Politics and Pleasure in Posthuman Times*. University of Minnesota Press, 2016.
Alexander, M. Jacqui. *Pedagogies of Crossing: Meditations on Feminism, Sexual Politics, Memory, and the Sacred*. Duke University Press, 2006.
Anderson, Amanda. *Bleak Liberalism*. University of Chicago Press, 2016.
Appadurai, Arjun. *Banking on Words: The Failure of Language in the Age of Derivative Finance*. University of Chicago Press, 2016.
Appel, Hannah, Nikhil Anand, and Akhil Gupta, "Introduction: Temporality, Politics, and the Promise of Infrastructure." *The Promise of Infrastructure*. Eds. Nikhil Anand, Akhil Gupta, and Hannah Appel. Duke University Press (2018), 1–41.
Armstrong, Nancy and John Marx. "Introduction: How Do Novels Think about Neoliberalism?" *Novel* 51.2 (2018): 157–165.
Banita, Georgiana. "Literature After 9/11." *American Literature in Transition*. Ed. Rachel Greenwald Smith. Cambridge University Press, 152–164.
Barad, Karen. *Meeting the Universe Halfway: Quantum Physics and the Entanglement of Matter and Meaning*. Duke University Press, 2007.
Baucom, Ian. *History 4° Celsius: Search for a Method in the Age of the Anthropocene*. Duke University Press, 2020.
Baucom, Ian and Matthew Omelsky. "Knowledge in the Age of Climate Change." *South Atlantic Quarterly* 116.1 (2017): 1–18.
Beal, Sophia, Michael Rubenstein, and Bruce Robbins, "Infrastructuralism: An Introduction." *Modern Fiction Studies* 61.4 (2015): 575–586.
Beatty, Paul. *Hokum: An Anthology of African-American Humor*. Bloomsbury, 2006.
——. *The Sellout*. Farrar, Straus and Giroux, 2015.
——. *Slumberland*, Bloomsbury, 2008.
——. *Tuff*. Anchor, 2000.
——. *The White Boy Shuffle*. Picador, 1996.
Bennett, Jane. *Vibrant Matter: A Political Ecology of Things*. Duke University Press, 2009.

Bennett, Joshua. *On Being Property Once Myself.* Harvard University Press, 2020.
Berlant, Lauren. *Cruel Optimism.* Duke University Press, 2013.
Best, Stephen. *None Like Us: Blackness, Belonging, Aesthetic Life.* Duke University Press, 2018.
Bewes, Timothy. "To Think Without Abstraction: On the Problem of Standpoint in Cultural Criticism." *Textual Practice* 28.7 (2014): 1200–1219.
Bjerre. Thomas. "Post-9/11 Literary Masculinities in Kalfus, DeLillo, and Hamid." *Orbis Litterarum* 67.3 (2012): 241–266.
Bonneuil, Christophe and Jean-Baptiste Fressoz. *The Shock of the Anthropocene: The Earth, History, and Us.* Trans. David Fernbach. Verso, 2016.
Borradori, Giovanna. *Philosophy in a Time of Terror: Dialogues with Juergen Habermas and Jacques Derrida.* University of Chicago Press, 2004.
Boxall, Peter. *Twenty-First-Century Fiction: A Critical Introduction.* Cambridge University Press, 2013.
Boyle, Kirk and Daniel Morzowski. "Introduction: Creative Documentation of Creative Destruction." *The Great Recession in Fiction, Film, and Television.* Eds. Kirk Boyle and Daniel Morzowksi. Lexington Books, 2013, xi–xxv.
Brown, Jayna. *Black Utopias: Speculative Life and the Music of Other Worlds.* Duke University Press, 2021.
Buelens, Gert, Samuel Durrant, and Robert Eaglestone, eds. *The Future of Trauma Theory: Contemporary Literary and Cultural Criticism.* London: Routledge, 2013.
Buell, Frederick. "Global Warming as Literary Narrative." *Philological Quarterly* 93.3 (2014): 261–294.
Buell, Lawrence. *The Environmental Imagination: Thoreau, Nature Writing, and the Formation of American Culture.* Harvard University Press, 1995.
———. *The Future of Environmental Criticism.* Wiley & Sons, 2005.
Butler, Judith. *Precarious Life: The Powers of Mourning and Violence.* Verso, 2004.
———. *Frames of War: When is Life Grievable.* Verso, 2010.
Canavan, Gerry and Andrew Hageman. "Array." *Paradoxa* 28 (2016).
Carpenter, Rebecca. "'We're Not a Friggin' Girl Band': September 11, Masculinity, and the British–American Relationship in David Hare's *Stuff Happens* and Ian McEwan's *Saturday.*" *Literature After 9/11.* Eds. Ann Keniston and Jeanne Quinn. Routledge, 2010, 143–160.
Carroll, Hamilton. "'Stuck between Meanings': Recession-Era Print Fictions of Crisis Masculinity." *Gendering the Recession: Media and Culture in an Age of Austerity.* Eds. Diana Negra and Yvonne Tasker. Duke University Press, 2014, 203–219.
Carroll, Hamilton and Annie McClanahan. "Fictions of Speculation." *Fictions of Speculation*, special issue of *Journal of American Studies* 49.4 (2015): 655–661.
Cazdyn, Eric. *The Already Dead: The New Time of Politics, Culture, and Illness.* Duke University Press, 2012.

Cervenak, Sarah. *Black Gathering: Art, Ecology, Ungiven Life*. Duke University Press, 2021.
Chakrabarty, Dipesh. "The Anthropocene and the Convergence of Histories." *The Anthropocene and the Global Environmental Crisis: Rethinking Modernity in a New Epoch*. Eds. Clive Hamilton, Christophe Bonneuil, and François Gemenne. Routledge, 2015, 44–56.
———. "The Climate of History: Four Theses." *Critical Inquiry* 35.2 (2009): 197–222.
———. *The Climate of History in a Planetary Age*. University of Chicago Press, 2021.
———. "Postcolonial Studies and the Challenge of Climate Change." *New Literary History* 43.1 (2012): 1–18.
Chaouli, Michel. "Criticism and Style." *New Literary History* 44.3 (2013): 323–344.
Charles, Ron. "Jonathan Franzen's New Novel." Review of *Freedom* by Jonathan Franzen. *Washington Post*. August 25, 2010.
Chase, Greg. "Of Trips Taken and Time Served: How Ward's *Sing, Unburied, Sing* Grapples with Faulkner's Ghost." *African American Review* 53.3 (2020): 201–216.
Cherniavsky, Eva and Tom Foster. "Permanent Crisis and Technosociality in Bruce Sterling's *Distraction*." *Journal of American Studies* 49.4 (2015): 711–729.
Chow, Juliana. "Partial Readings: Thoreau's Studies as Natural History's Casualties." *Anthropocene Reading: Literary History in Geologic Time*. Eds. Tobias Menely and Jesse Oak Taylor. Pennsylvania State University Press, 2017, 117–131.
Ciccariello-Maher, George. *Decolonizing Dialectics*. Duke University Press, 2017.
Clark, Christopher. "What Comes to the Surface: Storms, Bodies, and the Community in Jesmyn Ward's *Salvage the Bones*." *Mississippi Quarterly* 3.4 (2014): 341–358.
Clark, Timothy. *Ecocriticism on the Edge: The Anthropocene as a Threshold Concept*. Bloomsbury, 2015.
Colesworthy, Rebecca. "Capital's Abstraction." *Textual Practice* 28.7 (2014): 1169–1179.
Collins, Michael. "The Consent of the Governed in Ishmael Reed's 'The Freelance Pallbearers.'" *PMLA* 123.2 (2008): 422–437.
Connolly, William. "Extinction Events and Entangled Humanism." *After Extinction*. Ed. Richard Grusin. University of Minnesota Press, 2018, 1–26.
———. *Facing the Planetary: Entangled Humanism and the Politics of Swarming*. Duke University Press, 2017.
———. *The Fragility of Things: Self-Organizing Processes, Neoliberal Fantasies, and Democratic Activism*. Duke University Press, 2013.
Coole, Diane and Samantha Frost. "Introducing the New Materialisms." *New Materialisms: Ontology, Agency, and Politics*. Eds. Diane Coole and Samantha Frost. Duke University Press, 2010, 1–30.

Crosthwaite, Paul. "Is Financial Crisis a Trauma?" *Cultural Critique* 82 (2012): 34–67.
Crownshaw, Richard. "Agency and Environment in the Work of Jesmyn Ward." *Journal of American Studies* 50.1 (2016): 225–230.
Cunninham, Vincent. "Jesmyn Ward's Haunted Novel of the Gulf Coast." *New Yorker*. September 4, 2017.
Dancer, Thom. *Critical Modesty in Contemporary Fiction*. Oxford University Press, 2021.
Dango, Michael. *Crisis Style: The Aesthetics of Repair*. Stanford University Press, 2021.
Dawson, Paul. "The Return of Omniscience in Contemporary Fiction." *Narrative* 17.2 (2009): 143–161.
Dee, Jonathan. *The Privileges*. Random House, 2010.
DeLillo, Don. "In the Ruins of the Future." *The Guardian*. September 18, 2001.
DeLoughrey, Elizabeth. *Allegories of the Anthropocene*. Duke University Press, 2019.
Derrida, Jacques. *Specters of Marx: The State of Debt, the Work of Mourning, and the New International*. Trans. Peggy Kamuf. Routledge, 1993.
Dibley, Ben and Brett Neilson. "Climate Crisis and the Actual Imaginary: 'The War on Global Warming.'" *New Foundations* 69 (2010): 144–159.
Dickson-Carr, Darryl. *African American Satire: The Sacredly Profane Novel*. University of Missouri Press, 2001.
Dimock, Wai Chee. *Through Other Continents: American Literature Across Deep Time*. Princeton University Press, 2006.
———. "World History According to Katrina." *differences* 19.2 (2008): 35–53.
Donofrio, Nicholas. "Multiculturalism, Inc.: Regulating and Deregulating the Culture Industries with Ishmael Reed." *American Literary History* 29.1 (2017): 100–128.
Drew, Judith. "Identity Crisis: Gender, Public Discourse, and 9/11." *Women & Language* 27.2 (2004): 71–77.
Dubey, Madhu. "Racecraft in American Fiction." *Novel* 50.3 (2017): 365–374.
Duvall, John and Robert Marzec. "Narrating 9/11." *Modern Fiction Studies* 57.3 (2011): 381–400.
Eggers, Dave. *A Hologram for the King*. McSweeney's, 2012.
———. *Zeitoun*. McSweeney's, 2009.
Ellis, Cristin. *Antebellum Posthuman: Race and Materialism in the Mid-Nineteenth Century*. Fordham University Press, 2018.
English, James F. and Ted Underwood. "Shifting Scales: Between Literature and Social Science." *MLQ* 77.3 (2016): 277–295.
Farrier, David. *Anthropocene Poetics: Deep Time, Sacrifice Zones, and Extinction*. University of Minnesota Press, 2019.
Ferris, Joshua. *The Unnamed*. Back Bay Books, 2010.
The Financial Crisis Inquiry Report: Final Report of the National Commission on the Causes of the Financial Crisis.

Finch, Laura. "The Un-Real Deal: Financial Fiction, Fictional Finance, and the Financial Crisis." *Journal of American Studies* 49.4 (2015): 731–753.
Fisher, Mark. *Capitalist Realism: Is There No Alternative?* Zero Books, 2009.
———. *The Weird and the Eerie*. Zero Books, 2017.
Foucault, Michel. *The Birth of Biopolitics: Lectures at the Collège de France, 1978–1979*. Trans. Graham Burchell. Picador, 2010.
Franzen, Jonathan. *Farther Away: Essays*. Farrar, Straus, and Giroux, 2013.
———. *Freedom*. Farrar, Straus, and Giroux: 2010.
———. *How to Be Alone*. Farrar, Straus, and Giroux: 2002.
Frazier, Chelsea. "Troubling Ecology: Wangechi Mutu, Octavia Butler, and Black Environmentalism." *Critical Ethnic Studies* 2.1 (2016): 40–72.
Freeburg, Christopher. *Counterlife: Slavery and Resistance After Social Death*. Duke University Press, 2021.
Freedgood, Elaine and Cannon Schmitt. "Denotatively, Technically, Literally." *Representations* 125.1 (2014): 1–14.
Friedman, Gabriella. "The Social Life of Speculation." *American Quarterly* 71.1 (2019): 205–217.
Furlonge, Nicole. *Race Sounds: The Art of Listening in African American Literature*. University of Iowa Press, 2018.
Ganguly, Debjani. *This Thing Called the World: The Contemporary Novel as Global Form*. Duke University Press, 2016.
Ghosh, Amitav. *The Great Derangement: Climate Change and the Unthinkable*. University of Chicago Press, 2016.
Giroux, Henry. *Stormy Weather: Katrina and the Politics of Disposability*. Paradigm, 2005.
Goldberg, David Theo. *The Threat of Race: Reflections on Racial Neoliberalism*. Wiley-Blackwell, 2009.
Goyal, Yogita. "Introduction: The Transnational Turn." *The Cambridge Companion to Transnational American Literature*. Ed. Yogita Goyal. Cambridge University Press, 2017, 1–16.
Graham, Margaret Hunt. "*Freedom*'s Limits: Jonathan Franzen, the Realist Novel, and the Problem of Growth." *American Literary History* 26.2 (2014): 295–316.
Gray, Richard. *After the Fall: American Literature Since 9/11*. Wiley-Blackwell, 2011.
Greenberg, Judith, ed. *Trauma at Home: After 9/11*. Bison Books, 2003.
Griffiths, Matthew. *The New Poetics of Climate Change: Modernist Aesthetics for a Warming World*. Bloomsbury Academic, 2017.
Grusin, Richard. *Premediation: Affect and Mediality after 9/11*. Palgrave, 2010.
Guerrera, Lisa. "Can I Live?: Contemporary Black Satire and the State of Postmodern Double Consciousness." *Studies in American Humor* 4.2 (2016): 266–279.
Gupta, Suman. "Crisis of the Novel and the Novel of Crisis." *Canadian Review of Comparative Literature* 42.4 (2015): 454–467.
Halberstam, Jack. *The Queer Art of Failure*. Duke University Press, 2011.

Hamilton, Clive. "The Anthropocene as Rupture." *The Anthropocene Review*. 3.2 (2016): 93–106

———. "The Theodicy of the 'Good Anthropocene.'" *Environmental Humanities* 7 (2015): 233–238.

Haraway, Donna. *Staying with the Trouble: Making Kin in the Chthulucene*. Duke University Press, 2016.

Harman, Graham. "The Well-Wrought Hammer: Object-Oriented Literary Criticism." *New Literary History* 43.2 (2012): 183–203.

Harney, Stefano and Fred Moten. *The Undercommons: Fugitive Planning and Black Study*. Minor Compositions, 2013.

Hartman, Saidiya. *Lose Your Mother: A Journey Along the Atlantic Slave Route*. MacMillan, 2008.

———. *Scenes of Subjection: Terror, Slavery and Self-Making in Nineteenth-Century America*. Oxford University Press, 1997.

Hartnell, Anna. "When Cars Become Churches: Jesmyn Ward's Disenchanted America: An Interview." *Journal of American Studies* 50.1 (2016): 205–281.

Harvey, David. *The Enigma of Capital and the Crises of Capitalism*. Oxford University Press, 2010.

Heise, Ursula K. *Sense of Place and Sense of Planet: The Environmental Imagination of the Global*. Oxford University Press, 2009.

Higgins, David. *British Romanticism, Climate Change, and the Anthropocene: Writing Tambora*. Palgrave MacMillan, 2017.

Hoberek, Andrew. "Post-Recession Realism." *Neoliberalism and Contemporary Literary Culture*. Eds. Mitchum Huehls and Rachel Greenwald Smith. Johns Hopkins University Press, 2017, 237–252.

Horton, Zach. "Composing a Cosmic View: Three Alternatives for Thinking Scale in the Anthropocene." *Scale in Literature and Culture*. Eds. Michael Tavel Clarke and David Wittenberg. Palgrave MacMillan, 2017, 35–55.

———. *The Cosmic Zoom: Scale, Knowledge, and Mediation*. Chicago University Press, 2021.

Houen, Alex. "Novel Spaces and Taking Place(s) in the Wake of September 11." *Studies in the Novel* 36.3 (2004): 419–437.

Hsu, Hua. "No Compromises." *The New Yorker*. March 31, 2015.

Huehls, Mitchum. *After Critique: Twenty-First-Century Fiction in a Neoliberal Age*. Oxford University Press, 2016.

Hurley, Jessica and Jeffrey Insko, "Introduction: The Infrastructure of Emergency." *American Literature* 93.3 (2021): 345–359.

Intergovernmental Panel on Climate Change. *Climate Change 2007: Synthesis Report. Contribution of Working Groups I, II, and III to the Fourth Assessment Report of the Intergovernmental Panel on Climate Change*. Eds. R. K. Pachauri and A. Reisinger. IPCC, 2007.

———. *Climate Change 2014: Synthesis Report. Contribution of Working Groups I, II, and III to the Fifth Assessment Report of the Intergovernmental Panel on Climate Change*. Eds. R. K. Pachauri and L. A. Meyer. IPCC, 2014.

———. *Special Report: Global Warming of 1.5°C*. Eds. Masson-Delmotte et al., 2018.
Irr, Caren. *Toward the Geopolitical Novel: US Fiction in the Twenty-First Century*. Columbia University Press, 2013.
Iton, Richard. *In Search of the Black Fantastic: Politics and Popular Culture in the Civil Rights Era*. Oxford University Press, 2008.
Jackson, Chris. "Our Thing: An Interview with Paul Beatty." *The Paris Review*. May 7, 2015.
Jackson, Zakiyyah Iman. *Becoming Human: Matter and Meaning in an Antiblack World*. New York University Press, 2020.
Jameson, Frederic. *The Antinomies of Realism*. Verso Books, 2013.
———. *Representing Capital: A Reading of Volume One*. Verso Books, 2011.
Jemisin, N. K. *The City We Became*. Orbit, 2020.
———. *The Fifth Season*. Orbit, 2015.
———. *How Long 'til Black Future Month?* Orbit, 2018.
Johns-Putra, Adeline. "Climate Change in Literature and Literary Studies: From Cli-Fi, Climate Change Theater and Ecopoetry to Ecocriticism and Climate Change Criticism." *WIREs Climate Change* 7 (2016): 266–282.
Joy, Eileen. "Weird Reading." *Speculations* IV (2013): 28–34.
Kalfus, Ken. *A Disorder Peculiar to the Country*. Ecco, 2006.
Kaplan, Ann E. *Trauma Culture: The Politics of Terror and Loss in Media and Literature*. Rutgers University Press, 2005.
Karera, Axelle. "Blackness and the Pitfalls of Anthropocene Ethics." *Critical Philosophy of Race* 7.1 (2019): 32–56.
Keeble, Arin. "Marriage, Relationships, and 9/11: The Seismographic Narratives of *Falling Man*, the *Good Life*, and *The Emperor's Children*." *The Modern Language Review* 106.2 (2011): 355–373.
———. "Siblings, Kinship and Allegory in Jesmyn Ward's Fiction and Nonfiction." *Critique: Studies in Contemporary Fiction* 61.1 (2020): 40–51.
Keeling, Kara. *Queer Times, Black Futures*. New York University Press, 2019.
Keniston, Ann and Jeanne Quinn, eds. *Literature After 9/11*. Routledge, 2010.
Kim, Claire. *Dangerous Crossings: Race, Species, and Nature in a Multicultural Age*. Cambridge University Press, 2015.
King, Tiffany Lethabo. *The Black Shoals: Offshore Formations of Black and Native Studies*. Duke University Press, 2019.
Kingsolver, Barbara. *Flight Behavior*. HarperCollins, 2012.
Kinkle, Jeff and Alberto Toscano. *Cartographies of the Absolute*. Zero Books, 2015.
———. "Filming the Crisis." *Film Quarterly* 65.1 (2011): 39–51.
Kornbluh, Anna. *Realizing Capital: Financial and Psychic Economies in Victorian Form*. Fordham University Press, 2014.
———. "We Have Never Been Critical." *Novel* 50.3 (2017): 397–408.

La Berge, Leigh Claire and Alison Schonkwiler. "Introduction: A Theory of Capitalist Realism." *Reading Capitalist Realism*. Eds. Leigh Claire La Berge and Alison Schonkwiler. University of Iowa Press, 2014, 1–20.

Latour, Bruno. "An Attempt at a 'Compositionist Manifesto.'" *New Liyerary History* 41.3 (2010): 471–490.

———. *Facing Gaia: Eight Lectures on the New Climatic Regime*. Trans. Catherine Porter. Polity, 2017.

———. *An Inquiry into the Modes of Existence: An Anthropology of the Moderns*. Trans. Catherine Porter. Harvard University Press, 2013.

———. *Pandora's Hope: Essays on the Reality of Science Studies*. Trans. Catherine Porter. Harvard University Press, 1999.

Lawson, Andrew. "Foreclosure Stories: Neoliberal Suffering in the Great Recession." *Journal of American Studies* 47.1 (2013): 49–68.

LeMenager, Stephanie. "Climate Change and the Struggle for Genre." *Anthropocene Reading: Literary History in Geologic Time*. Eds. Tobias Menely and Jesse Oak Taylor. Pennsylvania State University Press, 2017, 220–238.

———. *Living Oil: Petroleum Culture in the American Century*. Oxford University Press, 2014.

Leong, Diana. "The Mattering of Black Lives: Octavia Butler's Hyperempathy and the Promise of the New Materialisms." *Catalyst* 2.2 (2016): 1–35.

Levine, Caroline. *Forms: Whole, Rhythm, Hierarchy*. Princeton University Press, 2015.

Lewis, Michael. *The Big Short: Inside the Doomsday Machine*. W. W. Norton and Company, 2010.

Lewis, Simon and Mark Maslin. "Defining the Anthropocene." *Nature* 519, 2015, pp. 171–180.

Lilla, Mark. *The Once and Future Liberal*. Harper, 2017.

Love, Heather. "Small Change: Realism, Immanence, and the Politics of the Micro." *MLQ* 77.3 (2016): 419–445.

Luckhurst, Roger. *The Trauma Question*. Routledge, 2008.

McClanahan, Annie. *Dead Pledges: Debt, Crisis, and Twenty-First-Century Culture*. Stanford University Press, 2017.

McGurl, Mark. "Gigantic Realism: The Rise of the Novel and the Comedy of Scale." *Critical Inquiry* 43.2 (2017): 403–430.

———. "The New Cultural Geology." *Twentieth-Century Literature* 57.3–4 (2011): 380–390.

———. "The Posthuman Comedy." *Critical Inquiry* 38.3 (2012): 533–553.

McInerney, Jay. *The Good Life*. Bloomsbury Publishing, 2007.

McKisson, Kelly. "The Subsident Gulf: Refiguring Climate Change in Jesmyn Ward's Bois Sauvage." *American Literature* 93.3 (2021): 473–496.

McKittrick, Katherine. *Dear Sciences and Other Stories*. Duke University Press, 2020.

McPhee, Martha. *Dear Money*. Houghton Mifflin Harcourt, 2010.

Madera, Judith. *Black Atlas: Geography and Flow in Nineteenth-Century African American Literature*. Duke University Press, 2015.

Mahon, Aine. "Achieving their Country: Richard Rorty and Jonathan Franzen." *Philosophy and Literature* 38.1 (2014): 90–109.

Manshel, Alexander. "Rise of the Recent Historical Novel." *Post45 Peer-Reviewed*. September 29, 2017.

Marcus, Sharon, Heather Love, and Stephen Best. "Building a Better Description." *Representations* 135.1 (2016): 1–21.

Marran, Christine. *Ecology Without Culture: Aesthetics for a Toxic World*. University of Minnesota Press, 2017.

Marshall, Kate. "The Old Weird." *Modernism/modernity* 23.3 (2016): 631–649.

———. "What Are the Novels of the Anthropocene? American Fiction in Geologic Time." *American Literary History* 27.3 (2015): 523–538.

Martin, Randall. *9/11 and the Literature of Terror*. Edinburgh University Press, 2011.

Martin, Theodore. *Contemporary Drift: Genre, Historicism, and the Problem of the Present*. Columbia University Press, 2017.

———. "Contemporary, Inc." *Representations* 142.1 (2018): 124–144.

Mattingly, Daniel. "Crash Fiction: American Literary Novels and the Global Financial Crisis." *The Great Recession in Fiction, Film, and Television*. Eds. Kirk Boyle and Daniel Morzowksi. Lexington Books, 2013, 96–110.

Matz, Aaron. *Satire in an Age of Realism*. Cambridge University Press, 2011.

Mbembe, Achille. *Critique of Black Reason*. Trans. Laurent Dubois. Duke University Press, 2017.

Melamed, Jodi. *Represent and Destroy: Rationalizing Violence in the New Racial Capitalism*. University of Minnesota Press, 2011.

Menely, Tobias and Jesse Oak Taylor. "Introduction." *Anthropocene Reading: Literary History in Geologic Time*. Eds. Tobias Menely and Jesse Oak Taylor. Pennsylvania State College Press, 2017, 1–24.

Michaels, Walter Benn. "Model Minorities and the Minority Model: The Neoliberal Novel." *The Cambridge History of the American Novel*. Ed. Leonard Cassuto. Fordham University Press, 2011, 1016–1030.

———. *The Trouble with Diversity: How We Learned to Love Identity and Ignore Equality*. Metropolitan Books, 2006.

Miller, Elizabeth. *Extraction Ecologies and the Literature of the Long Exhaustion*. Princeton University Press, 2021.

Mirowski, Philip. *Never Let a Serious Crisis Go to Waste*. Verso, 2013.

Mirzoeff, Nicholas. "It's Not the Anthropocene, It's the White Supremacy Scene. Or, The Geological Color Line." *After Extinction*. Ed. Richard Grusin. University of Minnesota Press, 2018, 123–150.

Moore, Jason. *Capitalism in the Web of Life: Ecology and the Accumulation of Capital*. New York: Verso, 2015.

Moretti, Franco. *Graphs, Maps, Trees*. Verso, 2005.
Morgan, Benjamin. "Scale as Form: Thomas Hardy's Rocks and Stars." *Anthropocene Reading: Literary History in Geologic Time*. Eds. Tobias Menely and Jesse Oak Taylor. The Pennsylvania State University Press, 2017, 132–147.
Morton, Timothy. *Dark Ecology: For a Logic of Future Coexistence*. Columbia University Press, 2016.
———. *The Ecological Thought*. Harvard University Press, 2010.
———. *Ecology Without Nature: Rethinking Environmental Aesthetics*. Harvard University Press, 2007.
———. *Hyperobjects: Philosophy and Ecology after the End of the World*. University of Minnesota Press, 2013.
Moten, Fred. *Black and Blur: Consent Not To Be a Single Being*. Duke University Press, 2017.
Moynihan, Sinead. "From Disposability to Recycling: William Faulkner and the New Politics of Rewriting in Jesmyn Ward's *Salvage the Bones*." *Studies in the Novel* 47.4 (2015): 550–567.
Muñoz, José Esteban. *Cruising Utopia: The Then and There of Queer Futurity*. New York University Press, 2009.
Murphet, Julian. "A Modest Proposal for the Inhuman." *Modernism/modernity* 23.3 (2016): 651–670.
Murphy, Patrick. "Pessimism, Optimism, Human Inertia, and Anthropogenic Climate Change." *ISLE* 21.1 (2014): 149–163.
Nash, Jennifer. "Intersectionality and Its Discontents." *American Quarterly* 69.1 (2017): 117–129.
———. "Re-Thinking Intersectionality." *Feminist Review* (2008): 1–15.
National Commission on Terrorist Attacks upon the United States. *The 9/11 Commission Report*, 2004.
Nayak, Meghana. "Orientalism and 'Saving' US State Identity after 9/11." *International Feminist Journal of Politics* 8.1 (2006): 42–61.
Nealon, Jeffrey T. "Realism Redux or, Against Affective Capitalism." *Neoliberalism and Contemporary Culture*. Eds. Mitchum Huehls and Rachel Greenwald-Smith. Johns Hopkins University Press, 70–85.
Negra, Diana and Yvonne Tasker. "Introduction: Gender and Recessionary Culture." *Gendering the Recession: Media and Culture in an Age of Austerity*. Eds. Diana Negra and Yvonne Tasker. Duke University Press, 2014, 1–25.
Ngai, Sianne. *Our Aesthetic Categories: Zany, Cute, Interesting*. Harvard University Press, 2012.
———. "Visceral Abstractions." *GLQ: A Journal of Lesbian and Gay Studies* 21.1 (2015): 33–63.
Nixon, Rob. *Slow Violence and the Environmentalism of the Poor*. Harvard University Press, 2011.
Outka, Paul. *Race and Nature: From Transcendentalism to the Harlem Renaissance*. Palgrave MacMillan, 2008.

Pfaff, Sarah. "'The slack string is just a slack string': Neoformalist Networks in *The White Boy Shuffle*." *Literature, Interpretation, Theory* 26 (2015): 106–127.

Plotz, John. "IS Realism Failing? The Rise of Secondary World." *Novel* 53.3 (2017): 426–453.

Povinelli, Elizabeth. *Economies of Abandonment: Social Belonging and Endurance in Late Liberalism*. Duke University Press, 2011.

———. *Geontologies: A Requiem to Late Capitalism*. Duke University Press, 2016.

Rambsy, Howard. "The Vengeance of the Black Boys: How Richard Wright, Paul Beatty, and Aaron McGruder Strike Back." *The Mississippi Quarterly* 61.4 (2008): 643–657.

Reber, Dierdra. "A Tale of Two Marats: On the Abhorrence of Verticality, from Laissez-Faire to Neoliberalism." *Novel* 51.2 (2018): 188–210.

Redfield, Marc. *The Rhetoric of Terror: Reflections on 9/11 and the War on Terror*. Fordham University Press, 2009.

Reed, Adolph. "The 'Color Line' Then and Now: The Souls of Black Folk and the Changing Context of Black American Politics." *Renewing Black Intellectual History: The Ideological Material and Foundations of African American Thought*. Eds. Adolph Reed, Kenneth Warren, Mahdu Dubey, William Jones, Michele Mitchell, Touree Reed, Dean Robinson, Preston Smith, and Judith Stein. Paradigm Publishers, 2010, 252–303.

Reed, Ishmael. "LeRoi Jones/Amiri Baraka and Me." *Transition* 114 (2014) 13–29.

Remnick, David. "The Financial Crisis and Climate Crisis" [podcast], available at https://www.newyorker.com/podcast/the-new-yorker-radio-hour/the-financial-crash-and-the-climate-crisis (last accessed May 27, 2022).

Rifkin, Mark. *Fictions of Land and Flesh: Blackness, Indigeneity, Speculation*. Duke University Press, 2019.

Roane, J. T. and Justin Hosbey. "Mapping Black Ecologies." *Current Research in Digital History* 2 (2019).

Robinson, Cedric. *Black Marxism: The Making of the Black Radical Tradition*. UNC Press, 1983.

Roitman, Janet. *Anti-Crisis*. Duke University Press, 2013.

Romm, Robin. "Nell Zink's '*Wallcreeper*'." Review of Nell Zink's *The Wallcreeper*. *The New York Times*. October 17, 2014.

Ronda, Margaret. *Remainder: American Poetry at Nature's End*. Stanford University Press, 2018.

Rosen, Jeremy. *Minor Characters Have Their Day: Genre and the Contemporary Literary Marketplace*. Columbia University Press, 2016.

Rosenberg, Jordy. "The Molecularization of Sexuality." *Theory and Event* 17.2 (2014).

Rothberg, Michael. "A Failure of the Imagination: Diagnosing the Post-9/11 Novel: A Response to Richard Gray." *American Literary History* 21.1 (2009): 152–158.

Saldívar, Ramón. "Historical Fantasy, Speculative Realism, and Postrace Aesthetics in Contemporary American Fiction." *American Literary History* 23.3 (2011): 574–599.

Schmidt, Christian. "Dismantling Blackness: The Degenerative Satires of Paul Beatty and Percival Everett." *Post-Soul Satire: Black Identity After Civil Rights*. Eds. Derek Maus and James Donahue. University of Mississippi Press, 2014, 150–161.

Schnellnhuber, Hans et al. *Turn Down the Heat: Why a 4°C Warmer World Must be Avoided*. International Bank for Reconstruction and Development, 2012.

Seltzer, Mark. *The Official World*. Duke University Press, 2016.

Serres, Michel. *Biogea*. Trans. Randolph Burks. Univocal, 2010.

———. *Times of Crisis: What the Financial Crisis Revealed and How to Reinvent Our Lives and Future*. Trans. Anne-Marie Feenberg-Dibon. Bloomsbury, 2014.

Seymour, Nicole. *Bad Environmentalism: Irony and Irreverence in the Ecological Age*. University of Minnesota Press, 2018.

Sharpe, Christina. *In the Wake: On Blackness and Being*. Duke University Press, 2016.

Shonkwiler, Alison. *The Financial Imaginary: Economic Mystification and the Limits of Realist Fiction*. University of Minnesota Press, 2017.

Simpson, Mark. "Lubricity: Smooth Oil's Political Frictions." *Petrocultures*. Eds. Adam Carlson, Imre Szeman, and Sheena Wilson. McGill-Queen's University Press, 2017, 287–318.

Singh, Julietta. *Unthinking Mastery: Dehumanism and Decolonial Entanglements*. Duke University Press, 2018.

Singh, Nikhil. *Black is a Country: Race and the Unfinished Struggle for Democracy*. Harvard University Press, 2004.

Smith, Zadie. *Changing My Mind: Occasional Essays*. Penguin Books, 2010.

Song, Min Hyoung. "The New Materialism and Neoliberalism." *Neoliberalism and Contemporary Culture*. Eds. Mitchum Huehls and Rachel Greenwald Smith. Johns Hopkins University Press, 2017, 52–69.

Spillers, Hortense. *Black, White, and in Color: Essays on American Literature and Culture*. Chicago University Press, 2003.

Spivak, Gayatri Chakravarty. *Death of a Discipline*. Columbia University Press, 2003.

Stankorb, Sarah. "Climate Fiction, or 'Cli-Fi,' Is the Hottest New Literary Genre." *Good Magazine*. March 22, 2016.

Stengers, Isabelle. *Cosmopolitics I*. Trans. Robert Bononno. University of Minnesota Press, 2010.

Stevens, Benjamin. "Medea in Jesmyn Ward's *Salvage the Bones*." *International Journal for the Classical Tradition* 25.2 (2018): 158–177.

Sylvanise, Frédéric. "An Interview with Paul Beatty." *Transatlantic* 31 (2013): 1–10.

Szeman, Imre and Jennifer Wenzel. "What Do We Talk About When We Talk About Extractivism?" *Textual Practice* 35.3 (2021): 505–523.

Tabone, Mark. "'The Ones Who Stay and Fight': N. K. Jemisin's Afrofuturist Variations on a Theme by Urusla K. Le Guin." *Utopian Studies* 32.2 (2021): 365–385.

Taylor, Jesse Oak. *The Sky of Our Manufacture: London Fog in British Fiction from Dickens to Woolf.* University of Virginia Press, 2016.

Taylor, Matthew. "At Land's End: Novel Spaces and the Limits of Planetarity." *Novel* 49.1 (2016): 115–138.

Thalos, Mariam. *Without Hierarchy: The Scale Freedom of the Universe.* Oxford University Press, 2013.

Thomas, Lindsay. "Forms of Duration: Preparedness, the *Mars* Trilogy, and the Management of Climate Change." *American Literature* 88.1 (2016): 159–184.

Tooze, Adam. *Crashed.* Penguin, 2018.

Trexler, Adam. *Anthropocene Fictions: The Novel in a Time of Climate Change.* University of Virginia Press, 2015.

Tsing, Anna. *The Mushroom at the End of the World: On the Possibility of Life in Capitalist Ruins.* Princeton University Press, 2017.

Tuana, Nancy. "Viscous Porosity: Witnessing Katrina." *Material Feminisms.* Eds. Stacy Alaimo and Susan Hekman, 2008, 188–213.

Turner, Jenny. "Prodigiously Intelligent and Odd." *The Guardian.* June 26, 2015.

Ullrich, J. K. "Climate Fiction: Can Books Save the Planet?" *The Atlantic.* August 14, 2015.

Vergès, Françoise. "Racial Capitalocene." *Futures of Black Radicalism.* Eds. Gaye Johnson and Alex Lubin. Verso, 2017, 160–180.

Vermeulen, Pieter. *Contemporary Literature and the End of the Novel: Creature, Affect, Form.* Palgrave MacMillan, 2015.

Versluys, Kristiaan. *Out of the Blue: September 11 and the Novel.* Columbia University Press, 2009.

Waldman, Amy. *The Submission.* Farrar, Straus and Giroux, 2012.

Walter, Jess. *The Financial Lives of the Poets.* Harper Perennial, 2009.

———. *The Zero.* Harper Perennial, 2007.

Ward, Jesmyn. *The Fire This Time.* Charles Scribner's Sons, 2016

———. *Men We Reaped.* Bloomsbury, 2013.

———. *Salvage the Bones.* Bloomsbury, 2011.

———. *Sing, Unburied, Sing.* Bloomsbury, 2017.

———. *Where the Line Bleeds.* Simon and Schuster, 2008.

Warren, Calvin. *Ontological Terror: Blackness, Nihilism, and Emancipation.* Duke University Press, 2018.

Warren, Kenneth. *What Was African American Literature?* Harvard University Press, 2011.

Weheliye, Alexander. *Habeas Viscus: Racializing Assemblages, Biopolitics, and Black Feminist Theories of the Human.* Duke University Press, 2014.

Wenzel, Jennifer. *The Disposition of Nature: Environmental Crisis and World Literature*. Duke University Press, 2019.
———. "How to Read for Oil." *Resilience: A Journal of the Environmental Humanities* 3.1 (2014): n.p.
Whitehead, Colson. *The Underground Railroad*. Anchor, 2018.
———. *Zone One*. Anchor, 2012.
Wilderson, Frank. *Red, White, and Black: Cinema and the Structure of U.S. Antagonisms*. Duke University Press, 2010.
Williams, Jeffrey J. "The Plutocratic Imagination." *Dissent* 60.1 (2013): 93–97.
Wilson, Sheena, Imre Szeman, and Adam Carlson. "On Petrocultures: Or, Why We Need to Understand Oil to Understand Everything Else." *Petrocultures: Oil, Politics, Culture*. Eds. Sheena Wilson, Adam Carlson, and Imre Szeman. McGill-Queen's University Press, 2017, 3–11.
Winter, Jerome. "Global Futurist Ecologies." *Literary Afrofuturism in the Twenty-First Century*. Eds. Isiah Lavender III and Lisa Yaszek. Ohio State University Press, 2020, 189–203.
———. "Scale Variance and the Concept of Matter." *The New Politics of Materialism: History, Philosophy, Science*. Eds. Sarah Ellezweig and John Zammito. Routledge, 2017, 200–224.
Wright, Michelle. *Physics of Blackness: Beyond the Middle Passage Epistemology*. University of Minnesota Press, 2015.
Wynter, Sylvia. "Novel and History: Plot and Plantation." *Savacou* 13 (1977): n.p.
———. "On How We Mistook the Map for the Territory, and Re-Imprisoned Ourselves in Our Unbearable Wrongness of Being, of Désêtre: Black Studies Toward the Human Project." *Not Only the Master's Tools*. Eds. Lewis Gordon and Jane Gordon. Paradigm, 2006, 107–169.
———. "The Re-Enchantment of Humanism: An Interview with Sylvia Wynter and David Scott." *Small Axe* 8 (2000): 119–207.
———. "Unparalleled Catastrophe for Our Species? Or, to Give Humanness a Different Future: Conversations." *Sylvia Winter: On Being Human as Praxis*. Ed. Katherine McKittrick. Duke University Press, 2015, 9–90.
———. "Unsettling the Coloniality of Being/Power/Truth/Freedom: Toward the Human, After Man, Its Overrepresentation – An Argument." *CR: The New Centennial Review* 3.3 (2003): 257–337.
Yusoff, Kathryn. *A Billion Black Anthropocenes or None*. University of Minnesota Press, 2019.
Zink, Nell. "Henry Adams, Expatriate Academics and 'A Dubstep Novel with a Bird'." Interview with Nell Zink, by Tobias Carroll. *Vol. 1 Brooklyn*, September 30, 2014.
———. *The Wallcreeper*. Dorothy, 2014.

Index

9/11, 1–4, 10, 111
  9/11 Commission Report, 2–4, 7–16
  criticism, 8–16
  in fiction, 2, 8–16
  and scale, 10–13
  and trauma theory, 13
  transnational renderings of, 15

acoustics, 73n32, 107, 163n22
Afrofuturism, 114, 135n24
Alaimo, Stacy, 30
Alexander, Jacqui M., 120
Animal Studies, 130–2
Anthropocene
  aesthetics of, 5–6, 21–5, 32–4, 117–18, 12
  naming of, 27, 64m24
  problems with, 4–5, 24–9, 35
  racialization of, 114–19, 127–33, 169–70, 177–8, 192
  and spatiality, 22–3
  and temporality, 24–5
anthropogenic climate change
  aesthetics of, 100
  and global weirding, 76–7
  Intergovernmental Panel on Climate Change, 77–9, 94–5
  economic impact, 78n3, 93–5
  and literary form, 80, 80n7, 89–90, 96–9
  and temporality, 83
  World Bank, 77n2
atmospheric reading, 106–9

Baucom, Ian, 8, 125–7
Banita, Georgiana, 12
Barad, Karen, 105n27
Beatty, Paul, 173–207
  Sellout, The, 172–7, 183–5, 190–4, 197–200, 202–3, 205–7
  Slumberland, 194–7, 204–5
  Tuff, 185–90
  White Boy Shuffle, 184–5, 195–6, 201–2
Bennett, Jane, 191
Bennett, Joshua, 132–3, 151–2, 159–60
Berlant, Lauren, 8–9
Best, Stephen, 175n1, 198
Bildungsroman, 96, 102
biopolitics, 190–2
Blackness
  and the anthropocene, 26–9, 35, 114–19, 192–4
  Black Studies, 28–9, 39, 114–33
  crisis of, 112–13, 145–6
  and death, 130, 131n18
  and ecology, 28, 39, 124–33
  and genre, 133–9
  and scale, 119–24
  and speculation, 114, 134–5
Boxall, Peter, 11
Brown, Jayna, 120, 124, 129n15, 134
Buell, Laurence, 80
Butler, Judith, 13n12

Cazdyn, Eric, 55–6
Chaouli, Michel, 33
Chakrabarty, Dipesh, 21–5, 82–3
Chow, Julianna, 53
Clark, Christopher, 165
Clark, Timothy, 33, 97–8
Colesworthy, Rebecca, 73–4
Connolly, William, 36, 63–4
contemporary
  crisis of, 2–5, 111–12, 142–3
  criticism of, 16–20
  and form, 7
  and literature, 5–6
Coole, Diane, 36, 58, 62, 67

crisis realism, 34
  and anthropogenic climate change, 77–8, 84–6, 92–3, 97, 103–4
  and financial crisis, 45–7, 62, 69–70
  and race, 113, 138–9
Crosthwaite, Paul, 62–3

Deepwater Horizon, 154–5, 166
DeLillo, Don, 1–4, 7–16
DeLoughrey, Elizabeth, 26–7, 115–16
Derrida, Jacques, 64n24
Dibley, Bem, 95
Dickson-Carr, Darryl, 199–200
Dimock, Wai Chee, 17n20, 20, 24–5, 144, 181
Dubey, Madhu, 204
dubstep, 107

ecocriticism, 79–80, 89
ecology, 6–7
Eggers, Dave
  A Hologram for the King, 48–56
  Zeitoun, 146
English, James, 30–1

failure, 46
Farrier, David, 26, 82
Faulkner, William, 159
Ferris, Joshua, 68–75
financial crisis
  2008 Subprime Mortgage Crisis, 43–75
  Financial Crisis Inquiry Commission, 43–5, 58–9, 65
  and literary form, 44–7, 55–6, 58–9, 70–5
  and temporality, 53–6, 61–2
Finch, Laura, 74
Fisher, Mark, 37–8, 101, 122n8
Franzen, Jonathan, 83–92
Frazier, Chelsea, 130n17
Friedman, Gabriella, 134, 136
Frost, Samantha, 36, 58, 62, 67

Ganguly, Debjani, 17
Ghosh, Amitav, 23n28, 107–8
Giroux, Henry, 145
Goyal, Yogita, 16n17
Graham, Margaret Hunt, 88
Gray, Richard, 13–14

Haraway, Donna, 83n13
Hartman, Saidiya, 113–14, 176
Hartnell, Anna, 145
Harvey, David, 55n14
Heise, Ursula, 98–9
Hosbey, Justin, 128–9
Horton, Zach, 21n25, 78n4, 119–20
Hsu, Hua, 182–3
Hurley, Jessica, 153–4
Hurricane Katrina, 141–2, 144–8

infrastructure, 153–4
Insko, Jeffrey, 153–4
intersectionality, 177–8
Irr, Caren, 18
Iton, Richard, 136n27, 187

Jackson, Zakiyyah Iman, 125, 130–2, 158
Jameson, Frederic, 53–5, 61
Jemisin, N. K., 110–14, 136–9

Keeble, Arin, 143n2, 148, 156
Keeling, Kara, 135
King, Tiffany Lethabo, 127–8, 186n13
Kingsolver, Barbara, 76–9, 92–101
Kornbluh, Anna, 61n23, 66

Latour, Bruno, 21, 32, 37, 63, 65–6, 73
LeMenager, Stephanie, 93, 167
Leong, Diana, 114–15
Lewis, Michael, 58–61
Levine, Caroline, 7
liberalism, 187–90
Lilla, Mark, 187–8

McClanahan, Annie, 44–7, 57, 73
McGurl, Mark, 23–4, 32, 66, 80
McKittrick, Katherine, 113n3, 118–19, 121, 139
McPhee, Martha, 56–9
Madera, Judith, 134
Marran, Christine, 12n11, 89–90, 95
Marshall, Kate, 101, 200
Martin, Theodore, 5–6
Marxism, 32, 42, 47, 64n24, 66, 182–3
materialism, 126
Matz, Aaron, 181, 201
Mbembe, Achille, 28
Menley, Tobias, 33
Michaels, Walter Benn, 182–3
Moore, Jason, 65n27

Moretti, Franco, 17–18
Morgan, Benjamin, 23–4
Morton, Timothy, 74, 83n13, 89, 91–2, 100–1, 106
Moten, Fred, 190
Murphet, Julian, 180–1, 201

Nash, Jennifer, 177–8
naturalism, 57–8
Negra, Diana, 51–2
Neilson, Brett, 95
neoliberalism
    and abstraction, 50–1
    crisis of, 54–6
    and ecology, 62–75
    Foucault on, 47–9
    and gender, 51–2
    and the market, 56–63
    and race, 51–2, 183–6
    and scale, 47–62
    and temporality, 54–6
    totality of, 52
new materialism, 62, 190–2
Nixon, Rob, 80, 195n24

O'Neill, Joseph, 14
oil, 154–5, 166–9, 193–4
ontological turn, 29n33

periodization, 24
postcritique, 19
Povinelli, Elizabeth, 115n4, 192

realism
    and 9/11, 8–14
    and the weird, 37–8, 81, 82n11, 100–1
Reed, Adolph, 184–5
Reed, Ishmael, 199–200
Rifkin, Mark, 135
Roane, J. T., 128–9
Robinson, Cedric, 187n15
Roitman, Janet, 9n5
Ronda, Margaret, 64n25
Rothberg, Michael, 14

Saldívar, Ramón, 189n18, 202n33
satire, 41, 180–1, 199–203
Seltzer, Mark, 18–20

Serres, Michel, 44, 66n29, 74
Sharpe, Christina, 38–9, 120–1, 128–9, 155, 169, 196, 206
Shonkwiler, Alison, 75
Simpson, Mark, 167–8
Singh, Julietta, 73n32, 107
Smith, Zadie, 11n9
Song, Min Hyoung, 191
Spivak, Gayatri, 17
Stengers, Isabelle, 113

Tasker, Yvonne, 51–2
Taylor, Jesse Oak, 33, 38, 81–2
Thalos, Miriam, 31
Thomas, Lindsay, 78,n4
transnational, 15–17
transscalar critique, 29–32
Trexler, Adam, 86, 92–3
Tsing, Anna, 65n26, 140
Tuana, Nancy, 193

Underwood, Ted, 30–1

Vergès, Françoise, 26, 192
Vermeulen, Pieter, 15, 54

Walter, Jess, 66–7
Ward, Jesmyn, 140–72
    Salvage the Bones, 140–1, 147–8, 150–1, 159–65, 168–72
    Sing, Unburied, Sing, 151–2, 154–8, 160–1, 165–72
    Where the Line Bleeds, 142–3, 148–50, 152–3, 158–9, 167
Warren, Calvin, 178
Warren, Kenneth, 174–6, 198–9, 206
Weheliye, Alexander, 123n11, 179, 190–1
Wenzel, Jennifer, 21, 40, 116, 167
Whitehead, Colson, 22–3, 28
Wilderson, Frank, 175n2
Woods, Derek, 22, 29–30
Wynter, Sylvia, 39, 113, 118, 121–4, 134, 176–7, 179n6, 186

Yusoff, Kathryn, 4–5n2, 27–9, 116–18

Zink, Nell, 101–9

EU representative:
Easy Access System Europe
Mustamäe tee 50, 10621 Tallinn, Estonia
Gpsr.requests@easproject.com

www.ingramcontent.com/pod-product-compliance
Lightning Source LLC
Chambersburg PA
CBHW070350240426
43671CB00013BA/2458